TRANSPLANTING RELIGIOUS TRADITIONS

TRANSPLANTING RELIGIOUS TRADITIONS

Asian Indians in America

John Y. Fenton

PRAEGER

New York
Westport, Connecticut
London

Library of Congress Cataloging-in-Publication Data

Fenton, John Y.
    Transplanting religious traditions : Asian Indians in America /
John Y. Fenton.
        p. cm.
    Bibliography: p.
    Includes index.
    ISBN 0-275-92676-1 (alk. paper)
    1. East Indian Americans—Religion. 2. East Indian Americans—
Cultural assimilation. 3. United States—Religion—1960—
I. Title.
BL2525.F46   1988
306'.6'089914110—dc19   88-15561

Library of Congress Catalog Card Number: 88-15561
ISBN: 0-275-92676-1

First published in 1988

Praeger Publishers, One Madison Avenue, New York, NY 10010
A division of Greenwood Press, Inc.

Printed in the United States of America

∞

The paper used in this book complies with the
Permanent Paper Standard issued by the National
Information Standards Organization (Z39.48-1984).

10 9 8 7 6 5 4 3 2 1

Contents

Tables

Introduction

The transplantation of Indian immigrant religious traditions to American soil was not deliberately planned. In the wave of immigration that began after 1965, Indians came to the United States for many purposes, but religion was seldom the primary reason.

Many Indian immigrants were not particularly religious when they arrived, and selected as they were by U. S. immigration regulations, most were secular, urban, modern, and technologically educated. The rudimentary religious observances that characterized the behavior of many before immigration continued in America. Others worshipped in the personal and familial ways to which they were accustomed in India but usually did not become concerned about preserving their cultures or their religious traditions until they had been in America for some years and had achieved an acceptable degree of financial security.

Oscar Handlin used the metaphor of "transplantation" to describe the experience of pre-World War II European immigrants to America:

> The immigrants lived in crisis because they were uprooted. In transplantation, while the old roots were sundered, before the new were established, the immigrants existed in an extreme

situation.   The shock, and the effects
of the shock, persisted for many years;
and their influence reached down to
generations which themselves never paid
the cost of crossing (Handlin 1951, p.
6).

According to Handlin, religion played a
crucial role in coping with the crisis caused by
the immigrants' "uprooting" from European
cultures.

Become immigrants and arrived in
America, peasants and dissenters
therefore alike struggled to reconstruct
their churches. In the manner of doing,
there were differences among the various
groups. But the problem of all was the
same: how to transplant a way of
religious life to a new environment
(Handlin 1951, p. 124).

Becker recently agreed that religion was indi-
spensable for European immigrants in America:

This experience was traumatic to at
least some degree for virtually all
immigrants--an uprooting from one's
hometown, kinfolk, the familiar round of
existence. It engendered loneliness, a
sense of loss, fear of the new and
unknown. Under these conditions, people
turned to their religion for comfort
and guidance. . . . Thus the migratory
experience helped place religion firmly
at the center of the immigrants' life, a
pattern that often endured well beyond
the immigrant generation (Becker 1988,
p. 1479).

However, for many of the Asian Indians who
arrived in the late 1960s and 1970s, religion
became of great importance only after a time lag
of ten to twenty years. And "how to transplant a
way of religious life to a new environment" is
still not "the problem of all." Religion is, of
course, one of the ways, an important one, in
which Indian immigrants maintain continuity with

their home culture. Some Indians say that they are more religious in America than they were in India, and being religious here is a much more consciously deliberate behavior than it would have been for them in India. But religion is less central in the adaptive strategy of many Indian immigrants than it was for the European immigrants in an era before "secularity" had eroded reliance on traditional religious orientations.

Most Indians did not come to stay but year after year, they did not return home. Eventually, they exchanged the mentality of sojourners making money for the time being for that of permanent residents. As the years passed and as children born in America came to maturity as Indian Americans, immigrants discovered that they had already put down new roots. Religious activity then began to change from a habitual, personal, and familial exercise into a conscious, deliberate effort. The beginnings of a second change in mentality also appeared as the Indian population took the first steps toward forming an Indian community. Accompanying this change, transplanting religious traditions moved toward the center of immigrant community concerns and religion is likely to become even more central over the next twenty years.

The title of Hugh Tinker's 1977 study of overseas Indians, The Banyan Tree, suggests the strong connections that often continue between overseas Indian cultures and their home culture. It also highlights the efforts overseas Indians often make to replicate the parent tree with satellite trunks, even when they are in quite different host societies.

The metaphor of "transplantation" suggests that shoots are taken from the parent tree, transported a considerable distance, and planted in new, often quite dissimilar, soils. Conditions in the new locations have much to do with how the "shoots" fare, and local growth can vary significantly from the original. How much of their cultures can and must be imported cannot be determined a priori. The transplantation process always involves a selection that never results in a complete duplication of the old-country form. In this respect Indians are no different from any other immigrants.

> Carrying their beliefs with them to America, the immigrants attempted to recreate their communal life of the Old World by implanting their traditional religion in America....But the immigrants' religion transcended their reconstruction of the ritual and institutional forms of the Old World faith (Miller and Marzik 1977, p. xv.).

As generations pass, the Indian religions transplanted into American cultural soil should look more and more like uniquely American variations of the parenting religious tradition. Although they can be expected to stress continuity with their origins, they will, inevitably, become native.

Modern Indian emigration to other countries has ancient precedents. The presence of numbers of Hindus and Buddhists was noted with frequency, for example, in the ancient Egyptian and Roman empires (Basham 1959, pp. 228-31; Thapar 1966, pp. 109-19). Buddhist religious traditions were exported from India to Sri Lanka, southeast Asia, and China by the beginning of the Christian era, and by the seventh century, to Korea and Japan. Somewhat more recently, Indian forms of Islam spread through southeast Asia from the fifteenth century.

The modern Indian diaspora began after 1835, when slavery was outlawed in the British empire. During the second half of the nineteenth century, several hundred thousand Indians traveled to the colonies of the empire as indentured workers to meet the new demand for manual labor, and large numbers remained overseas permanently. Other Indians paid their own way to the colonies to find employment in business or professional capacities (Tinker 1977). By 1980 Indians domiciled outside of India totaled approximately 14 million (Tandon and Raphael 1984, p. 3), but they constituted a majority of the local population only in Fiji and Mauritius. Indians formed large minorities in Trinidad and Guyana but in other countries they were generally less than 3 percent of the population. While the largest number of overseas Indians in 1980 was, as might be expected, in Asia (over 7 million), Africa had over 1.6 million, all of the Americas together had over 1.5 million, and there were over 800,000 Indians in Europe (Tandon and Raphael 1984, p. 2).

Indian immigrants are one of several new immigrant populations from Asia in America, and they are not the largest. Although Asians will remain a minority in America for the foreseeable future, their presence is already having a significant impact on the American religious scene. The religious situation in America has been fundamentally altered. American religion will never again be quite so completely dominated by the Christian and Jewish religious traditions as it has been in the past.

This study is focused on the religious traditions of Asian Indians of the Atlanta, Georgia, metropolitan area during the period from 1979 to 1988. The analysis includes an interpretation of Asian Indian religions in America to provide both a setting for the study and to contrast the transplantation of Indian religious traditions in Atlanta with urban areas that have much larger Indian populations. The primary data for the research consists of ninety-five open-ended interviews, extended participant observation on more than one hundred occasions, and analysis of 291 responses to a questionnaire administered during 1984 and 1985. Interviews and participant observation provided the basic evidence for this study. Responses to the questionnaire were used to give a broader empirical base and as a check for reliability of interviews.

Individuals were selected for interviews to ensure representativeness for the major gender, age, country and regional origin, religious, and organizational divisions and categories within the Indian population. Participant observation was employed as a research tool for major and minor gatherings among Indians in the Atlanta area spread over a nine-year period. The quality and quantity of information gathered in this fashion is reliable and representative for the Indian population, even though more information was collected about Hindus than about any other religious group.

Administration of the questionnaire presented special problems. Return rates for questionnaires given to immigrants in America from all countries are notoriously so low as to be without statisti-

cal value. A mailed survey of Indians in Chicago
by Elkhanialy and Nicholas (1976) had a very low
percentage of returns as did a 1984 study of
Indians in Atlanta by Rice, Kumar, and Taliaver.
Since a random sample was not feasible, I decided
to obtain a large, balanced, representative sample
instead. I administered the survey personally at
social and religious meetings of the Indian population until an adequate social base was obtained.
The survey broadens the data base of the research
and it is, I believe, a reliable indicator.
    The population that was surveyed with the
questionnaire has particular characteristics that
make it more reliable as a measure for some segments of the general Indian population of Atlanta
than for other segments. First of all, the survey
population is composed of first-generation immigrants who support the largest Indian organization and who attend meetings of Indian groups.
Second, the people who take part in these groups
are more active in Indian community affairs, and
they tend to be more affluent and better educated
than average. They have typically been in America
somewhat longer than average, and they are more
likely to be U.S. citizens than the Indian population as a whole.   The sample is probably somewhat
more religious than the average for the whole
Indian population, and because of the large proportion of Hindus and persons from Hindu backgrounds in the survey, the responses are much more
reliable for indicating <u>Hindu</u> attitudes and practices than they are for adherents of the other
Indian religious traditions.   Hindus   who
emigrated from India are also better represented
in the sample than Hindus of Indian extraction who
derive from other countries, such as Trinidad,
Fiji, or Guyana. Finally, the sample under represents the under employed and Indians below the
poverty line.
    The primary questions to be addressed in suc-
cessive chapters of the book are as follows:
    1. Who are the new Indian immigrants and what
is their situation in America? Why did they come?
How and to what extent have they fitted themselves
into the patterns of American culture?
    2. To what extent are Indian immigrants
religious? What does it mean when Indians who
admit that they perform daily individual worship

say that they are not religious? How do Indians express their religiosity individually and within families? What differences are there in the individual practices among the different Indian religious traditions?

3. For what reasons and to what extent do Indian immigrants participate in group worship? How do groups of immigrants carry on the Indian religious traditions? What is the role of religion in Indian ethnicity and in regional and pan-Indian institutions? To what extent is Indian religion divisive? On what bases have Indians been able to unite?

4. What meaning do temples and mosques have, and what functions do they serve for the Indian immigrants? Why are temples and mosques being set up now? Why is there more than one Hindu temple? To what extent is a plurality of temples divisive?

5. How do the expectations of Indian parents mesh with the desires of their children? Are Indian parents transmitting the religious traditions successfully? Do the children want to and are they likely to perpetuate the religious traditions? Are there significant differences between the first wave of Indian children and the next wave now entering adolescence? What is the future for Indian immigrant religious traditions in Atlanta and America?

TRANSPLANTING RELIGIOUS TRADITIONS

1
Asian Indians in America and Atlanta

There have been two waves of Asian Indian immigration to America. The history of the first, which ran from the turn of the twentieth century to the mid-1920s,[1] contrasts sharply with the second, which began after 1965 and is still under way. Few of the Indians who immigrated during the first period intended to remain permanently, and hardly any had special skills to offer. Further, hostile Americans of European extraction subjected Asians to racial discrimination, blocked off their access to economic advancement, restricted immigration severely, and eventually denied entry for Indians completely. These conditions made it very difficult for Asian Indians to sustain themselves and their culture. An account of the fate of Indian religious traditions under these circumstances is given briefly in the first part of this chapter.

The principal subject of this book is the successful transplantation of religious traditions from India to America that is now in progress. Indian immigrants in the second wave are in most ways much better prepared to succeed in America: They are highly educated, they come during a period of economic expansion, and American society is, for the most part, no longer hostile to their participation. The history of Indian immigrants during the current wave is predominantly a success story in which the religious traditions they brought with them are beginning to flourish.

EARLY TWENTIETH-CENTURY INDIAN IMMIGRATION TO AMERICA

Just under 7,000 Asian Indians immigrated during the first twenty years of this century. More than three quarters emigrated from northwest India, primarily from the Punjab, and perhaps 90 percent of the Punjabis were Sikhs. Almost all of the Punjabis obtained work as manual laborers, first in Canada and subsequently on the West Coast of the United States. Better educated professionals and businessmen from various parts of India, mostly Hindu and Muslim, settled in smaller numbers in San Francisco and Los Angeles, in New York City, and in the Mid West. There was also an annual average of 125 Indians, including students, who were in the United States on temporary visas from 1908 to 1920 (La Brack 1980, p. 67).

The Indians of rural California, predominantly Sikhs of the Jat (farmer) caste, took work as laborers in farming areas, wintering in such towns as Yuba City and Stockton in northern California and El Centro in the extreme south, and working during the growing season in the fields of the Imperial, San Joaquin, and Sacramento valleys. Most of these young men came just to earn money to send back to their families in India, and they expected to return home eventually. By 1920 some had accumulated enough money to lease or buy small farms. The majority did return to India, but most who remained became financially independent, and some became financially successful.

In the absence of Indian women and of the extended family structures that are so important in Punjabi culture, agricultural work "gangs" in California took on some features of substitute families. Gang members worked and lived together, saved collectively, and took responsibility for each other. Even after ten or fifteen years, when the men were no longer employed in work teams, relationships of mutual help and responsibility were often transferred to Indian cooperatives and businesses (La Brack 1985, pp. 101-10).

Although the much larger immigrant populations of Chinese and Japanese on the West Coast bore the brunt of racial prejudice, white American fear of the "Yellow Peril" made the lives of Indians precarious. After 1906 Indians were barred from U.S. citizenship on the grounds that they were non white, a decision that was confirmed by the decision of the U.S. Supreme Court in the Thind case of 1923. Uncertainty about the legal right of Indians to own land also made direct ownership of farms by Indians in California difficult. Canada blocked all future Asian Indian immigration in 1908, and the United States followed suit in 1917. On the West Coast Asians were excluded from private clubs, denied service in restaurants and hotels, and were often prevented from purchasing residential property (Jensen 1980, p. 298).

Indian political refugees in California organized the Ghadar (Revolution) party in 1914 to protest against racial discrimination in America and to agitate for the independence of India. Indians linked their difficulties in the alien social environment of California to the struggle for independence in India: Fighting against British rule was a way of maintaining a sense of identity and personal integrity in the face of prejudice and uncertain legal status in America (Juergensmeyer 1979). Although the revolutionary tactics proposed by Ghadar did not meet the approval of all Indian supporters, the party did help to unite Indians from different regions and religious traditions in the early years of immigration. After vigorous pressure from the U.S. government and prosecution of "revolutionaries" in 1917 after the outbreak of World War I, the Ghadar party was severely weakened.[2]

Agricultural work teams and the Ghadar party were important social institutions for Indians in California, but the institution of greatest importance for cultural survival was the (Sikh) Khalsa Diwan Society. Founded in 1910, the society built its first gurudwara (gateway of the "guru" or "teacher"), a place for worship, in Stockton, California, in 1915.

The Sikh religious tradition, which derives from its founding teacher, Guru Nanak (1469-1538), is largely an expression of Punjabi people and their culture. "Sikhs" are "disciples" of their spiritual guides, the ten gurus from Nanak to Gobind Singh (1666-1708). Although Sikh religiosity incorporates elements from both Hindu and Muslim devotional traditions, Sikhism developed its own unique religious structure as one of the major world religious traditions. Sikh spirituality is an intensely meditational and devotional worship of God without the use of images. Access to God is possible under the guidance and inspiration of the <u>Adi Granth Sahib</u>, a compilation of the teachings of the gurus, which serves as the spiritual authority in the stead of a living guru. Family and group worship center on reverence for the <u>Granth</u>, recitation of passages from the <u>Granth</u>, and the singing of <u>kirtan</u> (hymns), followed by a common meal that celebrates community solidarity and repudiates caste distinctions.

Guru Gobind Singh organized believers into the <u>Khalsa</u> (the community of the pure). Men belonging to the Khalsa take "Singh" (lion) as one of their names, while women take the name "Kaur" (princess). Men of the Khalsa are obligated to observe the five k's (<u>panch kaka</u>): unshorn hair (<u>kesh)</u> on the face and head, with the head hair usually covered by a turban; the wearing of a short dagger (<u>kirpan)</u>; khaki shorts (<u>kacch)</u>; a steel bracelet (<u>kara)</u>; and a comb (<u>kangha)</u>. Sikh men who observe the 5 k's are referred to as <u>keshadaris</u> (long-haired) while those who do not are called <u>sahajadaris</u> (those who are clean-shaven). The Sikh faith emphasizes this-worldly service and strong community rather than asceticism or withdrawal from the world. Sikhs are militant in defense of the faith and the Khalsa, and, in their many communities outside India, have been resistant to cultural assimilation.

The Stockton gurudwara was a place for regular worship and daily reading of the <u>Granth</u>. It was also a setting for the celebration of the major festivals of the year, for continuous readings of the <u>Granth</u> from cover to cover (a ritual called <u>akhand path</u>, "unbroken prayer"), for seven-day readings of the entire <u>Granth</u> (<u>saptah path</u>), "seven prayer"), and for the performance of weddings, initiations, and funerals. The gurudwara provided a sense of cohesion for the Sikh and the wider Indian population as well (La Brack 1980, pp. 110-17).

In Sikh tradition no priesthood is needed to mediate between human beings and God. In practice, however, congregations in India generally employ a granthi (a professional reader of the Granth). Since no granthis were available in America, the Stockton gurudwara elected granthis from among their own number, rotating the office from one person to another. The quality and traditional character of worship varied according to the abilities and inclinations of the person chosen. Because the Sikh population in California was scattered, Sikhs living far away from Stockton usually attended the gurudwara only for the major religious festivals of the year. As a partial accommodation to American cultural pressures, most male Sikhs had discontinued displaying some or all of the five k's by the 1920s.

So few Indian women immigrated to America before 1946 that some Punjabi men married non-Indian women. In southern California most of these women were Mexican-American, and they were Roman Catholic.[3] Since they could not understand Gurmukhi (the language of the Granth) or Punjabi, non-Indian spouses could not participate to any great extent in Sikh religious tradition. The children of these interethnic marriages were even less involved, and if they were religious, the children tended toward the religious faith of their mothers rather than the Sikh tradition of their fathers (Leonard 1986).

Between 1920 and 1940 about 5,400 additional legal and illegal immigrants were added to the Indian population, but overall, the population decreased because 4,500 Indians returned to India. Some had always been sojourners with the intention of remaining only long enough to earn money. Others went to India participate in independence movements. But many other Indians found life in America too difficult. By the early 1940s the Indian population in America dropped to roughly 2,400, about 1,400 of whom lived in California. By 1946 the Indian American population had decreased to less than 1,500 persons. The cultural and religious traditions of Sikhs in California fell into decline.

In the period prior to the independence of

India (1947) relations between Hindus and Sikhs in
the Punjab were generally close. In fact, it was
not uncommon for families in the Punjab to have
both Sikh and Hindu members. They were included
in the Sikh community in Stockton, and for a
generation or more, Muslims and Hindus attended
social and religious functions at the gurudwara.

In 1917 Muslims, who made up about one third
of the pre-World War I Indian immigrants in California (Jacoby 1956, p. 13), formed the Muslim
Association in Sacramento. The purpose of the
association was as much social as religious. A
Mosque Association was only established in 1944.
Outside California, in cities such as Detroit,
Indian Muslims joined Muslims from other countries
to establish mosques.

The few hundred Hindus in California came from
different regions of India, had good educational
backgrounds, and tended to live in urban areas.
Before the 1950s most of their organizations, such
as the pan-Indian Hindustani Welfare Society in
southern California, were temporary. Hindus performed puja [worship, literally, "doing honor"] in
their homes occasionally, and there was a small
temple in San Francisco and one in Los Angeles.
While some Hindus made connections with the
Vedanta Society in California, others became Uni-
tarians. The few Hindus located outside California were scattered across urban America.

Due to a combination of political pressure
from various American and Indian American lobbying
groups and the need for the United States to have
good relations with independent India, an annual
immigration quota of 100 persons for Indian immigration was secured in 1946 that made Indians
eligible for naturalization. Although only 6,000
new Indian immigrants were admitted during the
subsequent twenty years, the quota had symbolic
and actual value for Indians in America: Brides
could be obtained from India, families could be
reconstituted, travel home to India was once
again possible, and American land could be owned
with a clear legal title. Nine years after the
new legislation an Indian American was even elected to the U. S. Congress.[4]

The independence of India and the resumption
of Indian immigration together with the increasing
financial success among Sikh cling-peach orchard

farmers in northern California helped to regen-
erate Sikh religious activity in a modest way
after World War II (La Brack 1980, pp. 184-201).
The center of Sikh population shifted away from
Stockton to the Yuba City/Maryville area, where
the India Society of Yuba and Sutter Counties was
organized in 1947. Sikhs in the Imperial Valley
bought an abandoned Buddhist temple in El Centro
in 1948 to use as a gurudwara.

The traditional conservatism of the new immigrants helped to revive orthodox Sikh practices,
including the display of the five k's among men.
Tension developed, however, between long-term
residents in the partially accommodated Sikh
tradition in California and the newcomers with
their Punjabi village traditions. As the newer
immigrants began to obtain leadership roles, the
gurudwaras in California became more traditional
and attendance became almost exclusively Sikh. The
wives and children of mixed marriages in effect
were excluded from participation.

The partition of India into Muslim (Pakistan)
and non Muslim nations (India) reawakened dormant
religious divisions within the Indian population
in California. The Mosque Association founded in
1944 became a place of worship that attracted
Muslims from other countries. And although most
Indian Muslims in California derived from the
section of the Punjab that became part of India,
their identification with international Islam
increased their social distance from other
Indians. Hindus started organizations to celebrate holidays, to entertain, and to facilitate
meeting other Hindus in the 1950s, but religious
functions in these associations were incidental.

The immigration of Asian Indians to the United
States before 1946 occurred under conditions that
made a stable long-range transplantation of religious traditions virtually impossible. Except for
rural areas of California, Indian immigrants were
too scattered across urban centers of California,
the Mid west, and New York to be able to develop
sustainable religious institutions. Indians were
the objects of racial discrimination. Their total
numbers were never very great, and very few women
were included. Most of the immigrants in rural
California were poorly educated and initially
spoke poor English. Sikhs did develop a religious

center in northern California, but by the 1940s the population was nearly depleted.

After the introduction of immigration quotas and the restoration of naturalization rights in 1946, the Sikh tradition began to be reinvigorated. After 1965 most of the difficult conditions of the earlier period were corrected or improved, and the chances for successful transplantation of religion were much higher. In the ten years following 1965 Sikh immigrants in the Yuba City/Maryville area not only built a new gurudwara, but were able to reconstruct a stable facsimile of Punjabi-village extended-family structures with endogamous marriages (La Brack 1980, pp. 272-91). Under new conditions the Sikh religious community of northern California became self-sustaining and vigorous.

The 1987 Indian population of Yuba City/Maryville, about 99 percent Sikh, was estimated to be 9,000 (Vora 1987), and in 1986 there were three gurudwaras in the area. There were also sizable Sikh communities and gurudwaras in the Los Angeles and San Francisco Bay areas (La Brack 1986).

THE NEW INDIAN IMMIGRANTS

Immigration policy changed for many reasons. To many Americans, it seemed consistent with the ideology of America as the leader of the "free world" to treat all nations with a more even hand. Liberalized immigration regulations were also consonant with more open American attitudes toward foreigners and a growing shift from the melting pot image of American society to greater tolerance for cultural pluralism and ethnic diversity. After World War II the United States played a role of diplomacy of much broader international scope, which was given urgency by American cold-war rivalry with the Soviet Union. A more open and less racially based policy of immigration was part of a greater American cooperation with the countries of Asia required to keep them free of Soviet influence. Preferential admissions also attracted highly trained immigrants who were assets in the American economy.

The Hart-Celler Act of 1965 abolished the national-origins quota system and halted the exclusion of people from the Asia-Pacific Triangle. The eastern hemisphere of the world was allowed 170,000 immigrants annually with a limit of 20,000 for each country. Within the quota preferential treatment was given to immediate family members and highly trained professionals, such as engineers, physicians, scientists, professors, teachers, and businessmen. The Western Hemisphere Act of 1976 extended the new system to western hemisphere nations.

Currently, in 1988, the total annual quota is 270,000 persons, with a maximum of 20,000 admissions from any one country. Beyond the quota limits admissions are possible for spouses, parents, and unmarried children of U.S. citizens under age twenty-one. Because of the large number of refugees admitted after the Vietnam War, about 60 percent of all Asian immigrants were admitted outside the quota limitation by 1981. Fifty-two percent of European immigrants and 28 percent of South American immigrants were also brought in beyond the quota limitations (Gardner, Robey, and Smith 1985, p. 9).

The percentage of immigrants to the United States who came from Asian countries increased dramatically after 1965. Whereas immigrants of European birth were 58 percent of all immigrants and Asians constituted only 5 percent for the period from 1931 to 1960, the European contribution had dropped to 19 percent and Asian immigrants had increased to 34 percent for the period from 1970 to 1979. For the years 1980 to 1984 the Asian influx had grown to 48 percent, while the European portion had shrunk to 12 percent (Gardner, Robey, and Smith 1985, p. 2).

The Time and Size of the Immigration

Immigration since 1965 has occurred under conditions very different from the first wave. The total numbers are now over half a million, and especially in urban areas, the Indian population is large enough to develop institutions capable of maintaining Indian cultures and religions. The immigrant population is composed of roughly equal numbers of males and females so that it is possible to have normal nuclear families. Travel to and from India is almost routine, and new immigrants arrive each year, so that immigrant culture is continuously replenished from the home culture.

The 1980 U.S. Census figures for the Asian population of the United States are given in Table 1. The six largest immigration groups are listed in order of decreasing size.

Table 1

Asian American Population, 1980 U.S. Census

National Origin	Number of persons
Chinese	812,178
Filipino	781,894
Japanese	716,331
Asian Indian	387,223
Korean	357,393
Vietnamese	245,025
Total Asians	3,300,044

Source: 1980 U. S. Census, PC 80-1-C1, Table 160.

The Population Reference Bureau (Gardner, Robey, and Smith 1985) estimated that in September 1985 the Asian Indian population of the United States was 525,600 (an increase of 35.7 percent above the 1980 figure) out of a total Asian American population of 5,147,900. The same bureau also projected (assuming no changes in immigration laws) that the Asian Indian population would be 1,006,305 (160 percent above the 1980 figure) out of a total Asian American population of 9,850,364 in A.D. 2000. In 1980 Asian Indians were the fourth largest Asian American population. Filipinos will be the largest Asian immigrant group in A.D. 2000, while Asian Indians are forecasted to drop to fifth position behind Koreans. From being 1.5 percent of the total U.S. population in 1980, Asian immigrants will increase only to 4 percent by A.D. 2000 (Gardner, Robey, and Smith 1985, pp. 38, 5, 37).

As Table 2 shows, 70.4 percent of the Asian Indians counted in the 1980 U.S. Census were foreign-born and 29.6 percent were born in the United States. With an Asian Indian population of 4,725, Georgia had a higher percentage (37.5 percent) of native-born Indians than the nation as a whole and a smaller percentage of Asian Indians who were foreign-born, but not born in India (10.9 percent), than the country as a whole (17.2 percent). In Atlanta a larger proportion of the foreign-born Indian population came directly from India than for either the state of Georgia or for the country as a whole. If one were to project the Atlanta Indian population for 1988 along the same parameters as those used by the Population Reference Bureau for a national total for 1985, one would expect the figure to be about 3,700 persons. Local Indians believe the correct number to be about 5,000 currently.

India was the country of origin for 87.9 percent of respondents to my questionnaire administered in Atlanta from 1984 to 1985. The remaining 12.1 percent emigrated from eleven different countries, the United Kingdom and Canada being the most frequent countries of origin. Others emigrated from Zambia, Trinidad, South Africa, Pakistan, Bangladesh, Kenya, Uganda, West Germany, Tanzania, and Malayasia.

Immigrants from India came predominantly from urban areas and, like most recent immigrants to America, they now live overwhelmingly in urban areas. Ninety-two percent of the six largest Asian immigrant groups (Japanese, Chinese, Filipino, Korean, Asian Indian, and Vietnamese) live in standard metropolitan statistical areas (Gardner, Robey, and Smith 1985, p. 12). U.S. Census figures for 1980 show that the largest number of Asian Indians (84,000) was concentrated in the New York City metropolitan area (with 24,000 living in

Table 2

Asian Indian Population and Nativity

by Country, State, and City

Nativity	United States	Georgia	Atlanta, SMSA*
Born in India			
	206,087 (53.2%)	2438 (51.6%)	1533 (60.5%)
Foreign-born, not born in India			
	66,530 (17.2%)	517 (10.0%)	(not reported)
Native-born			
	114,606 (29.6%)	1770 (37.5%)	(not reported)
Total:			
	387,223	4725	2533

Source: 1980 U.S. Census, PC 80-1-C1, Table 161; PC 80-1-C12, Table 94; PC 80-1-D12, Table 195.

Note: * The Atlanta Standard Metropolitan Statistical Area includes fourteen counties.

Queens). California had 60,000 Indian residents
(primarily in Los Angeles and San Francisco),
while there were 34,000 in Chicago and more than
10,000 each in Washington, D.C., Detroit, Philadelphia, and Houston. Twelve other cities had
Asian Indian populations between 2,500 and 6,000.
The 2,533 Asian Indians in the Atlanta metropolitan area in 1980 constituted 21.2 percent of the
11,825 Asian immigrants in Atlanta and .12 percent
of the total Atlanta population. Outside Atlanta
in Georgia there were 361 Asian Indians in Augusta, 163 in Columbus, 145 in Macon, and 153 in
Savannah.   Charlotte, North Carolina, had over
1,400 Asian Indians and there were 353 in
Chattanooga, Tennessee. There were Asian Indian
populations exceeding 500 persons in Birmingham,
Alabama; Columbia and Greenville, South Carolina;
and Memphis, Tennessee.

    Table 3 gives the 1980 U.S. Census estimates
(based on a sample) for the period of immigration
of Asian Indians from India. The dramatic increase nationally after 1965 is readily apparent.
The percentage increase in Georgia and Atlanta
starts to match the national percentage increase
only with the 1970-1974 figures.

    In 1980 almost half (43.7 percent) of the
Asian Indians born in India had been in America
five years or less, 33.1 percent had lived here
for six to ten years, and 14.8 percent for ten to
fifteen years. Only 8.4 percent had been in the
United States for more than fifteen years.   For
Atlanta the figures are similar: 43 percent in
America for one to five years, 34.5 percent for
six to ten years, 12.2 percent for ten to fifteen
years, and 10.2 percent for more than fifteen
years.

Table 3

Period of Immigration of Asian Indians Born in

India in the United States, Georgia and Atlanta

Period	Number of persons					
	United States		Georgia		Atlanta SMSA	
		percent increase		percent increase		percent increase
Before 1950	2,772		17		11	
1950–1959	5,268		67		46	
1960–1964	9,169		133		100	
1965–1969	30,545	333%	304	228%	187	187%
1970–1974	68,201	223%	805	265%	529	282%
1975–1980	90,132	132%	1,112	138%	660	125%
	206,087		2,438		1,533	

Source: 1980 U. S. Census, PC 80-1-D1-A, Table 254; PC 80-1-D12, Table 195.

A More Receptive America

Indians arriving in America in the 1950s and early 1960s were sometimes the object of racial prejudice. Although there seems to have been no fixed pattern, Indians in the southern states were sometimes classified as non whites and segregated like American blacks. As a second-generation Indian American reported:

> My parents came here when there was still that era when you had to go to the back of the bus. You had to go to separate bathrooms. . . . When my dad entered a bus, the driver told him to go to the back. He then got off the bus. But that kind of stuff [makes you] think, where do you belong in this society?

As a counter example, I know of a case during the 1950s in which seminary students in Dallas, Texas, sneaked an American black into the white section of a segregated movie theater by putting a turban on his head and passing him off as an Indian. There were so few Indians in the South that although they were perceived to be different, they were often racially unclassified. One male immigrant published an account of being refused food at a downtown Atlanta lunch counter in the early 1960s:

> "No, we don't serve coloreds," says the waitress. You demand to see the manager. He is all apologies; the waitress did not know we were foreigners. The dinner will be on the house, he says. Who cares, you respond. And you and your friends walk off in righteous indignation (Chawla 1981).

An Opened Society

The Civil Rights Act of 1965 was passed in the same year as the Hart-Cellar Act, so that by far the great majority of Indian immigrants enjoyed the benefits of its provisions on their arrival, and especially since affirmative action programs have been put in place, they have rarely been subjected to blatant forms of racial discrimination. Discrimination that does occur is generally more subtle, and some cases of purported discrimination may be misperceptions by Indians due to differences in cultural practices. One woman opined:

> If there are two of us applying for a job and there are two of us who are equally intelligent, who have equally good backgrounds, I always feel it would be the local American who would get a preference because he had something going more than I had, and that is the culture, their physical appearance. Their ability to communicate with people will always be stronger, so I feel I always have got to prove a little bit extra to make up for those points. I have always to be a little bit higher and do something a little bit extra to get that position.

Very few of the Indians with whom I talked reported any clear - cut discrimination they had experienced because they were Indian, but many reported incidents that were ambiguous--apparent slights that may have been due to racial discrimination. Consistent vandalism at Hindu temple sites, such as in Pittsburgh, may or may not be racially or religiously motivated. "Dot Busters" attacking Indians in Jersey City and the murder of an Indian in Hoboken, New Jersey, (Perry 1987a, 1987b; Hudson 1987) may be isolated occurrences. Discrimination suits have occasionally been reported in Indian immigrant newspapers, especially in the last few years.[6]

Discrimination against Indians may at times be more a question of life-style and consumption habits than an ethnic issue. The non drinker and non partying person, for example, is sometimes at a disadvantage in competing for high-rank positions in large corporations. As the wife of one middle-rank executive in a large corporation reported,

. . . possibly my husband has reached
the highest he can go. . . . There is no
hiring discrimination. . . . The only
problems we've had are when, say, like a
group from the office is going out to
eat or something, or for a party. We are
the only misfits for the simple reason
that we don't choose to drink [alcohol]
or eat. . . . Some other Indians would
not have that problem because they do
[drink].

Indian businessmen sometimes have cause for complaint. As one businessman said in 1981:

To develop some sort of a normal
business relation for an American--it
would take about one year. It takes
me two years. . . . I do understand
that being the first-generation Indian
in this country I am going to come to
face with that problem over and over
again. . . . It's in a very subtle form.
It is discrimination from two sides.
It's not from whites only. I get it
also from blacks. We are neither black
nor white, so you stand somewhere in
between, and, well, also it's a blessing
in disguise so you can expect both
situations. . . . Once you start knowing
people and once you go out for lunch one
or two times, then you can talk to them
freely and openly. Otherwise, it would
be difficult. There is a certain
prejudice against me, for example, in
the city of Atlanta, when a black
contractor is competing against me.

On the other hand, several Indian informants suggested that many Indians repress evidence of discrimination because they do not want to feel insecure in America. For example, one Indian told me that the movie actor Peter Sellers's comic caricature of Indians was actually a takeoff on Pakistanis. Even if this were true, most Americans would not know the difference between Pakistanis and Indians.

This man's dissatisfaction with American news media is fairly general among Indian immigrants:

> Most of the times when there have been articles on any sort of doings in India, they are negative type. I wish they would open up a little more and try to go into a little more length than how India is poverty and in India people have starvation. This is not the only news, and that's what they show, or Hare Krishna. I've heard lot of derogatory remarks, all negative remarks from my [American] colleagues about Rajneesh and they don't think it's right. And I don't blame them too because, a lot of times, personally, I don't think this is done the right way. . . . The point is that we have a lot of good things too. . . . Most of the American people, including those living in Atlanta, and everybody else learn from what they see on TV and what they read in newspapers. So their impression is people asking you, "Did you ever see a car before you came to this country?" Or things like, "Did you ever have electricity or inside plumbing?" You know, lots of those things.

Some Indian Muslims are concerned that American media bias against Middle Eastern Muslims (cf. Haddad and Lummis 1987, pp. 158-64) may affect them negatively:

> Consciously or unconsciously, there has been so much propaganda in the world that downplays the good in Islam and up-plays the bad in it. . . . So, for example, when a person in Italy hijacks a plane, . . . he is called a Japanese guy or a Greek guy. But if the person is from Lebanon, for example, he is called a Muslim. To me, it is equating a bad act with a religion rather than a bad act with a person of a particular national origin. . . . I get mad at the news media who report on Islam because

> they seem to know nothing about Islam
> intellectually, and they should.

Sikhs have received adverse publicity from accounts of the assassination of Prime Minister Indira Gandhi and the alleged involvement of Sikhs in various terrorist acts, but under the circumstances there is surprisingly little evidence of any general American prejudice against Sikhs. To some degree, Americans appear to immigrants to be just unconcerned:

> Many people, they don't know anything
> about other countries. The main reason
> is they don't need to because they are
> so much self-contained. So they don't
> need to. Whereas foreigners, they know
> more about this country because they see
> this country as more prosperous, more
> elegant, more prominent places to see in
> this country. So they want to learn
> more about other countries.

Racial and religious prejudice against Indians might possibly reemerge under the right conditions, but overall, the American experience of Asian Indians since 1965 has been positive.

Clothey's 1978 Pittsburgh study (1983, p. 167) indicated that about half of the respondents found Americans "friendly" and "respectful" toward Indians. Small fractions (15 percent or less) found Americans ignorant about India, not willing to accept Indians on a personal level that goes beyond professional acceptance, and just over 6 percent reported instances of discrimination against themselves personally. Vempathy (1984) suggested that there are patterns of subtle discrimination against Indians.

Undoubtedly, the Civil Rights Act and its accompanying enforcement mechanisms contribute heavily to the positive reception of Indians by Americans. The civil rights movement and the various black power movements that succeeded it helped Americans in general to become more tolerant, not only of black cultural differences from whites, but also of the cultural differences of other ethnic groups. The opening up of opportunity in American society for blacks helps all nonwhite groups. Indians were prepared to take advantage of the opportunities and have done much better occupationally than blacks. Only 14 percent of blacks hold managerial, professional, or executive positions in America, compared to 48.5 percent of foreign-born Asian Indians (Gardner, Robey, and Smith 1985, p. 31). Indians have also imitated black civil rights movement models, for example, in forming a political action group to represent Indians that was successful in getting an "Asian Indian" ethnic category included in the 1980 U.S. Census (Fisher 1980, pp. 117-33).

Whether or not Asian Indians are a legal minority (Fisher 1980, pp. 128-33), employers often believe that hiring Indians helps to satisfy affirmative action and equal opportunity requirements. Indian women are sometimes hired because they can be counted both as minority and as female. The American women's or feminist movements to some extent have made better jobs available for Indian women, and at least for women in the work force, they probably affect Indian women's conceptions of their social roles.

America and India, 1965-1986

Fluctuating diplomatic relations between the United States and India have not affected immigration laws or rates of immigration and seem to have had no material effects on Indian immigrants in America. Although relations between the two countries were quite good at the beginning of the 1960s, they have subsequently fluctuated. American military support of India's rival, Pakistan, has, for example, been a continual problem for India.

The introduction of Indian "export" religions, such as the Hare Krishnas and Transcendental Meditation, to America began at about the same time as the new immigration. At least for a time these devotion and meditation movements increased young Americans' consciousness of and their positive appreciation of India. It seemed to some young people that Indian religions might have a superior mystical quality that had somehow been lost in the western religious traditions. Coverage of India in the American media has increased markedly in the last few years with films, television series, the 1985-1986 Festival of India programs in the United States, and increased news coverage of momentous as well as tragic events in India.

While secularization in India, particularly in urban areas, is growing, the Hindu and other native Indian religious traditions are in many ways resurgent. After independence, any Indian feelings of religious inferiority to Christianity left over from the colonial period rapidly evap-orated. In fact, Indians are likely to claim that Indian religious traditions are spiritually superior to those of the West and that Indian culture offers a needed antidote to western materialism. India has continued to develop, to urbanize, to modernize, and to westernize during the last twenty years. And although India is unevenly developed, it is not an underdeveloped country. Indian-Americans often feel that the American news media suppress the positive aspects of India. One woman remarked:

> We feel they really don't show India. The India that's shown is always the old population, the poor people in the streets. They show the back of the picture, but never the front too. The front: The number of people that are coming out of the colleges. They're working so hard. They've brought the country from a total agrarian country to the twentieth century.

The Atlanta Situation for Asian Indians

Atlanta seems to be an especially benign loca-tion for Asian Indians. A general impression is conveyed by this man's experience:

> I came as a student. I worked for about three months in Indiana, and my cousin was here. It was summer vacation, and he said, "Come on down over here." And I hadn't seen him for about four or five years. And I came down here and stayed with him. . . here in Atlanta. I liked the city, and he said, "There is a very

good school, Georgia Tech. Why don't you apply for admission?"...I liked the city so much, so I never thought of moving out of it.

The city's ability to work out black and white relations has helped to set up a favorable situation for Indians. There is also an ideological tie between the civil rights movement, especially the Southern Christian Leadership Conference, and the satyagraha movement (literally, "grasping the truth," nonviolent resistance) for Indian independence that was led by Mohandas K. Gandhi. As is well known, Martin Luther King, Jr., borrowed freely from Gandhi's thought and techniques (Dikshit 1975). References to this connection are part of the political rhetoric from local city government, especially under the mayorality of Andrew Young since 1980, and Indians participate in the Martin Luther King, Jr., Center for Non-Violent Social Change's celebration of Gandhi's birthday each August. A special Gandhi room in the Martin Luther King, Jr., Center for Research in Non-Violent Social Change was set aside on Gandhi's birthday in 1983. Indians are, however, sensitive to racial differences and to relative prestige based on race. They usually locate residentially in white rather than black neighborhoods of the city. Many Indian women also use forehead dots, partly to follow Indian customs, but also to prevent being mistaken for members of other ethnic groups.

Native American attitudes toward Indians range from acceptance to nearly complete ignorance. There are no neighborhoods in Atlanta where Indians constitute the majority of the inhabitants, and Indians in Atlanta are not very visible. Probably, Atlantans become most aware of Indians while shopping at the DeKalb Farmers' Market (which carries many imported produce items for the Asian and Central American immigrant market, attracts large numbers of Asian customers, and employs Asian workers).[6]

The American experience of Asian Indian immigrants contrasts sharply with the experience of Asian Indians in Great Britain and Canada. Indian and Pakistani immigrants have frequently been met with hostility and violence in Great Britain

(Bhatti 1980, pp. 51-58; cf. Gilroy 1982). The roughly 250,000 Indians in Canada are concentrated primarily in Vancouver (with a large Sikh population) and the Toronto-Montreal urban corridor. Racist behavior in Canada increased in the 1970s, and violent attacks against Indians and their property were commonplace in 1977-1978 (Haddad 1983, p. 180; Mukherjee 1981). Buchignani, Indra, and Srivastiva (1985, Chapter 12) offered several reasons for Canadian prejudice against South Asians. The primary factor, they suggest, is Canadian ethnocentrism--a high sensitivity to racial and cultural differences from the dominant English and French population reinforced by stereotypes and misperceptions of South Asians. The number of immigrants increased suddenly in the 1970s at the same time that there was an economic downturn and a great increase in competition for jobs. Resentment of immigrants seems to be highest in economically hard times. Ramcharan (1982, p. 90) suggested that Indian immigrants did not fit the ascribed economic status for new immigrants--being trained for middle- and upper-level jobs, they did not start at the bottom as expected and were resented by Canadian-born children of earlier immigrants who had not yet done as well economically. Newspapers gave considerable and often biased coverage of South Asians, while at the same time taking editorial stands against increased immigration. The Canadian federal government also indicated that it considered immigration a problem, and until recently, government agencies have been rather ineffective in redressing complaints of racism and prejudice. Overt racist behavior against South Asians has apparently declined since 1978, but lack of equal access to employment opportunities remains a problem.

Given the twentieth-century history of civil rights problems in the United States, it seems probable that the better situation for Indians in America as compared to Canada is due to the civil rights movement and to resulting equal opportunity legislation, to effective affirmative action programs, and to greater American economic prosperity during the last generation rather than to any greater racial tolerance among Americans as compared to Canadians. However, Asian Indians are also something of an anomaly in American culture with no long-term, clearly demarcated place in the racial and ethnic structure of American society. A businessman testified to the nonrecognition exhibited by some of his customers: "People still call me here and ask me whether I am a Cherokee Indian or what Indian I am. So they don't know about India much." One long-time Indian Canadian woman, now a resident in the United States, put it this way:

> One is less visible in the U.S. as an Indian than in Canada. Because in Canada, if you're Indian, you're seen immediately as East Indian and not as an individual. And you're carrying, even if you are just arrived from Delhi-- you're immediately seen as having this baggage of stereotypes. Whereas here the Indian is exotic. Maybe he is slowly acquiring the baggage, but it hasn't happened yet.

In contrast to Americans, Canadians share, at least to some extent, the heritage of the British Empire, which in the period before Indian independence unambiguously relegated Asian Indians to inferior social status.

A POPULATION PROFILE

Asian Indian immigrants left their homelands for a variety of reasons, but the chance for a higher standard of living was paramount. And because they were for the most part highly trained, technical people, there was every prospect that they would be able to achieve their goals.

Why They Came

Probably the most important reason Indians come to America is the prospect of greater material prosperity combined with better working conditions, enhanced chances of advancement, and a wider range of financial and investment opportunity. One man summed it up this way:

[There was] something inside that says
that, all right, we can go there and get
a better business than what we are doing
here. . . . I would say it's more
economic than anything else. There are
more opportunities in this country, and
once you establish yourself, you have a
better standard of living. . . . What
are considered to be everyday routine
items here--some of them are considered
to be luxuries back home in India.

A Gujarati (from northwest India) offered this
explanation:

One of the reasons why Gujaratis, you
see more emigrating and going to
different countries etc., is--I was
going to say they are the people who
were in business to begin with. Most
Gujaratis are the business people. They
are always betting, in the sense that
they were willing to take risks, going
overseas to Africa. . . . something
inside that will say, all right, we can
go there and get a better business than
what we are doing here. I remember,
say, for example, my father saying that
when I came here, somebody says that
"Your son is going 10,000 miles away.
How do you feel about it?" My father
says, "Well, I came from a small town
called A___ to Bombay for the betterment
of my life. It took more time to reach
from A___ to Bombay in those days than
what it takes from Bombay to New York
now. The distance has really become
short today." He was absolutely in
favor of my coming.

Secondary reasons for immigration include opportunities for additional education and Indian
perceptions of America as a land of freedom and
opportunity.[8] More than 6,000 Indians came to
America and Canada as refugees after they were
expelled from Uganda in 1972 (Nanji 1974, p. 151).
The freedom sought is to some extent a release
from the familial, cultural, caste hierarchical,

and business restraints of Indian society. The "open society" looked like this to one woman:

> I found out that there are a lot more opportunities anywhere whether you are a student, whether you are a worker, whether you sit at home. But there are more opportunities to grow as a person in this country than anywhere. It is better than in my country.

Sometimes, parents came for the sake of the children. A second generation student told me:

> Parents take all responsibility for [the children] and sacrifice for them. My father gave up a potentially much more powerful and prosperous career in India to come to America for our sakes.

A first-generation parent expressed similar concerns for the children:

> My children's education is most important at this time. So we made the move, the biggest move in our life, bringing them to a foreign country. The system of education in this country is marvelous, and I want them to get that benefit. Afterwards, if they want to settle here, I don't have any objections. . . . But me and my wife prefer to go back. I mean, that's how we feel today.

A significant number of the immigrants came originally on student visas but managed to change later to permanent resident status. Of 290 persons responding to my questionnaire survey in Atlanta in 1984 and 1985, 26 percent (mostly men) had been students at the time of immigration.

One former student attributed his coming to Atlanta to sheer chance:

> I closed my eyes, had the map [of the United States] in front of me, put my finger down, and it landed on Georgia. The honest answer! Then, in Georgia you

think of the capital, right? The capital of Georgia is Atlanta. And the technical school under Atlanta was Georgia Tech--and then why Georgia Tech? Let me take another trial. Then Civil War, Underground Atlanta, <u>Gone With the Wind</u>, and Portman, John Portman, building the Peachtree. I am a civil engineer, and I have a bachelor's degree in civil engineering. So this idea of John Portman building the Peachtree Plaza that we read about in the American magazines then. Civil wars, historical background. Honestly! That's how I came. The only other place I had an offer was Denver. But I chose this by the exotic way.

Atlanta has many work opportunities for highly qualified Indians. From 1970 to 1985 the nonfarm job growth rate each year was ahead of the national average, and the Atlanta economy has been healthy even when other sections of the country were in economic recession. Networking also accounts for the move of some Indians to Atlanta. Prospective students contact current students at, for example, the Georgia Institute of Technology.[9] Physicians facilitated the coming of other physicians from the same Indian medical school. A few university professors have also brought in former graduate students. To a certain extent people already here arrange for kin to move to Atlanta. It should be noted that the <u>religious factor</u> plays little or no role in motivating Indians to immigrate to America and none in their moving to Atlanta.

Who They Are

Although it is clear that the majority of Indian immigrants in America are from Hindu backgrounds, reliable figures for their religious affiliation are not available. Using the estimated 1985 Asian Indian population of 525,600 given by Gardner, Robey , and Smith (1985, p. 38) as a base, I will hazard some guesses about the 1985 religious affiliation of the immigrants as

follows: In 1985 about 65 percent   (342,000)   of
the   Indian   immigrants   to America   had   a   Hindu
family   background, and 16 percent (84,000) had   a
Muslim background.   Cole and Sambhi (1978, p. 162)
estimated   a   figure of 100,000   Sikhs   of   Indian
origin in the United States (primarily on the West
Coast)   and   100,000   Sikhs   in   Canada.   Melton
(1987a, p. 744) also gave a high figure of 250,000
Sikhs in America for the mid-1980s.   Jensen (1980,
p. 296) estimated that Sikhs constituted 30 to   40
percent of the Asian Indian population in California.   I estimate much lower, namely,   that   Sikhs
were   10 per cent or less of the   Indian   American
population (52,000 perhaps).   Christians may have
been   as high as 5 percent of the total   (26,000).
The Federation of Jain Associations in North America   ("Ohio Jain Federation" 1987) claimed   25,000
Jains   in North America, but I project   the   lower
figure   for Jains of about 3 percent of the   immigrants   in the United States or 16,000 persons   in
1985.   Naby   (1980) estimated   that   there   were
2,000   Parsis (Zoroastrians) in the United   States
in   the late 1970s, while Lopate (1986)   suggested
7,000   in North America.   An American estimate   of
5,000 would seem apt.   In addition, there are   300
to 400 Jews from India (Pais 1987) , and there may
also be 100 or more Indian Buddhists.
     Except for immediate family members of   people
already   in   America,   the   1965   immigration   law
favored the immigration of the highly skilled   and
highly educated. Highly trained persons in "criti-
cal"   professions   in   short   supply   were   given
preference: engineers,   physicians,   scientists,
professors,   business   men--who were   urban,   educated, and   English   speaking.   It is common   for
Indian immigrants to acquire additional   education
after   arrival in America.   The 1980   U.S.   Census
estimated that 52 percent of Indians over   twenty-
five   years   of   age had four   years   or   more   of
college education, both in the country as a   whole
and   in   Georgia. From the   Indian   population   in
Georgia   72 percent of the men and 34   percent   of
the women had four years or more of college.   The
population   polled by   my Atlanta survey   in   1984
and 1985 had more education than the Census   indicated, with 82.9 percent having at least a college
degree   and   58 percent   having   education   beyond
college.[10]   Because   the   immigration   laws   give

preference to immediate family members of permanent residents, most future immigrants from India and other Asian countries will be brought in on the basis of kinship rather than training. Future immigrants are thus less likely to be high- ly qualified than immigrants of the previous twenty years.

Just over 48 percent of foreign-born Asian Indians in America had jobs as managers, professionals, or executives compared to 24 percent for white Americans and to 23 percent for native-born Asian Indians (However, only 29 per- cent of the native-born were part of the labor force.[11] [Gardner, Robey and Smith 1985, p. 30]). Technical, sales, and administrative support occu- pations accounted for 28 percent of the foreign- born, and 7.8 percent were in service occupations. U.S. Census 1980 occupational figures for foreign- born Asian Indians in Georgia were similar to those for the country as a whole, except that technical, sales, and administrative support jobs were 6.4 percent higher than the national average.

The 1984 to 1985 Atlanta survey showed 15 percent of the Indians in health, 36 percent in applied sciences, 19 percent in business, and 10 percent in educational occupations. Students made up 11.5 percent, and 3.6 percent were "other," unemployed or retired. The 25.9 percent who were students at time of immigration are now employed in health, applied science, business, and educa- tion. These results are in broad agreement with the 1980 Census figures for Georgia, with 47.8 percent of the Indians in managerial and professional occupations and 34.4 percent in tech- nical, sales, and administrative support jobs. Only 26 percent of the survey respondents were students at the time they immigrated. Since the time of entry, 40 percent of the survey respon- dents (including former students) had changed occupations, with the greatest rate of change (59 percent) being from business to other occupations. Most adult women in the survey are also employed. Only 4.3 percent of respondents (all were women) listed themselves as homemakers. The Census for Georgia indicates that 46.7 percent of Indian females sixteen 16 years of age and over were in the work force in 1979.

Very few, if any, religious professionals from

any of the native Indian religious traditions immigrated to America in the first decade after 1965, and very few would have been among the professions favored for admission to the United States. Until quite recently, Indians from these traditions have usually found it necessary to rely on their own nonprofessional resources for religious and ritual leadership. The earliest Hindu temple with a resident full-time priest (in Pittsburgh), for example, was dedicated in 1976. The number of religious professionals is still small but is gradually increasing.

While the 1980 U.S. Census estimated median family income in America in 1979 for the population as a whole to be $19,917, the median family income for Asian Indians was $24,993, better than any of the other large Asian American nationalities (except for the Japanese at $27,354). Asian Indian earnings were well above the median for the entire population, but they were probably below the average income for college graduates in America, especially because in 48.7 percent of the Indian families there were two workers, and in 9.5 percent there were three or more workers. In Indian families with only one worker, median income was $21,784; with two workers, it was $26,928 (see Dutta 1986). In Georgia the Census showed Asian Indian median family income to be higher than all other Asians, including the Japanese.

Financial success has so far eluded some immigrants. People in the survey population on temporary visa, 96 percent of whom had been in America five years or less, had much lower incomes, with 76 percent reporting family incomes under $20,000 per year. The U.S. Census indicated that some 8.6 percent of the Indian families in Georgia (forty-five families) who immigrated between 1970 and 1980 had incomes below the poverty level in 1979. The householder was in the labor force in 57.3 percent of these families in Georgia; in 16.7 percent of the families females were the householders with no husband present. A woman with five children widowed after seven years in America and near poverty level explained her plight:

My husband died, now, it's almost close
to two years. And I have five children.

> And I have to support them and I don't
> have time to go anywhere. . . . I work
> two jobs. . . . In the morning I work
> seven til three in the hospital; come
> back. Three thirty I go back and start
> four o'clock till nine thirty. And I
> don't have time.

Nationally, 7.4 percent of Asian Indian families were below the poverty level. But about three quarters of these families had immigrated during the previous five years. For the white population 7 percent were below the poverty level. Only 4.5 percent of the Indian population were receiving public assistance (excluding social security) compared to 5.5 percent for the native white population. Overall, the national figures show that Asian Indians are doing well financially, especially if one considers that almost half had been in America five years or less at the time of the Census.

Respondents to my Atlanta survey in 1984 and 1985 reported much higher incomes. Fifty two percent reported annual family incomes of $40,000 or more, and 32.8 percent stated their income to be $50,000 or more. Nationally, the Census indicated that only 11.3 percent of Asian Indians earn over $50,000 annually; but in Atlanta 12.4 percent in the survey reported family incomes over $75,000.

ACCULTURATION AND CHANGES IN LIFE-STYLE

Most Asian Indian immigrants to the United States have with comparative ease become part of the skilled American work force. Habits of hard work, strong savings and investment patterns, and business acumen have enabled many who have been in America a decade or more to become financially successful. While respondents to my Atlanta questionnaire had higher family incomes than for the Indian population as a whole, for this group, and presumably for the general Indian population, family income is higher the longer the immigrants have been in America. Questionnaire results are that 91 percent of Atlanta respondents resident in America over fifteen years had an annual family

income of at least $40,000 in 1984 and 1985.
Favorite Indian investments tend to be motels,
general real estate, business, and stocks and
bonds.

According to the Census, 77.5 percent of
Georgia Indians immigrated since 1970. In 1975,
27.2 percent lived in another state with over 40
percent having moved from the northeastern section
of the United States and just under 40 percent
coming from other southern states. Indians who
have been in America for some years tend to change
residences from apartments in central Atlanta to
homes in suburbia. In 1988 these families typically live in very new homes in new developments
outside the interstate perimeter highway.

Most Indians live in nuclear rather than extended families, although the Census for Georgia
reported relatives other than spouses and children
resident in 38.6 percent of Indian households.
Adjusting to the American context is often easier
for people who are in the work force, as this
exchange makes clear:

> Q: Do you miss the kind of neighborhood
> contacts I assume you were accustomed to
> in India?
> Wife: I do.
> Husband: Well, it's actually a big
> city. This is a big city and big cities
> are all the same, every place. . . .
> Wife: . . . But if you are in the
> house. Well, I do not work outside the
> home, so then I find that you get
> lonely. But it has never been
> depressing, never to that extent. No.

Immigrants from countries other than India, such
as this woman who was widowed after immigrating,
sometimes have more negative feelings:

> Everybody had their own business,
> everybody who come there--not like here
> where you just work for somebody. . . .
> I never worked for anybody in my life,
> and just when we came here I start. And
> it was hard in the beginning because
> there [in East Africa] we had our own
> business and our own property, and

> people worked for us. So when you have
> your own property and you have to leave
> and go and start a beginning, it's kind
> of hard. We don't have any problem
> there, and we don't work that hard like
> we work here. Here it's hard to work.
> . . . For a lady, it's hard here.

Two children per family is typical. Very few families have more than two children. In Atlanta,
according to questionnaire respondents in 1984 and
1985 who were parents, 70 percent of the children
were under sixteen years of age. As the children
grow older, the interests of Indian parents tend
to change from financial and/or educational pre-
occupations to greater concern for life quality,
including the selective preservation of Indian
culture.

Living in American houses has required some
minor adjustments for Indians. The Hindu custom of
keeping the kitchen area pure, for example, is
impossible to practice when the door from the
carport or garage to the kitchen is a major entrance to the house. Again, for Hindus, rooms
with wall-to-wall carpeting cannot be made
ritually clean. Taking a shower remains more
popular than bathing in a tub. This continues
(especially Hindu) notions that cleansing water
should flow from the purest part of the body (the
head) toward the least pure (the feet) and away
from the body and that one should not sit in water
that has washed off body impurities. Indian homes
in Atlanta are furnished like the homes of native
Americans. Hardly anyone sits on the floor with
any regularity other than for religious ritual
occasions. And even sitting on the floor for
these occasions has become uncomfortable for many
immigrants because they have become unaccustomed
to it. Husbands take part in housework and child
care to a greater extent than in India, but they
generally confine their participation to "male
roles", such as cutting the grass or putting out
the garbage, although they cook and wash the
dishes when necessary. The isolation of the sub-
urbs is a problem:

> The funniest thing is people don't know
> who are the neighbors here. I know only

> this neighbor. I don't know about the
> other neighbor. It's the funniest
> thing. We love to know each and
> everybody. But if they don't
> reciprocate, it's hard. And that's the
> way American life is.

Some women who are not in the work force find
life in America lonely:

> Sometimes, you know, I feel homesick,
> sometimes bored. But really, you know,
> I don't want to go for work. Because if
> I go to work, I can't take care of my
> family properly. . . . But sometimes,
> you know, I am far away from my family,
> so I really feel homesick. . . . I come
> from a joint family. This is the first
> time that we will have a family like
> this, husband and wife.

Except for choosing marriage partners, the
Indian caste system has become almost non functional in America. But even in urban India, caste
restricts the range of potential mates much less
than it did a generation ago.[12] Achieved status
indicators, such as education, income, and community and occupational leadership, tend to replace ascribed social status. Indian immigrants
obtain marriage partners in many cases by arranged
marriage or partly arranged marriage, although
free-choice or "love" marriages are also common,
especially when both of the potential mates are
already in America.
     Brides and grooms for Indians in America are
frequently obtained from India through family
arrangements. A male Indian physician described
the marriage process:

> Sometimes. . . when they come here, they
> come as single persons, they come as
> students. Then, during their first two
> years, they finish their course, they
> get a job, and by that time the pressure
> starts coming from their parents, you
> know, that it's time that they go back.
> They can come back, but go there and get
> married and then return. That is one

main reason why they go back there. Get
married and then come back. If they
meet here primarily, then they would
rather stay. It is more economical to
get married here and then, at their own
pace of time, they can go and visit
their folks.

Matrimonial advertisements placed in Indian
newspapers by a mediator (usually close kin) for
both men and women are one of the ways contacts
are made for arranged marriages. Potential mates
may be in America, India, or other countries. Two
examples from India Abroad ("Classifieds," 1986),
a New York weekly, indicate the range of appeals:

Sister invites correspondence from well
qualified professionals for younger
sister, 27, slim, beautiful, doing
residency Delhi. Please reply with
returnable photograph.

Correspondence invited for 30 years old,
MS Computer Engineer, green card holder,
from fair, good-looking graduate. Tamil
Iyer girls below 26. Send details with
returnable photo.

While the first advertisement makes no mention
of language, caste, or religion, the second speci-
fies language (Tamil), caste, and religion (Iyer
is a Brahman Hindu caste or jati). Unless stated
in the advertisement, it is assumed that the
candidate has never been married. As the second
advertisement makes clear, having a green card
(permanent residency in the United States) is
regarded as a positive attraction for a potential
marriage partner who could also obtain permanent
residence certification by means of the marriage.
Marriages to green-card holders or citizens have
occasionally been fraudulent, with the nonresident
partner entering into the marriage solely for
immigration purposes and subsequently abandoning
the spouse. U.S. Representative Mazzoli estimated
in 1986 that one third of marriage-based petitions
for immigration (from all countries) involve fraud
of some kind (U.S. Congress 1986). A small minority of immigrant Indians (several dozen in

Atlanta) is married to non-Indians. First-generation immigrant Indian men marry non Indians more often than do Indian women.

The Census indicated that 71 percent of Indians in Georgia fifteen years of age or older were married in 1980 (compared to a national average for the whole population aged fifteen or older of 60 percent now married). It is probable that 95 percent of Indians over thirty years of age are married. Most first-generation Indians strongly disapprove of divorce. But nationwide, 2.1 percent of the Indian population fifteen years old or older in 1980 was divorced (compared to 5.1 percent divorced for the nationwide population as a whole aged fifteen years or older) (Bureau of the Census 1984, pp. 10, 67-68, Tables 255, 264). Persons divorced in Atlanta ran slightly higher at 3.2 percent. In addition, 1.3 percent of the Indians were separated. The Atlanta survey indicated that most divorces occur during the first five years of marriage and the first few years of residence in America. Marital adjustment stress is presumably highest at this point. The number of widows and widowers among Indians is very small due to the relative youth of the population.

INDIANS OR AMERICANS?

Overseas Indians may appear to some observers to be sojourners rather than true immigrants, even after several generations, because they tend to maintain their ethnic differences, they do not necessarily integrate into the host culture, and as in the East and Central African former British colonies, they may depart when the economic circumstances are no longer favorable. In my view the actual situation of overseas Indians has been more complex. How overseas Indians relate to their host cultures varies greatly with the local circumstances. In the East and Central African British colonial situation Indians had financial success but no power, and they were sandwiched into a status hierarchy above Africans but below Europeans. There was no possibility of integrating as a group into African ethnic groups other than through intermarriage, a process, even if feasible, that would have meant the eventual disapppearance of Indian culture. The Africanization of East and Central African economies after independence was and is inevitable, so Indians, most of whom were engaged in business, had little hope for a successful future if they remained in those countries. Thus, it is arguable that their large-scale departure was due more to the circumstances than to a general trait shared by all or most overseas Indians (See Tandon and Raphael 1984; Thompson 1974, pp. 46-52).

Some, perhaps most, Indian immigrants did come to America initially as migrants or sojourners with the intent of returning home eventually. Some do in fact come only for specific reasons (for example, education, medical treatment), and they return when there is no longer reason to stay. Even Indians who are true immigrants maintain strong ties with primary and extended families in India and often send money home.[13] Said one immigrant: "My parents are really old and they do not have an independent earning of their own. And I support them financially." Unmarried males typically return to India for brides, and very large numbers of Indians return to India for visits at least once in five years. Parents and other kin visit in America and sometimes immigrate.

Many Indians say that they wish someday to return permanently to India, but most have in fact continued to stay and will remain in America. They are nostalgic about India and tend to maintain idealized conceptions of life there. But they also experience inner conflict between the material prosperity they enjoy in America and "the Indian spirit." Sometimes, as for this Muslim father, the conflict centers around the future for the children:

> We may stay or we may not. . . . We have to see how the community things develop in this country, how does it flourish. . . . If we have enough strength of mind, we can retain all the identity we want. But we cannot say about the coming generation--how they are going to get it. . . . If we see that the identity is getting lost and we don't care about that, then we might stay.

And if we care about that, we won't.
. . . It will take another couple of
years--three or four years--before we
can say.

One person suggested that "Indians love India
abstractly and hate it concretely. They hate
America abstractly and love it concretely." The
desire of some Indians to retire in India
eventually is also in tension with their ties to
their children who will undoubtedly remain in
America. According to one recent immigrant, when
Indians get together socially, they talk primarily
about "back home." Until the very early 1980s
Indian motion pictures were screened occasionally
in movie theaters or halls. These screenings were
supplanted by video cassette players, which I
found in most Indian homes as much as five years
before VCRs became common in native American
homes. Indian movies are so popular in part because they give a chance for immigrants to "return
home" to the "imaginary India" projected by Bombay
films. Indians in Atlanta, as in other cities,
import Indian popular and classical culture and
entertainment both from other places in North
America and from India. Live musical and dance
performances by Indian stars are most popular, but
performances and plays are also produced by local
talent. There has been an Indian music radio
program in Atlanta each Friday night for more than
ten years, and there are also half a dozen Indian
restaurants and about the same number of Indian
groceries. While the former attract many non-
Indian customers, the clientele for the groceries
is primarily Indian. A restaurant manager opined:

I think the existence of so many Indian
restaurants means that Indian food is
getting popular. It's not cutting into
business. I think I appreciate the idea
because the more Indian restaurants are
there, I think people will tend to know
about Indian food, Indian culture.

The groceries rent out Indian movie video
cassettes,[14] and offer music records and tapes,
clothing, utensils, calendars and other goods from
India. They regularly advertise their sales using

mailing lists of Indian customers obtained from a variety of sources, including the largest pan-Indian organization, the India American Cultural Association. Clothey's survey (1983, p. 171) of Pittsburgh Indians showed that 98 percent listened to Indian music, 85 percent read periodicals intended for Indians in America, 53 percent read Indian periodicals, and 79 percent are teaching their native Indian language to their children.

The ambivalence about remaining in America that Indian immigrants express face to face was much less evident in their written responses to the questionnaire in Atlanta. Of the 265 persons out of 291 answering the question, 78 percent indicated that they intend to remain in America. The intent to remain increases with greater time in America and with rising income. Recent arrivals with temporary visas and lowest income showed the least desire to stay.

As reported by the 1980 Census, naturalization rates for Indian immigrants were low (24 percent nationally and 27.4 percent in Georgia). But this figure is not a reliable indicator because 43.7 percent of the Indian immigrants had been in America less than five years and were thus not even eligible to become citizens. It is fairly common practice among Indians for one spouse to naturalize while the other retains Indian citizenship. Naturalization rates are gradually increasing, but the reason Indians become citizens is generally practical. One long-term resident noncitizen expressed the question this way: "Is it necessary to do what I want to do?" One woman who is a citizen decided:

> that we would live here for long, for good, because primarily for our children--that if there is any country where I would like to raise my children, it would be here. Because, number one, that they themselves have something in them that could be best brought out in a free society where really there are democratic values, where people are treated on their merit and talents, not entirely on their race or religion. This is our experience. . . . The not only academic studies and opportunities, but

> life opportunities, for good life, for a
> wider horizon as you say, that I would
> like to live here and give my children
> the best of everything. So that was
> why! Number two, . . . if we are not
> citizens, we can't have both. If we want
> to take active part in politics, we
> cannot. And we just want to have our
> say in everything. . . . And then, if
> you are here, and if you are going to
> live here for good, why not have the
> full advantage of life here as a
> citizen? Why should you have second-
> class citizen treatment?

Being an American citizen does make sponsorship of
close kin for immigration easier. An Indian immigration lawyer explained:

> If I'm an immigrant and I have been here
> five years and I acquire U.S.
> citizenship, then I can sponsor my
> brother and my sister. And if my
> brother gets immigration, then at least
> he can bring his family, and so the
> effect of sponsoring one person is
> geometric in the sense that you are not
> sponsoring one person, you are
> sponsoring a whole family. . . . The
> primary reason I have found out for
> immigrants becoming naturalized is
> because they want to sponsor. . . . If
> you are a citizen, it's not just
> brothers and sisters, it is your
> parents, and your married children--so
> you can see why you would want to become
> a citizen.

For 1978, for example, 91 percent of the persons
immigrating to America from India were admitted
under the regular quota. Of the 9 percent (1,678
persons) admitted beyond the quota, 3 percent were
parents and 3 percent were spouses of U.S. citizens. Children of citizens or of spouses of
citizens accounted for another 1 percent, while
all others were another 2 percent (Chandrasekhar
1984, p. 89).

In the Atlanta survey in 1984 and 1985, 36.6

percent of the respondents indicated that they were citizens, and an additional 5.7 percent were in the process of naturalizing. Indians are also participating in the American political process, especially since 1984, not only by voting and participating in campaigns, but also by financial contributions (see Kalkunte 1986 and Dutta 1986, pp. 83-84). The Indian cochair of the Michael Dukakis campaign for president, Ramesh Kapur, has claimed that Indian participation in the political process has greatly increased for the 1988 presidential election (Venkateshwaran 1988).

After ten to twenty years in America Indian immigrants, like previous immigrants, are culturally betwixt and between--no longer Indian, but not yet fully American. One woman saw this as a problem of balance:

> I've tried to take the good of both sides. I cannot possibly be totally Indian here. Nor can I be totally American. That would go against the grain of me because I see good in what I came from, and I would like to pass that on to my children.

Optimism about being both Indian and American was expressed by another woman:

> I feel that becoming citizen has not changed the Indian in us. The way I feel and think about certain things, about human relationships, about outlook on life, traditions, philosophy, religious philosophy, culture, my ideas of raising children, family--in these matters I would go ahead and say we both are still Indian in the bigger core of our heart. In other outside matters like clothing, dressing, food, we have changed. . . . So we have our feet in both this culture and that culture. In this home there will be Indian food. Of course, there will also be American, Italian, Mexican--whatever we enjoy.

Some families have returned to India. And while some who returned remain in India permanently,

others, as in the following account, returned to
America because they could not readjust:

> [Our return] . . . kept delaying because
> one of the other brothers kept coming
> here and I had to take care of them
> going to school. At one point we did
> get clear of that, so come 1972 we
> decided we were returning home. . . . It
> just took us two years to find a job
> that I wanted to do, so in '74 we left.
> We packed up everything, sold
> everything, and just went to India. So
> even after twelve years in this country
> my mind was set that I was returning
> back. And my goals had expanded. . . .
> So I went to the Institute of Management
> in _____. So we did spend a year there,
> and a year of being on our own
> completely altered everything. . . . Now
> we were far away from everybody, and we
> were away from our home for the first
> time, and we were taken away and
> deprived of all the community we were
> used to--and I was at the top place! It
> was running through double standards.
> . . . [Even after returning to his home
> environment, it was a problem depriving
> his] . . . family of the small things in
> life, which, maybe you will think
> unimportant. But to me, to walk in a
> store and not only to buy sugar, but to
> be able to select a brand. . . . I
> couldn't throw a party on a offhand
> basis. I couldn't do any of the things
> I was used to--things that I had
> adjusted to when I was in America. We
> came back in '75 with the whole idea of
> adjusting and making America our home.
> . . . It was hard for a year, two years,
> but it finally worked out all right.

Another had a somewhat similar experience:

> So we took a trip back. But we came
> back, you know. My father wanted me to
> stay. I returned and a couple of years
> later I went back again, again with the

idea of staying. But the more I stayed
here, the less I wanted to settle in
India. . . . Every time I go back the
question arises: Can I have a nice
house? A nice car? Can we have
television? And I would find it
difficult to practice business there.
Indian practice of business is quite
different.

First-generation Indian immigrants acculturate
without assimilating: At work they adopt American
practices and cultural habits, but at home and at
gatherings of Indian ethnic organizations they
retain many Indian practices. To do otherwise
would be to lose touch with their culture. Adults
often state a preference for Indian food, but
they eat American food at work, including meat
(except observant Muslims). At home they
generally eat Indian food, although American-style
pizza is a great favorite. Many Indians still
consume the evening meal late, two to three hours
later than most Americans would eat, with the meal
marking the end rather than the middle of a social
visit. Indians who have changed diets drastically
sometimes have to retrench when visited by
parents, as this young couple discovered:

Q: Do you eat beef or pork?
Wife: Yes, a little bit.
Husband: You are not going to tell my
Mom, are you? . . . It creates, like a
couple of years ago, my mother-in-law
came, and everytime they came we
literally had to clean out the fridge.
Wife: You have to hide.
Husband: As a matter of fact, they are
complete vegetarians, and even asking
about meats at the dinner table upsets
them.

Many Indian men indulge in light social drink-
ing, but women are much less likely to drink
alcoholic beverages in public. As for tobacco
consumption . . .

Wife: Indians, they smoke. Indian
ladies don't smoke.

> Husband: Ladies, never.
> Wife: Very seldom. Very, very seldom.
> Like maybe . . .
> Husband: One in 10,000.
> Wife: Yes. Something like that.

A very high percentage of Asian Indian immigrants have good to excellent English language ability. The Census indicated that only 7.3 percent of persons eighteen years of age or over who immigrated to America between 1970 and 1980 spoke English not well or not at all. English is spoken at work, but Punjabi, Gujarati, Bengali, or other Indian languages are spoken in the home. In 73 percent of the population immigrating to America between 1970 and 1980, all members of the family spoke the native language at home, according to the 1980 Census. (Second-generation children are in fact more likely to understand the native Indian language passively but to be unable to use it effectively themselves.) Indian women who are not in the work force acculturate less than those who are. Nonworking women and elderly persons also account for most of the immigrants who speak English poorly. One husband explained:

> Most of the Indian community members living in Atlanta, or most of the United States, most of them are English speaking. Some of their wives perhaps don't speak as well. My wife, for example, she understands a little bit. She can converse a little bit, but she had a high-school education. That's about it. But I think that she can get by with Hindi on the national level [with Indians from different regions] or broken English.

NOTES

1. Although the U.S. Immigration and Naturalization Service lists one Asian Indian immigrant in 1820 and a total of 660 immigrants during the whole of the nineteenth century, La Brack (1980, p. 44) has argued with considerable plausibility that all or most of the Indians reported were in

fact persons of European descent who came to America from India.

The most extensive studies of Indian immigrants before 1965 are by Bruce La Brack and Joan M. Jensen. Most of the published research about Indian immigrants in this period concerns the largest population, the Indians of California. See the bibliographical entries for Rabindra C. Chakravorti, Yusuf Dadabhay, Rajani Kanta Das, Gary R. Hess, Harold S. Jacoby, Mark Juergensmeyer, H. Brett Melendy, and Lawrence A. Wenzel.

2. On the last day of a trial of seventeen Indians (and others) for violating the Neutrality Act in 1918, a Sikh defendant shot and killed a Hindu defendant in the courtroom. A policeman immediately shot the Sikh dead (see Muthanna 1975, p. 425).

3. Some Indians, especially students, married women of European descent. Marriages between Indians and American black women were confined largely to Muslims in Detroit.

4. Representative Dalip Singh Saund, a California Sikh, served three terms in Congress.

5. Incidents of discrimination, such as not being given large enough raises, not being promoted, difficulty renting houses, and being socially isolated, were reported by 70 out of 159 respondents to a questionnaire (3,812 were mailed out) by Elkhanialy and Nicholas (1976, pp. 41-50) in the Chicago area in 1976. For additional allegations of discrimination against Indians, see Chandras 1978, pp. 86-90 and Parthasarathy 1982.

6. A telephone survey conducted in 1987 by two Emory University students, Sanjay Gandhi and Jim Hinson, suggests that persons in affluent north Atlanta neighborhoods are likely to have some personal acquaintance with Asian Indians (75 percent of the survey), to expect them to be middle or upper class (89 percent), and to be professional or white collar workers (75 percent). Summary perceptions of Asian Indians included "hard working," "honest," "fill vital roles," "small, but growing," and almost no negative comments.

7. The mystique of "going to America" is quite widespread in India. During my 1967 sojourn in India, almost all of the Indians I came to know

reasonably well eventually asked me, "Can you help me get to America?"

8. Student networking of this sort occurs in other parts of the country also, as I observed, for example, at the Pennsylvania State University and the University of Washington in Seattle during the 1960s and 1970s.

9. With regard to the alleged "brain drain," one Indian scientist suggested, "We are not missed in India." Affluent overseas Indians stimulate the Indian economy to some extent through money sent back to their families in India, by their investments in India, and by their business dealings with Indian firms (see Dutta 1986, p. 83).

10. The probable reason for the supposedly poorer performance of native-born Indians is that some 70 percent of the native-born children of post-1965 Asian Indian immigrants were below age fourteen in 1980 (Gardner, Robey, and Smith 1985, p. 15).

11. One informant claimed, "We don't ask the caste or say the caste. We know that we are Hindus. Actually, I don't know which caste I belong to. In our family nobody asks that. You are not supposed to say right out or ask."

12. According to Shavid Javi Burki's estimates (cited in Owen 1985, p. 13), remittances sent home to Pakistan from labor migrants to other countries enabled the Pakistani economy to grow at 5 percent per annum throughout the 1970s rather than at the rate of 2 percent that would have been expected without the remittances. Lipton and Firn (1975, pp. 114-15) estimated that $42.3 million in remittances of this type were made from the United Kingdom to India in 1970. A survey of New York City Indians by Thottathil and Saran (1980, p. 240) yielded an estimate that 30 percent of Indian families were sending about $100 per month home and that 26 percent were sending more than $100 per month. Extrapolated for 95,000 families in the entire United States in 1980 this estimate would suggest almost $64 million in remittances sent home annually. See also Helweg 1979, pp. 89-93.

13. In 1987 Indian groceries consulted in Atlanta stocked from 2,500 to 5,000 different video cassette motion pictures, which rented for

as low as $1 per week. Store operators estimated
that families rent three cassettes per week on the
average. The majority of films were in Hindi, but
there were also Malayalam, Telegu, Tamil, and
Punjabi films. Rental of Indian movie cassettes
is also popular among immigrants from China,
Southeast Asia, and the Middle East. This
information was collected for a class report in an
undergraduate class at Emory University by Naveed
Sabir during the spring of 1987.

2

Individual and Family Religion and Culture

The present chapter examines religiosity among Indian immigrants as individuals and as members of family units. First-generation immigrants often find it easy to continue personal praxis as it was in India.

RELIGIOUS BEHAVIOR IN THE INDIAN POPULATION

In the questionnaire administered to Atlanta Indians 80.5 percent of those answering in the sample responded yes to the question, "Are you religious?" (missing values = 14). There were no significant differences between men and women. But many of the respondents who indicated that they are not religious also reported that they do individual worship, prayer, or meditation. From the people who responded that they were <u>not religious</u>, 23.5 percent indicated that they do some kind of <u>individual worship</u>, <u>prayer</u>, <u>or medi-tation daily</u>! From this same group of people an additional 11.8 percent reported that they do individual worship at least once weekly, another 9.8 percent carry out individual worship at least once a month, and 19.6 percent at least once each year. In all, thirty-three of fifty-one respondents (64.3 percent) in the sample clearly felt that it was possible to deny that they were religious even while admitting that they occasionally perform individual worship (see discussion in the following section).

While it is clear that people may take part in group worship for a variety of reasons (some of which are not primarily religious), individual worship is a practice in which one engages primarily for religious reasons. Even though these thirty-three respondents understood the term "religious" differently, it seems reasonable to argue that anyone who engages in individual worship should be considered a religious person. If we then add the daily, weekly, and monthly worshippers, 92.4 percent of the Indian survey population in Atlanta could be considered at least nominally religious. Only 6.7 percent of the entire sample (26 of 291 persons) and just 35.3 percent of respondents who indicate they are not religious (18 persons) never engage in individual worship.

This line of argument need not imply, and surely does not entail, a high degree of religiosity within the Indian population any more than nominal religiosity would suggest intense spirituality for the American population in general. I am claiming merely that almost all Indian immigrants in the sample participate at a personal level with at least some degree of assent to, and support of, systems of symbols that relate human needs to sacred realities. That is, almost all Indian immigrants are to some degree religious. (Fenton 1983, pp. 7-23). Since Gallup (p. 173) reported in 1985 that 90 percent of the American population were willing to indicate a religious preference and that eight out of every ten Americans claimed that religion is very important in their lives, we can say with assurance that Indian immigrants are at least as religious as native Americans.

A survey conducted in 1978 in Pittsburgh by Clothey (1983, p. 168-69) showed partially similar results. In that study 76 percent indicated that they were religious. However, Clothey found that 10 percent more of the women than the men claimed to be religious and that the more highly educated respondents and respondents who entered the United States as students were less likely to say that they were religious than immigrants who were less well educated and who entered under classifications other than as students.

The ambiguity some Indian respondents experienced with the word "religious" vanished when they were asked, "Are you more or less religious now than when you entered the United States?" Almost 98 percent of the sample (284 out of 291 questionnaires) responded, with 26 percent affirming they were "more religious," 18 percent testifying that they were "less religious," and 56 percent reporting "no change." Immigration to America appears, by itself, to have had little effect on religiosity. Individual worship practices are, for the most part, easy to transplant from one culture to another, and almost all of the people interviewed said that the manner in which they practice individual worship had not changed since immigration. But people did tend to respond that they are "more religious" as the age of their oldest child increased (until about age twenty).

Some form of individual worship, prayer, or meditation was carried out daily by 52 percent of all respondents, at least once weekly by 19 percent, and at least once a month by 12 percent. Indian women perform daily worship at a rate 11 percent higher and weekly worship at a rate 3.7 percent higher than men. The percentage of men who never engage in individual worship is higher than for women.

It was quite difficult to design a question about religious belief that was suitable for a population with so many traditional and regional variations. After testing, the question asked was, "Do you believe in a Higher Reality (e.g., Brahman, Ishvara, Allah, Sat Nam) as the basis of meaning and value?" Although the question was very general and possibly a bit vague, 75.4 percent agreed or agreed strongly. Even so, several Christians disagreed or disagreed strongly, apparently because the term "God" was missing from the list of examples in the question.

These measures show that the Indian population of Atlanta is fairly religious. In fact, it is more observant than I would have expected based on my interviews alone. It is possible that the anonymity afforded by the questionnaire elicited more honest answers than some interviewees gave to me face to face or even than Indians are likely to give to each other directly.

With the exception of Indian Christians who have a natural connection to Christian churches, the religiosity of Indian immigrants in Atlanta is largely unaffected by the religion of native Americans. Some Hindus and Jains reported that they have visited Christian churches for worship a few times; but Christian attempts to convert non-Christian Indians have so far not been very substantial, and non-Christian Indians have had very low interest in conversion. None of the non-Christian Indians I interviewed admitted that Christian churches had any influence on them. The following polite refusal is fairly typical of Hindu resistance to conversion:

> One time the Jehovah Witnesses came here in my neighborhood. . . . I let them sit here. We both listened. We told them what we were. We told them, "We respect your religion, but we are Hindus and we are going to remain that way. With that understanding if you still want to discuss with me, I am very willing, open, and you are invited." . . . They stayed for about an hour and a half discussion. After that they never came back when I told them we would not change.

Efforts to bring Korean and Chinese immigrants into Atlanta churches have been more successful. Christian missionary outreach is, in this case, facilitated by the presence in Atlanta of a large number of Korean and Chinese Christians whose special worship services in their own languages also attract non-Christians.

HINDUS

Less than half (119) of the 291 people in the Atlanta survey reported that they adhere to a specific religious tradition. Among these, only 73 people acknowledged that they were Hindu (455 men and 24 women). Of the remaining respondents, 104 indicated that they were religious but did not belong to a specific religious tradition,

while 54 responded that they were neither religious nor an adherent of a specific religious
tradition.   (Fourteen persons in the survey did
not answer these questions.) Survey results are
shown in Table 4.

Table 4

Three Groups of Respondents

GROUP 1	GROUP 2	GROUP 3
number of persons:		
(73)	(104)	(54)
religious	religious	nonreligious
traditional	nontraditional	nontraditional
high individual worship	high individual worship	low individual worship
high group worship	low group worship	very low group worship

Survey results indicated that behavior at the
level of individual religiosity in Group 1 and
Group 2 is very similar. Much greater differences
become apparent in group oriented types of
religious behavior. Group 3 individuals are less
religiously observant both as individuals and as
participants in religious groups. They are also
much more likely never to participate in any
religious kind of behavior than are members of
Groups 1 and 2.
     Group 2 behavior differs very little from
Group 1 behavior on most indicators of religiosity

at the level of individual observance. The rate of participation in group worship for Group 2 is much less than Group 1 although it is still much higher than for Group 3. The rate of positive responses for Group 3 to questions about individual religiosity is much lower than the other two groups. But not everyone within Group 3 is religiously nonobservant. There are persons within Group 3 who worship individually daily, and there are those who participate in group worship. (Some of the people who responded that they were "not religious" even though they perform worship individually daily would fit more naturally in Group 2 if it were not for the ambivalence they felt toward the label "religious.")

There are adequate reasons to assume (even though direct indication was not given in the questionnaire responses) that most, if not all, of the 158 people in Group 2 and Group 3 do in fact come from Hindu backgrounds, that is, their parents or grandparents were Hindu and their communal ties are Hindu.[1] The constituency and the family names on the mailing lists for most of the groups to which the questionnaire was administered (except those groups chosen primarily to balance the sample in terms of religious representation) were culturally Hindu. I also know by personal acquaintance that most respondents in these groups are of Hindu origin, and I have talked with some of the individuals in the survey who did not name their religious traditions (all were from Hindu backgrounds).

The questionnaire responses of the three groups of people I have argued to be of Hindu background can be illuminated by relating them in a loose fashion to trends in contemporary Hindu religious tradition both in India proper and overseas. Modernizing reform movements within Hindu tradition began to appear prominently during the nineteenth century. Where these movements, such as the Arya Samaj, have caught on in overseas Hindu communities, a more conservative kind of Hindu movement has sometimes developed as a reaction. In Fiji, as in some other overseas Hindu communities, such as Guyana (Wilson 1983; Jayawardene 1968; Burghart 1987a), the conservative movement is sometimes called Sanatana Dharma (eternal duty/religion). I will label the reformist movements "neo-Hindu" and the more conservative trends "traditional Hindu." In addition to these two trends, there is also a trend toward secularization in which the term "Hindu" serves largely to refer to the communal cultural tradition from which one's family derived and with which one is more or less identified in contrast to Indian Christians or Indian Muslims. This trend will be referred to as "cultural Hinduism."

Traditional Hinduism includes both a more old-fashioned kind of person who would tend to employ fairly lengthly ritual processes primarily in the Sanskrit language as a frequent (usually at least twice daily) personal religious practice, as well as individuals who have adopted simpler, less time-consuming types of personal worship but who would still identify themselves as following one of the "orthoprax" (astika) Vedic Hindu subtraditions. Some contemporary Hindus might report themselves as "not religious" because they understand themselves as "not very religious"; that is, they do not spend anywhere nearly as much time in worship as did the older generations. Among the immigrants, many of the more traditional worshippers who stress lengthy ritual detail belong to the older generation. Some modern Hindus, such as this woman, remember the old traditions as something their grandparents or parents practiced:

> As a family, we do not believe in orthodox puja. We do sit and pray before my children go to bed or take their food. We all say certain shlokas, stanzas in Sanskrit. It's a tradition. And whether the children follow or not, they recite it with us. Also they attend whenever we go out to perform puja. . . . We do not do regular puja. When I was not working, every day, every morning, after taking baths I would light up the lamp, a typical Indian lamp in which you put ghee and wick and light. I would pray for some time. I used to read one chapter of [Bhagavad] Gita every day, sitting before God. But I don't do those, you know, actually bathing or doing those marks [on the image].

> That's a typical traditional way. . . .
> I have seen my grandmother doing all
> that--taking two hours every morning,
> bathing each god and doing a certain
> mantra, a certain yellow mark on this, a
> red mark on that, dressing up gods and
> doing arati [offering light], and
> reading, and all that. But my father
> would sit in a chair and meditate, you
> know. He would close his nose, touch
> his nose here, and do pranayama, deep
> breathing [breath control exercises].
> And he is a devotee of Ramakrishna.
> . . . So in my particular family I have
> inherited both traditional upbringing,
> religious upbringing, and, what shall I
> say, philosophical, in which you don't
> do ceremony. But you think of God and
> meditate and read books on philosophy
> and religion.

The principal thrust of neo-Hindu movements
has been reform of religious tradition, recovery
of its original thrust, and the contemporary re-
expression of the Hindu spiritual message in a
universal form. Some of the basic tenets of neo-
Hinduism may derive from the Muslim theology of
religions (W. C. Smith 1957, pp. 19-30). In the
Muslim view all peoples have had true prophets
whose messages were true revelations of God, and
all were in basic agreement with each other.
However, over time the prophetic message became
distorted, resulting in the development of the
different sectarian religions.[2] The true prophet
(Muhammad in the case of Islam) rereveals and
restores the original message. In a slightly
different form and with numerous variations, this
theology has found expression in nineteenth and
twentieth century religious movements and has
become part of the contemporary common Hindu
ideology. The Muslim theory coheres basically
with indigeneous Hindu theories, such as is expressed in the Bhagavad Gita (4:1-4) pronouncement
that the "lost" original, universal revelation is
now being restored by a guru (in this instance, by
Lord Krishna). Among its tenets is the belief
that the message of Hinduism is timeless, not a
product of history, and that it is the original

content of all true spirituality. The true contemporary teacher re-presents the ancient truth of Hindu spirituality and of all true spirituality, shorn of the merely sectarian tradition that has been added to it. A woman who follows one of the modernist Hindu movements explained how people who join the movement can retain their old religious affiliation, but in a way that is reinterpreted by the leader of the movement. The leader recovers the original spirit that has been lost:

> He makes you a better follower of your own religion because, you know, your own religion taught you the same thing. . . . He normally uses the Bible to teach them. And he pulls out the same words, but they have a different connotation when he tells you what they really mean. . . . But the meaning as told you by a preacher today is so different from what was written by the followers of Christ 2,000 years ago.

A male follower of a different contemporary Hindu movement sees Hindu and Christian religious traditions as fundamentally the same:

> I had a few Christian friends from college. I used to go to a Baptist church. I went there for two years or so, almost regularly. She [wife] was in India at the time. Just to know what a Christian is. . . . And surprisingly, I think Hinduism and Christianity are the same. . . . Basically, the bottom line is the same what they are teaching. . . . We both are talking about two different shades, but the object itself is the same. When you try to put anybody else's god down, you are actually not, because all gods merge into one. . . . When I say Christianity, I'm not saying as a general [statement covering all Christians], but maybe Southern Baptists.

True spirituality transcends specific religious traditions and religion as such. As the spiritual essence of all religions, it is always the same. It is objective, not merely subjective. Since it is Truth, spirituality is based on reason, and it is perfectly compatible with modern natural science. Because contemporary guru reformers are recovering the original truth and criticizing the religious traditions that have illegitimately grown up around it, "religion" and "religious" have, for some Hindus, become terms of disrepute. Even the term "Hindu," for some, means "sectarian," and therefore Hinduism cannot be universal or eternally true.

It should now be clear why some neo-Hindus would deny being Hindu (one ought to transcend mere Hinduism). It is undoubtedly because of this ideology that a large number of Hindus who completed the Atlanta questionnaire affirmed that they were religious but declined to identify themselves as Hindu. The term "Hindu" was understood in a proscriptive sense as a religious form that should be spiritually transcended.[3]

Most respondents (who affirmed that they considered themselves religious) took the term "religious" in a generic sense.[4] But a few respondents interpreted the term "religious" in a proscriptive or pejorative sense. They denied that they are religious because being religious is not consistent with being spiritual. Religion for them means belief and practice that are merely historical, socially divisive, exclusive, and sectarian. Adherence to eternal truth requires a very generalized sort of faith that transcends these forms of religion. From their point of view they are being neither inconsistent nor untruthful when they state that although they are not religious, they do engage in individual worship. Agehananda Bharati (1972, p. 294) referred to such moves from ritual to "emotive tokens" like "spirituality" as a continuing form of "Sanskritization" within the Hindu tradition that has precedents as early as the criticism of Vedic rituals contained in the Upanishadic scriptures.

Several informants suggested to me that many Hindus who do participate in specific religious traditions do not like to admit it. It is not fashionable to acknowledge publicly that one is traditional or sectarian. One Hindu graduate student explained:

> If you ask a Hindu what he is, certainly
> chances are better than fifty-fifty that
> he will never say he is a Hindu. He
> will go around about talking about what
> he is not and what he does not believe.
> So it takes half an hour to say who he
> is.

Reticence about admitting that one is Hindu is
also tuned to attitudes Hindus expect Americans to
have. When Americans inquire, one Hindu woman
says that she replies:

> that I am Unitarian. In my heart I am
> not really lying. . . . Because many
> people misunderstand when I say that I
> am Hindu. If I told them that I have an
> idol in my altar, they would think I am
> a foolish person who is praying to
> stones. So I usually avoid it.

The term "cultural Hindu" refers to Indians
with a Hindu family background who have low observance of religious practices and whose identification with the Hindu religious tradition is
primarily cultural or communal. For some people
with Hindu backgrounds the designation "Hindu" is
cultural rather than religious:

> What makes me a Hindu? I'm Hindu by
> birth. That is what, when I say "I am
> Hindu," I'm Hindu by birth. Like, I
> say, I have not followed Hinduism
> myself. So from that point of view, no,
> I am not [Hindu]. . . . I did not
> participate in any festivals [as a
> child] because I am Hindu. I
> participated in the festivals because it
> was fun. . . . I am not a religious
> person, but I see myself as a Hindu
> simply from my morals that I was raised
> in and my mentality. That keeps me
> Hindu.

Most of the secularized Hindus in the survey
are represented in Group 3. But the respondents
in Group 3 with high rates of individual worship

are more likely neo-Hindus who object to the term "religious" rather than secular Hindus who are really nonreligious. Individuals in this group may or may not be religiously observant. Taken as a whole, this group participates in religion both individually and in social gatherings at a rate significantly lower than the first two groups. Very few are totally nonobservant. But both men and women in Group 3 score lower for all of the measures represented in Table 5.

Responses to the Atlanta questionnaire show that individual worship, prayer, or meditation is practiced daily by 58.3 percent of respondents who identified themselves as Hindu (Group 1) (75 percent of the women, 50 percent of the men) and at least once each week by an additional 20.8 percent (with the same rate for men as for women). Some of the Hindu men (8.3 percent), but no women, indicated that they never do individual worship.

Rates of individual worship, prayer, or meditation in Group 2 (religious but nontraditional) are quite similar to Group 1 but with no appreciable difference between the practices of men and of women, except that all of the persons who never worship individually were men. Individual prayer, worship, or meditation can, of course, be carried out without utilizing traditional ritual forms and without having to rely on a formal institutional basis. The greater differences between Groups 1 and 2 appear at the level of group worship. While some of the women (25 percent) in Group 3 (nonreligious and nontraditional) never perform individual worship, they were still more likely to worship individually than were men in Group 3. For Hindus generally, Clothey's Pittsburgh investigation indicated that 45 percent engaged in daily meditation.

Table 5

Hindu Religiosity

	Group 1	Group 2	Group 3
	Traditional Hindu (%)	Neo-Hindu (%)	Cultural Hindu (%)
Individual worship daily	58.3	58.4	23.5
Never	5.6	4.0	35.3
More religious	34.7	29.0	7.4
No change	48.6	58.3	68.5
Believe in Higher Reality (agree and agree strongly)	84.3	78.4	49.0
Fasting, weekly and monthly	34.8	24.3	11.4
Never	43.5	50.5	83.0
Affirm work as duty (agree and agree strongly)	80.7	55.1	23.9

Table Five

(continued)

	Group 1	Group 2	Group 3
	Traditional Hindu (%)	Neo-Hindu (%)	Cultural Hindu (%)
Shrine in home	84.7	68.0	57.4
Worship at shrine	79.7	64.0	60.8
Arrange pujas always or mostly	64.8	50.5	26.0
Never	9.9	19.4	42.6
Attend group worship once monthly	60.0	35.4	22.7
Never	5.7	15.7	35.9

Individual worship may take different forms within the Hindu religious tradition. The most traditional form of devotion is puja, worship of the deity after its presence has been invoked and offering a series of services and gifts. Most Hindus I consulted normally carry out abbreviated forms of individual worship, although a few practice yoga for extended periods. According to one man,

> We do puja every day . . . separately.
> I am the first one. . . . Before I
> leave, before I have my breakfast, and
> after I get ready, I do my puja. I have
> my breakfast and go. And next is my
> wife. . . . It is very short. It takes
> about five minutes . . . <u>mantras</u>. . . .
> My mother . . . spends about an
> hour. . . . My daughter, she takes part
> some of the time, when we are completing
> Diwali, or something like Durga puja.

Perhaps two thirds of the Hindus in Atlanta have
religious roots in the various traditions associated with the personal deity, Vishnu, and with
Rama and Krishna, who are his descent forms
(<u>avatara</u>).   For those who worship these deities
(or those associated with the god Shiva or the
Mother Goddess) prayers, the singing of hymns,
recitation of scripture, repetition of the name or
names of the deity, or visualizations are the
typical forms of individual worship. For some
persons concentrating upon a single object or even
concentrating without an object for support of
the concentration, or recitation of syllables such
as <u>aum</u>, or mantras (stanzas from Hindu scriptures)
to aid concentration would be usual for individual
meditation.   There are also Hindus who practice
Transcendental Meditation, which they have learned
in America.
     For some Hindus the object of the religious
life is identification with or merging of the
deepest inner self (<u>atman</u>) with ultimate reality
(the <u>Brahman</u>). A male graduate student explained:

> I always consider mental peace the
> ultimate wealth a person could possess.
> You can have everything, but if you
> don't have mental peace, it doesn't
> amount to anything. <u>Shanti</u> [peace].
> Yes. . . . To a large extent, I do
> believe in rebirth and things like that.
> Being a nice person in this world to
> help you out to work on an ultimate
> goal, <u>moksha</u> [liberation]--I believe in
> that.   I differentiate between getting
> yourself into a rigid set of do's and

don'ts. I don't believe in that. But being a good person in general eventually should contribute towards your betterment along the cycle of . rebirth and ultimately to the final goal. I believe in that.

The recitation of scriptural passages is a standard part of Hindu worship, but the reading of sacred scriptures, while no doubt a religious activity when it is done, is more typically an ingredient in modern forms of individual worship, as the following exchange with an adult Hindu male makes clear:

> Q: Do you read any religious scriptures regularly?
> A: No. I don't.
> Q: Would you call yourself a religious person?
> A: I would.

On the other hand, some modern Hindus, like this woman, both recite and read scriptures:

> Every day. I pray, read Ramayana or any religious book. . . . I have some free prayer. Also, I have slokas [scriptural stanzas]--which I know the meaning real well. I don't like to chant without knowing the meaning. I read books sometimes, hymns too-- philosophical books of the Ramakrishna Mission.

The Bhagavad Gita (3:12-13, 9:27) stresses that food must be offered to God before it is eaten. Some kind of religious interlude before meals is a fairly common practice:

> I don't know the right word for it, but what we do is just take a part of the food and give it to the particular deity. I don't know if there is a name for that. We do it all of the time. I do a light, you know [arati, offering the light of fire]. . . . After that you just distribute it.

Q: So there is some sense that the food you eat normally is also prasad [an offering to God returned to the devotees as a gift]?
A: Right.

A young man gave a similar account:

We don't do any puja. We pray together [recite mantras] in front of the murti [image]. And sometimes we put the prasad there. And after that we eat. . . . This offering to God . . . if you take it as prasad, that means that prasad is not yours. It is God's. So that you have the feeling that you are wrongly eating somebody else's [food]. You are not eating your own food. So it eliminates selfishness, I think.

Almost 35 percent of the Hindus said they were more religious at the time of the survey (1984 to 1985) than when they had immigrated, with men and women about equal. Just under 21 percent of Hindu men but only 8.3 percent of the Hindu women said that they were now less religious. Approximately 15 percent more of the women than men claimed that their degree of religiousness had not changed since coming to America. A higher percentage of people in Groups 2 and 3 reported no change, and a much smaller percentage of people in Group 3 stated that they were more religious. Most interviewees, like the following, claimed that their patterns of personal worship have not changed:

It is not very elaborate. . . . We normally say prayers both in the morning and in the evening. . . . And if there is a special occasion . . . we tend to do something special on that day. But as a regular . . . routine, we just recite certain mantras. . . . I have not made any changes that I would not have made in India. In India there was nobody breathing on my neck, you know, and trying to make sure that I am doing what I should be doing. And the same thing applies here.

A unmarried male student suggested that even students seldom change patterns of individual worship:

> At least 90 percent of them with whom I have come into contact--I would not say it was all families and everybody else-- but the people I have come into contact with, at least 90 percent try to maintain the same amount of prayers that they used to do in India.

Hindus agreeing or agreeing strongly that they believe in a Higher Reality as the source of meaning and value were 84.3 percent compared to 75.5 percent of the entire survey sample. (Some Hindus affirm an impersonal nondual ultimate reality. Others are monotheists, while still others believe that the one God manifests itself in many different forms.) To my surprise, Hindu women agreed or agreed strongly at a lower rate than men. Indians in Group 2 agreed or agreed strongly at 78.4 percent. The lack of significant difference between Groups 1 and 2 is consistent with the theologies of both traditional and neo-Hinduism and the religious participation of both Groups 1 and 2. That just under half of those who are both nonreligious and nontraditional (Group 3) agreed or agreed strongly indicates lower religiosity even for individual belief.

Hindu women often fast one day in a week or a lunar month to fulfill a vow (vrata) made to a deity in supplication for a particular blessing (Wadley 1983). Wives frequently fast to secure the continued health of their husbands or families. One woman testified:

> You have to do it for a certain period of time. And at the end of that you promise something and you do that. See, for a certain period of time you say, I don't drink this, I don't do this, for a six month period of time. And at the end, when you finish the vrata you do certain things. . . . Vrata is for a period of time, a longer period of time. It can be a year or two years, five years, six years, ten years, or even six

months, six weeks. But it's a longer
period, not [just] one whole day.

When asked, "If at all, how often do you fast
for religious purposes?" 20.3 percent of Hindus
(Group 1) responded "at least once a week," 14.5
percent "once a month," and 21 percent either
"once in six months" or "once a year." Only 17.8
percent of the Hindu men compared to 25 percent of
the women fast for religious purposes weekly. The
figures for at least once a month are 11.1 percent
for men and 20.8 percent for women. Just under
half of the Hindu respondents never fast, and 9.2
percent more of the men never fast than of the
women. Rates of fasting for religious persons in
Group 2 were somewhat lower than for Hindus, and
they were markedly lower for persons in Group 3.
A woman who does not practice fasting stated:

> My husband's niece is here, and she just
> came from India visiting us. And she
> fasts every Monday. . . . Every day of
> the week belongs to a different god. So
> Mondays are Siva's. I think she is
> doing it to please Siva. So, I haven't
> had a chance to ask her why. . . . She
> just chose to, I think.

Another question on the survey was, "Do you
consider your study or work to be a kind of religious duty or vocation (e.g. , as <u>dharma</u> or as
<u>karma-yoga</u>)?" Karma-yoga is a prominent teaching
in the <u>Bhagavad Gita</u> and elsewhere in the Hindu
scriptural tradition. The doctrine refers to the
conception that people should do the work (karma)
that is given to them purely out of a sense of
duty to do their part in the universe while remaining unattached (yoga) to the rewards or results of the work. Dharma, in this context,
refers basically to the same understanding of work
as a vocation done out of a sense of duty rather
than for reward. As one Hindu woman described her
husband, "He likes to help everyone, to do things
for people. He works as a kind of devotion. He
can't lie . . . and everything must be done well."
Of the whole survey population, 54.7 percent of
respondents agreed or agreed strongly that they
consider their work a kind of religious duty. But

those   who said they were Hindus agreed or   agreed
strongly at the much higher rate of 80.6   percent.
Group 2 respondents agreed and agreed strongly   at
a   rate   of 55 percent (significantly   lower   than
acknowledged Hindus), while those persons in Group
3 agreed and agreed strongly at only 23.8 percent.
The   prevalence of the sense of work   as   vocation
thus declines sharply with the change from   expli-
cit   identification with the Hindu tradition to   a
more   general   sort   of   religiosity   or
"spirituality," and it declines even more markedly
for   those who say that they are   nonreligious   as
well.   Women in Groups 1 and 2 agreed and   agreed
strongly   only slightly less than men.   But   among
those who are both not religious and do not belong
to   a   specific religious   tradition   (Group   3),
55.6 percent of the women agreed or agreed strongly compared to 15.2 percent of the men.
     Astrology   is still employed by   some   Hindus,
although younger persons sometimes use it less, as
a woman related:

> My father was   a very   good astrologist.
> . . . He has taught me the whole   thing.
> He has my whole life charted in a   book.
> So,   it's   very   traditional.   Some
> families   believe   it,   and   some don't.
> . . . I   believe that . . . there   are
> certain periods which just are not   good
> for   me.   The   time   is   bad   so   I   be
> cautious.   I don't if I   still   believe
> it.   My husband used to believe   it.   I
> don't know whether he believes it now or
> not.

Clothey   (1983, p.   169) indicated that 21   percent
of   his Hindu respondents in   Pittsburgh   followed
the advice of an astrologer.
     Except   for   the few Hindus   who   continue   to
perform   elaborate traditional puja   in   Sanskrit,
popular   Hindu   individual forms   of   worship   are
simple,   they can be carried out in   private,   and
they require no special arrangements.   A household
shrine   is   an aid rather than a   requirement   for
worship.   Habits   of personal   worship   that   are
unobtrusive and do not conflict with the   requirements   of employment can rather easily   be   transplanted from the Indian context to America.

Images in Hindu homes may be used merely as a focus for symbolic worship, but many Hindus invoke the deity's presence into the image for the duration of worship. Shrines are sometimes located in the living or dining room but are more often set up in a back room or in a closet. The shrine typically contains representations or symbols of one or more deities and sometimes a portrait of a guru. Some are fairly simple -- a table or chest on which metal images a few inches high, or pictures, are displayed, together with a device for burning incense sticks. The most elaborate home shrines take up a whole room. Some shrines are large chests enclosing a dozen or more murti (images of deities) with some of the murti more than a foot in height. According to questionnaire responses, 67.2 percent of the whole Indian population have shrines in the home, and 67 percent reported that someone in the family worships there. Most of the Indians with shrines are Hindu, Jain, or Sikh, although Muslims often and Indian Christians occasionally set a place aside in the home to be used exclusively for prayer. Under most circumstances Hindus are more likely to have shrines in the home than people from other religious traditions. For the Indian population as a whole, most of the families without shrines in the home had low incomes ($20,000 or less) and were on temporary visas. But among Hindus (Group 1), even families with low incomes had shrines in 81.8 percent of the cases, and 60 percent of the homes of Hindus on temporary visa had religious shrines. Religious but nontraditional respondents (Group 2) reported shrines in the home at about the same rate as Group 1, while Group 3 respondents had home shrines at a rate 10 percent lower than for the survey population as a whole. A 1978 Pittsburgh survey (Clothey 1983, p. 169) indicated that 56.9 percent of respondents maintained shrines in their homes.

Religious shrines were reported to be in 84.7 percent of the homes of Hindu respondents, and in 79.9 percent someone worshipped at the shrine. The percentage of women Hindu respondents who worship individually is higher than for Hindu men, and most Hindu informants suggested that women are much more likely to worship at the shrine than men are.

Among the three groups of respondents, women vary from men at significant points. For all indicators of religious behavior women were always as much and they were often more observant than men. Women worship individually at a higher rate than men, and in Groups 1 and 2 there were no women who responded that they never performed individual worship. Women fast much more than men in Groups 1 and 2 and a smaller percentage of women than men in Group 3 never fast. Women in Group 3 were three times more likely to regard their work as a form of duty than men, considered themselves more religious now than at the time of immigration at twice the rate for men, and arrange pujas for special occasions at almost twice the rate for men. In all three groups women indicated that they participate in group worship 25 percent more frequently than men in the corresponding groups.

Opinion varied as to whether or not a Hindu woman can worship by proxy on behalf of the whole family, or whether each individual must do his or her own worship to derive any spiritual or material benefits. Popular opinion and tradition suggest that women do puja more frequently than men. In agreement one woman said:

> It's a Hindu tradition. The lady of the house prays for everybody. Then, as parents grow old, the children say that our parents are praying for us. . . . It is a family tradition, a pattern in Hindu society. Even if the father was not praying when he was working, he prays when he is retired. As you grow older, somehow prayer takes an important part in your life.

One Hindu woman explained:

> The woman does it every day. They pray and they offer. . . . It is basically a woman's responsibility and she is doing it for the whole family. . . . I remember, when I was young, I got this thing from my mother. She was the second daughter in the family, and she was entrusted with this responsibility

by my grandmother. She used to do it every day twice, and every Thursday. And she used to fast and thirst the whole of Thursday until the evening she finished the puja. . . . Someone in the family does it, it's all right.

A Bengali woman explained her shrine:

Lakshmi [Goddess of Good Fortune] puja is done in most of the Hindu houses of Bengal. . . . They do it every Thursday. . . . I do it every Thursday in my house. . . . I have a small room and I have all of the images there, and I do it every Thursday. . . . But the rest of the pujas . . . always the man does it.

Some women suggest that women pray both for the family and for themselves:

Even in my bed [in the morning] I do two or three shlokas. Whenever I do some work, I pray to God first and then do the work. . . . And when I go to sleep, I pray before I go to sleep, two or three minutes. It's not much. But that's what I can do. . . . I do it myself. But when I pray, I just pray for the whole family. You know, like thanks for the whole family. So, you know, it's combined. It's an improvement for my life too.

Other Hindus suggested that no one can worship by proxy for another person. As one man explained:

If you have a hunger, you have to eat to take care of your hunger, right? And if I am hungry, I tell my wife, "OK, you eat on my behalf." I won't be content. I'll still be hungry. So, it's individual--what you do, you will get back. But if I don't pray that's my choice, right?

Even some "nonreligious" (Group 3) Hindu women would find a shrine desirable in the home under the right circumstances: "My mother has one in her room. . . . I am not a very religious person, but when we build a new house I would definitely make a nice permanent place for a shrine."

Of seventy-one Hindus responding, 23.9 percent "always" and 40.9 percent "most of the time" arrange pujas or other religious observances for birth, birthdays, moving into a new house, new business ventures, and so forth. There were no significant differences between male and female responses. A surprisingly low 9.9 percent "never" make such arrangements. Religious/nontraditional respondents (Group 2) arranged puja for such occasions less often than Hindus while people in Group 3 arrange puja infrequently and close to one half never arrange pujas.

Almost all family and group religious observances take place on the weekend to fit in to the American work schedule even when, by the lunar liturgical calendar, they would normally fall within the work week. Until the opening of the India Cultural and Religious Center in Atlanta in 1984, pujas were performed in homes or rented halls for annual calendar events dedicated to various Hindu deities. Sometimes several families celebrate these occasions together:

> Puja is a religious ceremony. And when somebody is having an inauguration of a new house, somebody gets a baby, somebody has some nice raise, or something good is happening, Indians like to celebrate and attribute it to God. And they want a little ceremony with it where they can invite friends.

Some of these ritual observances continue in private homes despite the existence of the cultural center and, since 1986, of a temple room in the cultural center.

Most Hindus in Atlanta know the Hindu religion as a "little tradition," that is, as it was practiced in their home and/or immediate locale in India. They know little of variant practices and beliefs from other regions of India or of Hindu subtraditions with which they have no direct acquaintance. Popular hymns are well known, and the Bhagavad Gita is generally popular, but with the exception of a few who are well versed, Atlanta Hindus know only fragments of the "great tradition" represented by the Sanskrit scriptures, commentaries, and theologies.

Many Hindus in Atlanta and elsewhere in America do not know how to perform traditional Sanskrit puja. In their home setting someone in the extended family or the neighborhood might have been a trained ritualist able to assist the family in carrying out its ritual obligations. Also, until very recently, no religious professionals or priests were available. To meet their needs at least some of the time, a few local Brahmans perform puja for others as a favor, usually without accepting payment. According to one of the men who performs the ritual, some clients call on him primarily because they do not understand the ritual:

> They say we do it without knowing exactly what it is because they have no knowledge of Sanskrit or anything like that. They just follow the rituals. . . . We have got many scriptures that tell you the things of puja, but nobody tells you the interpretation of the puja. And that is why they think that once in a while they ask me to do it. Then they can understand the deeper meaning behind it. . . . And secondly, on occasions like this they can call more people who are interested in a certain activity who also enjoy being there. And that's the reason why they ask me to come: most of the time for their own instruction.

In agreement, one householder who has made use of this priest's services said:

> Much of the time when you go to India and attend even one of the Satyanarayana pujas or most of the temples with priests, I guarantee that none of the listeners understand. You just do it more or less mechanical. But nobody questions why or what's the meaning or what does this say.

While some of these temporary priests learned their priestly role before immigrating, others had to teach themselves in America. The rituals that are performed are sometimes more abbreviated than they would typically be in India.

One of the acting priests also adds a local set-in-America story (katha) to the traditional stories concerning the benefits of fulfilling vows to perform the ritual:

> At the end of each Satyanarayana puja you tell the stories from the five chapters of the Satyanarayana. And each one tells you how important it is, you know, for you to worship Satyanarayana even when you are very prosperous to maintain the prosperity; and if you are not prosperous, to obtain prosperity. But either way you need Satyanarayana puja. And that is the kind of stories-- that one man did not do it, and he became very unhappy. And one person did it, and he became very happy. So, that kind of thing. . . . But, you know, I did a sixth chapter of my own in Sanskrit based on a small, little incident here. . . . _____, his family was going in a boat. And suddenly the boat started drowning. And the children were screaming, and everyone was screaming. And they were in the middle of the waters, and they were very much worried about it. And his wife thought suddenly at that time that "If we all come out in a single piece in this boat, then I will do Satyanarayana puja. And I will find someone who does it, but I will get it done." . . . So she did that, and suddenly the boat came around, and there was no casualty . . . and everyone came ashore. . . . I put the entire incident in Sanskrit . . . poetry and added the sixth chapter of my own: how a family came out just by doing a ritual.

This nonprofessional priest also gives short ex-

planations in English if children are present in
the attempt to make the rite relevant for both
adults and children.   The most active ad hoc
priest performs Satyanarayana puja (as thanks for
safely passing a crisis or for success in a new
venture) and grhavastu puja (for inaugurating a
new house) most often. One person for whom the
rite has been performed described it:

> He does, like, call all the gods. And
> it purifies the house. Like in India
> when, like when you buy the land, then
> you will actually do it [puja] in the
> ground.   Before you are building that
> house, you will do the puja. That's the
> tradition. That's a different picture.
> But this is, you do the puja, bless the
> house, and everything.

The priest has also done Lakshmi puja for success
in business for the coming year in homes and, on
one occasion in a large hall, he directed dozens
of families so that they could perform the ritual
for themselves. He has also performed puja for
the quickening of a child, for the first birthday,
for the long life of a child, for investiture of
Brahman boys with the sacred thread, for weddings,
and for death. Many of the traditional samskaras
(rites of passage through the stages of life) are
no longer performed (they are also generally in
decline in urban India).

Professional priests are sometimes brought to
Atlanta for weddings or other special rituals from
other American cities with larger Hindu populations, such as Pittsburgh. Itinerant gurus and
swamis (mendicant religious teachers) often perform puja during their visits also. Some families
perform pujas with the assistance of audio or
video cassettes that explain the ritual acts they
should perform to accompany the recorded Sanskrit
stanzas.

Moving into a new house is sometimes solemnized by boiling milk or putting out water and
rice for the spirits of the place. Some families
break coconuts as a sacrifice for something good
that has happened:

> Thursday, Friday. . . . When you have

> something like good work done, we get
> these [coconuts], and we pray to God for
> whatever good has been done and just
> sacrifice that [break the coconut]. [It
> is] . . . a thanksgiving . . . on very
> good occasions.

Only a few persons have told me that they commemo-
rate their fathers on the anniversary of their
death, but since the Indian population here and in
the rest of the United States is relatively young,
parents are in most cases still living.

Holi is a joyous festival in India with some
similarities to Mardi Gras or to Halloween. Typically, people throw colored water on each other,
and some forms of role reversal are acted out
(women taking men's roles, servants becoming
bosses, and so forth.) In Atlanta many Hindus,
like this woman, celebrate Holi in a subdued
fashion:

> Holi is, of course, a lot of people
> getting together and a festival that
> . . . you somehow don't feel the urge to
> do it here. Your neighbors don't
> understand what the significance is.
> It's not really that you can join them.
> So . . .

Divali, the festival of lights, on the other hand,
is celebrated with regularity. Divali occurs in
November or December and includes decorating the
house inside and out with lights. Thus, it fits
right in with the symbolism of Christmas and Hanukkah.

> Q: Do you celebrate Christmas?
> A: Yes, we do. You know, the candles
> and the little puja. And we try to
> invite some of our close friends, and
> mostly it's small affairs . . . espe-
> cially for the children. [My son]
> . . . we let him know what it is all
> about and he really catches on the ex-
> citement of it. . . . I've got some
> fireworks at home and used those. And
> the neighborhood children came. They
> enjoyed it too.

> Q: So, do you have lights in front of
> the house and maybe in the yard as well?
> A: No. We do not go that far.   Well,
> here it's sort of . . . So we put up
> candles all around the house inside.
> Q: And I suppose that some of your
> neighbors might think it's Christmas
> lights?
> A: Nobody has questioned yet.

Many Hindus also celebrate Christmas in addition.
While for some Christmas is a secular celebration,
for others it is regarded as the birthday of one
of the descent forms (<u>avatar</u>) of God: "My mother
always celebrates it just like a Hindu festival
with sweets and things. Light the lamp and pray
to Jesus Christ." For some Hindus Thanksgiving
takes over the function of harvest festival (despite the fact that harvest does not occur in the
fall in many sections of India):

> We have a special dinner. We don't have
> meat or turkey. But we let the children
> know that this is a Thanksgiving dinner.
> We treat it as a harvest festival. . . .
> The [fall] harvest in Gujarat is in
> October-November. So Thanksgiving serves
> much the same purpose.

JAINS

The Jain religious tradition begins (in this
era) with the enlightenment of its founder
Vardhamana (from the sixth to fifth centuries
B.C.E., roughly contemporary with Siddhartha
Gautama, the Buddha), titled "Mahavira" (great
hero) or "The Jina" (the conquerer), who is believed to have overcome the limitations of human
life by crossing over or making a ford (he is
called "Tirthankara" or "ford maker") from this
life to release from birth, death, and suffering.
During worship, Jains usually arrange uncooked
rice grains in a design that represents the major
tenets of the Jain path to liberation (<u>kaivalya</u>)
in summary form. The bottom two thirds of the
design consists of a right-handed swastika the
rotating wheel of which represents the world of

birth, change, and death. At the top of the design is an upturned crescent below a dot that represents release. Between the swastika and the symbol of release are three dots denoting right faith, right knowledge, and right conduct, the means by which human beings may pass from this world to the realm of eternal peace (kaivalya).

The Jain path to liberation requires a life of absolute nonviolence (ahimsa) toward all living things (which is conceived more radically than in any other religious tradition), absolute truthfulness, absence of greed, chastity, frequent stringent fasting, twice daily confession, meditation, and renunciation of all attachments. The standards for Jain monastic conduct are quite severe. Officially, lay persons should vow to obey similar regulations, but in practice the official path, even in India, remains an ideal followed by only a few lay persons (Jaini 1979, p. 188).

Jain individual and family worship or puja is structurally similar to Hindu puja. Often the home will contain a small shrine with images of Mahavira and other Jinas, which function as aids in visualizing the goal of liberation. Some Jain sects do not employ images in worship. Rising before dawn, the traditional Jain salutes the Jinas, ponders his religious duties and whatever vows he or she has taken, bathes, dons clean clothing, and accompanied by a sense of peace of mind and dedication to the Jina ideal, offers a series of gifts to the Jinas represented by the images and ends by waving lighted lamps before the images (as in Hindu puja).

While the number of Jain respondents to the Atlanta questionnaire was too small to be of much evidential value, interview responses as well as questionnaire returns suggest that Jains in Atlanta are more religiously observant at the individual level than other Indians. Of nine respondents who identified themselves as Jain, 89 percent stated that they do individual worship daily, and the other 11 percent indicated that they worship at least once each week. This is the highest frequency for individual worship for any of the Indian religious traditions included in the survey (some Jains interviewed thought these figures might be high). Some Jains perform both the morning and the evening traditional worship, but most carry out an abbreviated puja either in the morning or in the evening.

All respondents reported shrines in their homes, and 89 percent indicated that someone in the family worships at the shrine. Five out of seven Jains interviewed also had shrines in their homes. Fasting, a characteristic practice of traditional Jain religiosity, was observed by 11 percent of the Jain participants in the survey once each week, 11 percent once a month, 22 percent once per year. The remainder never fast. Almost all Jains interviewed said that they and their families fast at least one day annually in observance of Mahavira's birthday (Mahavir Jayanti). A few women fast one day a week, but this may be as much a Hindu regional way of insuring the family's health and well-being as a specifically Jain practice. On the other hand, Jain respondents indicated that they arrange pujas or other religious observances always or most of the time for birth, birthdays, moving into a new house, new business ventures, and so forth at about the same rate as do Sikhs and Hindus (67 percent). A Hindu nonprofessional ritualist occasionally performs puja for Jain friends. Jains regard their work as a vocation or form of duty at a rate comparable to Hindus (71 percent). Reportedly, many Jain men are no longer strictly vegetarian, especially when they eat outside the home, and some drink alcoholic beverages.

Differences between the Digambara and Shwetambara Jain subtraditions have become of little functional value in Atlanta, and only private distinctions are made between Jains who do and those who do not employ images in worship. Some Jains in Atlanta have drifted away from the tradition. Some are not religious. One said he might become a Unitarian eventually. Another became attracted by a Hindu movement, as he explained:

> We are now kind of aloof from Jain, basically because we don't have any exposure, and also back home Jainism is one of the hardest religions to practice. It has so much restriction on diet, as well as you have to lead austere life, compared to _____

[another Indian tradition].

Perhaps 80 percent of the sixty to one hundred families of Jains in the Atlanta area derive from the state of Gujarat in northwest India, and most of the remainder are North Indian. Gujarati Jains identify closely with regional Gujarati culture and, in Atlanta, celebrate some annual festivals together with Gujarati Hindus. Jains from other North Indian areas tend to follow suit.

SIKHS

As was discussed in Chapter 1, the Sikh religious tradition is based on devotion to the one God whose guidance is present in the <u>Guru Granth Sahib</u> rather than in any living teacher. Sikhs in Atlanta who possess a copy of the <u>Granth</u> set it up in a shrine room devoted solely to that purpose. Sikhs are supposed to rise before dawn, bathe, and recite the Japji, a famous prayer from the <u>Granth</u>. As is also the case in India, the wife usually leads the <u>path</u> (prayer) and reads from the <u>Granth</u> for worship in the home. One woman explained that she does it for her family:

> I do feel when I'm doing it, I'm doing it for my son and for my husband. . . . But I feel they are doing it for me too. . . . When my husband prays, I feel it is not one-sided. . . . I feel he prays for us too. It is not one way.

Traditionally, one is supposed to worship in the home before the <u>Granth</u> both in the early morning and in the evening. It sometimes proves difficult to find the time to do this in America, especially if both the husband and the wife work. One Sikh family was convinced by parents to put the <u>Granth</u> in their home even though the two working parents could not keep this schedule. The wife said that the parents' rationale was as follows:

> It doesn't <u>have</u> to be in the morning. As long as you can do it any time of the day, it would be OK. And on the weekends now, we do it in the morning

and in the afternoon. . . . There is
nowhere that it is written [in the
scriptures] that if your schedule
doesn't permit it, it doesn't say you
can't pray another time. It's just
because this situation never occurred
[before now]. It's not necessarily a
"concession" [to the American schedule].
I wouldn't use that terminology. I
would think the nature of the schedule
has never been perceived before, and the
need has not been perceived. And there
were enough people in the home [in
India] to do it mornings and evenings.
If there was no need, it never occurred.
So it's just a "modification," I would
say.

Since only fourteen Sikhs identified themselves in the Atlanta survey, results are of
limited statistical value, but they are roughly in
line with opinions about religious observance
solicited through interviews. By most measures of
religiosity in the survey Sikhs did not differ
significantly from other Indians, although they
did not practice daily individual worship as often
(64 percent daily; 29 percent at least once each
week) as Jains, Hindus, and Christians. There
were shrines in the homes of 42.9 percent of the
Sikhs in the survey. While none of the respondents claimed to perform pujas for all occasions
that might call for it, 43 percent said that 7
they did so most of the time, 50 percent "not
often," and 7 percent "never." Individual worship
has to be squeezed into busy schedules:

Q: Do you do devotions every day?
A: I try to for a few minutes or even
in the car. We do it in the morning when
we leave the house [on the way to work].
Q: You do not need any special place to
do it?
A: Not really. But we do try to sit in
front of the Guru Granth Sahib at night
and do prayer for five or ten minutes at
least.
Q: And sometimes, I believe you said
that on weekends the family joins in as

well.
A: Definitely.

The observance of the five k's (long hair, comb, khaki shorts, short dagger, and steel brace- let) by men is a particularly salient cultural trait of Sikh tradition that advertises unmis- takably (and in a way that draws attention in America) that they are different (see La Brack 1979, pp. 135-7). Americans, particularly in rural areas, often do not know what the five k's signal, and they sometimes mistake Sikhs for Arabs. But even in urban areas in the American South, keshadhari (long-haired) Sikh men and boys draw attention to themselves. Many Sikh men have modi- fied observance in America, trimming their beards, shaving their faces clean, or cutting the hair. One told me that it was inconvenient, given the kind of manual labor he has to perform. Another gave the excuse that it frightened children. A man who was not wearing the steel bracelet said that he had lost it and was waiting until he could go to the Golden Temple in Amritsar to replace it (even though it had been lost about eight years). This form of personal religious observance is not undertaken lightly or without deliberate choice, as a Sikh woman explained:

> Q: Does it make any difference to you whether or not Sikh men are bearded and wear the turban?
> A: To me, yes. It may not to other people. . . . I am really proud of it. . . . Everybody asks me why my husband is wearing a turban and why my son is. . . . Men have to go through this looking physically very different in other countries [outside India]. And they feel that people are not necessarily looking at them positively or that they always have a negative association with their physical appearance. . . . My feeling is that it is very important from the point of view of religion and very important to our family. You know, they want to preserve the culture. . . . Yes, to be recognized from two miles away could be positive or

it could be negative. [So I tell my
husband] . . . people don't necessarily
look at him because he looks bad, but
because of how handsome he looks. [My
boss said] . . . "I think he is awfully
handsome, but I think he would be more
handsome if he took the turban off."
[Others said] . . . "Oh, I think his
turban really adds to his royal
appearance." So, there are different
ways of perceiving it. . . . To be
different is not easy. . . . But you
have to believe in it and be proud of
it. . . . [The men who have removed the
beard, and so forth] . . . do comment
that "As a woman you don't have to feel
the pressure." . . . And that's true.
. . . When I visited San Francisco
[where there is a large Sikh population]
. . . it was great to be walking in the
streets and not being noticed. . . . He
could go to the beach with a little
scarf on his head and run all day long
and not be noticed or be stopped to
answer questions.

As is certainly the case for almost all Indian
immigrants of all religious traditions, family
ties are extremely important. But the emphasis on
family need not exclude religious values and often
includes them:

Q: What is most important to you to
preserve from your cultural tradition?
A: The family closeness, the feeling of
belonging in the family, and the caring;
the role of parents; the child's role
toward parents. If I could teach that
to my child, that would be the most
important priority on my agenda. . . .
Q: Anything else?
A: There are always going to be good and
bad things. But to preserve the strong
ties. Again, it is coming down to the
family issues, I guess.
Q: Did you assume that Sikh traditions
were already involved?
A: The religious ties? Yes. It would

be very important. But the reason I put
that second on my priority list is that
I feel it would come automatically.
. . . To me, religion would be one of
the things to bring the family together.

There are no professional priests in Sikh
religious tradition. One local man has obtained a
license to perform marriages and has celebrated
them for the local community on occasion. During
the marriage ceremony, the couple circumambulates
the Adi Granth four times while hymns are recited.
Women visiting from India have also solemnized
Atlanta weddings a few times. A very limited
number of marriages of Sikh men have been with
native American women. The Sikh population in
Atlanta has been stable at forty to fifty-five
families since 1977.

MUSLIMS

Indian Muslims in Atlanta fall into two
groups. Sunnis, who constitute perhaps 80 percent
of Muslims worldwide, believe that Muhammad was
the last spiritual guide and that there have been
no successors. The Shi'ah believe that there has
been a succession of spiritual guides after the
death of the Prophet Muhammad.

Sunnis

On the one hand, Islam is the religious tradition
based on the revelation of God to Muhammad beginning about 610 C.E. incorporated in the Qur'an and
Islamic praxis (shari'ah). On the other hand,
Islam is believed by Muslims to be the true religion, the primordial revelation revealed to the
first human being, Adam, and subsequently to the
true prophets (including Moses and Jesus) of every
people. From the point of view of Muslims, Islam
is both the primordial and the final world religious tradition. As the final religion, Islam
is the recovery of the original will of the one
omnipotent God in a clear, unmistakable form that
calls for the submission (islam) of all creatures
to their Creator. Expressing standard Muslim
theology, one Muslim emphasized that creatures

below human status are already Muslim:

> Like the planet has to go around the
> sun, and the blood circulation in the
> human body will continue, and the person
> will be born and grow and die and
> everything . . . everything in   this
> universe as created, and all inanimate
> and animate objects, all are basically
> Islamic. They follow a certain rule.

Anyone   who   witnesses   aloud   to   the
Oneness/Unity of God and to Muhammad as the Messenger of God is regarded as a Muslim (one who
submits to God's will). The witness (<u>shahadah</u>) is
always included in the prayers incumbent upon an
observant Muslim five times each day. Prayer is a
direct interchange between each person and God.
No priests or other intermediaries are necessary,
and images of God are forbidden. In addition,
Sunni (from <u>sunnah</u>, the example of the prophet
Muhammad) Muslims are required to give alms to the
needy, to observe a total fast during the daylight
hours of the lunar month of Ramadan, and if prac-
ticable, to make the pilgrimage to Mecca in Saudi
Arabia at least once in their lifetime. These
five pillars (witness, prayer, alms, fasting, and
pilgrimage) are the framework for human submission
to God.

Underdevelopment of American Muslim economic
and political power (Abdul-Rauf 1983, p. 277)
probably contributes to the fact that American
Islam has so far received very little public no-
tice as an <u>American</u> religious tradition, despite
the presence of an estimated 2 to 3 million Muslims (Haddad and Lummis 1987, p. 3; Lovell 1983,
p. 93). Americans are in general ignorant about
or poorly informed about Islam (Haddad and Lummis
1987, p. 160). But with 25,000 to 35,000 new
immigrants arriving each year, it is estimated
that Muslims will outnumber Jews in America soon
after the turn of the twenty-first century (Haddad
and Lummis 1987, p. 3).

Muslims are unlikely to forget that they are
and will for the foreseeable future remain a minority in America. In a predominantly Muslim
country business often stops for midday prayer,
and there is strong majority sanction to perform

the prayer, but this is often not the case in countries where Muslims are in a minority. Interviews indicate that Muslims in India also observe the five daily prayers to a lesser extent than they would in Pakistan or Bangladesh. When a Sunni Muslim prays, it is obvious to non-Muslims since it involves standing, kneeling, and prostration while facing in the direction of Mecca. Even practicing the basic requirements of prayer has the potential of provoking reactions of curiosity at best and, at worst, of fear, as this medical doctor noted:

> I think you are always conscious when you are foreign and a minority. Atlanta is an excellent place to live, but you still become aware of it. . . . especially when you are strictly observing, practicing. . . . Sometimes you want to dress in your own clothes. . . . Islam is a religion which lives around the clock. If you are a Muslim and are out two or three hours, it's time for prayers and you've got to go to wash. . . . For example, if you are going down Peachtree Street and it's time for prayers. . . . If it was back home in _____, I'd probably go to a little park or there would be a mosque around, and I would go to pray. Here you cannot do that. In fact, if you do, people would think you are strange. They don't know what you are doing.

The five prayer periods during each day provide the observant Muslim with a structure for the inner religious life. The content of salah, Muslim prayer, is largely fixed and generally takes about twenty minutes to complete. For example, the periods for the beginning of the daily prayers between September 28 and October 1, 1982, were as follows: first at 5:59 a.m.; second at 1:28 p.m.; third at 5:10 p.m.; fourth at 7:33 p.m.; fifth at 8:58 p.m. An adult male described the way the daily prayers provide the rhythm of his life:

> See, in the morning when you get up, before the sunrise, you go to pray. So

when you pray, you concentrate your mind
and drag it away from all evil things,
and sort of, you take a vow that
whatever you are going to do the rest of
the day will be based on honesty, peace,
and without any bad attitude. So by the
time you've continued this, by one
o'clock or two o'clock in the day-to-day
life, in the hourly life, your mind
gets diverted--so that by that time the
second prayer comes in. So if you are
really somehow diverted, human needs,
like that, there is something wrong here
and there. You might have told a couple
of lies here and there . . . sometime
you might have got angry. . . . Second
prayer comes, where again, if it has
diverted it will come back. So that's
the process. It goes on.

Only eight persons identified themselves as
Muslims in my Atlanta survey, a return too small
to be of independent evidential value. The results are, however, generally in accord with the
surveys of Muslim immigrants conducted by Haddad
and Lummis (1987, pp. 25, 29, 167) in the midwestern, eastern, and northeastern United States
and with opinions proffered elsewhere (Lovell
1983, p. 100). Only two of the eight respondents
indicated that they pray five times daily.
Another two stated that they pray at least once
daily. The other four pray at least once each
week. One half had places set aside in their
homes, which they reserved exclusively for prayer.
The results of the survey of Haddad and Lummis
(1987, p. 29) show that 24 percent of their respondents (who immigrated from many different
countries at different periods) often pray five
times each day, and another 21 percent sometimes
pray five times a day. The data accord with one
Atlanta Muslim's view of immigrant Indian observance:

A lot of people, they are young, and
listen, they are not religious in their
motivations. . . . There are so many
Muslims. Maybe 30 percent are following
[Islamic practices]. . . . There are a

lot of people who don't.

But other Indian Muslim immigrants estimated
that at most 5 percent of the Muslim population in
America perform salah five times a day. That
prayer is required five times each day is well
known and not in dispute among American Sunni
Muslims. Some get around the problem by
scheduling their lunch hour to coincide with the
midday period for prayer. Muslims who are con-
scientious can usually find a way to pray at midday despite the indifference of their employers to
their religious needs:

> [When the midday prayer is late], I
> could easily pray after 5 p.m. [When
> earlier], it will coincide with my lunch
> hour. . . . I come home most of the days
> . . . but, otherwise, I can go to a
> place and pray.

Other Muslims skip the prayer while they are at
work. A student living in a college dormitory
skips the midday prayer so as not to attract undue
attention. Another college student arranged to
have an off-campus apartment rather than a dormitory room expressly to make her observing the
prayers less noticeable and thus less difficult to
practice.

Half of the Muslims in the Atlanta survey
observe the fast during the month of Ramadan all
of the time, while three out of eight observe the
fast most of the time. The Haddad and Lummis survey (1987, p. 29) indicates that first-generation
immigrant Muslims are more likely to observe the
fast than they are to pray five times each day:

> A good religious man should offer five
> times prayer in a day. He should not
> miss any prayer. And he should go to
> the mosque, if possible, on Friday,
> every Friday. . . . So maybe I cannot, I
> may not be able to make all of those
> things, though I think that one day I
> will be able to make them. . . .
> Q: In the house do other people do their
> prayers?
> A: Yes.

Q: Do some of them do them as much as
they are required?
A: Yes.
Q: Do you fast all during the day in
Ramadan?
A: Sometimes I do; sometimes I can't.

The end of the Ramadan fast is observed with a
feast of celebration called Eid al-Fitr that is
one of the occasions when the largest number of
Muslims in Atlanta are likely to congregate together. Eid al-Fitr is also the traditional time
to pay the zakat ("almsgiving"). Computing the
amount of alms due is quite complicated, but in
general it should be about 2.5 percent of gross
income. By customary tradition alms worth at
least a few dollars for each family member should
be given before Eid al-Fitr, often to needy Muslims, but sometimes also to nonMuslims who are in
need. It is Muslim tradition to conceal one's
generosity to others. The Eid celebration at the
end of the Ramadan fast is one of the religious
high points of the year:

> After finishing your thirty-day fasting,
> you eat your food and share it with all
> of your neighbors. If there are any
> poor, first you take care of them, and
> when they have eaten, then everybody
> eats. Your superiors, your inferiors,
> you become the same. You try to embrace
> them which means you belong to the same
> community. . . . we feel we are all in
> one community, you know.

The ideal of Muslim unity and equality under
God expressed symbolically at Eid al-Fitr is
realized much more forcefully in the reunification
of the "house" of Islam in the pilgrimage (Hajj)
to Mecca. Pilgrimage to Mecca by Indian immigrants in Atlanta is fairly common, and a local
travel agency offers a full Hajj tour package.
Many Muslims are well off financially and can
afford to make the journey, often arranged in
conjunction with return trips to India.

> The basic process [of Hajj] means you
> should be away from everything. Nothing

should be more important to you than God
and the hereafter. . . . And it is
expected after Hajj that you must
continue a life like that. . . . You
should be able to control your senses,
which get diverted here and there.

Whether or not immigrant Muslims are more or
less observant in America is a matter of some
dispute. Half of the Muslims in the Atlanta survey
said that they were more religious than they were
at the time of immigration and one quarter
indicated that they were less religious.

In the survey of Haddad and Lummis (1987, p.
25) 45 percent of Muslims from all countries
indicated that they had become more religious in
the last four years. Some Muslims believe that
Indian Muslims are in general less observant in
America than they would be in their home
countries. The Haddad and Lummis survey (1987, p.
168) indicates that the percentage of Pakistanis
and Indians who considered themselves religiously
very active varied from as low as 13 percent on
the East Coast to as high as 67 percent in the
Midwest. For the Midwest a much higher percentage
of Indians and Pakistanis considered themselves
religiously very active than did Muslims born in
America or who immigrated from other countries.
The percentage of Pakistanis and Indians who
scored themselves as somewhat deviant with respect
to required behavior (for example, consumption of
alcohol) was also much lower than for Muslims from
other countries or born in America. One Atlanta
Muslim saw the situation this way:

Some people, they are fanatic Muslims.
Wherever they go, they are fanatics.
And some Muslims are liberal. I think
they are a little bit relaxed [in
America], all the fanatic Muslims too.

But other Muslims think they are more religious:

My observation is that when you take
people and bring them here, the people
that are coming to the mosque were not
as religious back home as they are now.
. . . I know Muslims are, to a certain

extent, very conscious of their religion here.

Another Indian man, while acknowledging that Muslims in general may be less observant in America, argued that they are more observant here than elsewhere because there are mosques in Atlanta:

> Unfortunately, we are saying that it should be and quite a few people do observe these five pillars. But you will find some people who don't pray five times a day, although they would like to. But, you know, either their job or interest in something else, or their business, something keeps them away from it. . . . I would say that if you took a hundred people from here and sampled them with a hundred people from a place where there is no mosque or activity, such as in Atlanta, you will find that there is more religiousness in Atlanta.

Haddad and Lummis (1987, p. 25) reported that only 5 percent of the Muslims in their survey considered themselves not very religious. All respondents testified to their belief in a Higher Reality as the source of meaning and value. Belief in the basic tenets of Islam remains very strong, even among persons like this individual who is not very observant:

> I am not a very religious-minded man. But I know very little. I believe on faith. I have faith, and I believe in Muslim religion. And I believe in Al'lah, and I believe everything.

A more observant and religiously active Muslim also expressed strong faith in the way of Islam:

> To me, the religion makes sense. Without taking you away from becoming successful in this world by honest means, it focuses on something which is the hereafter. If you believe in the

hereafter, then the road to take is that
[Islam].

Like other Indian immigrants, Muslims
accommodate to American culture in varying
degrees. American cultural festivals that can be
interpreted as nonreligious and that celebrate
family ties are especially popular. These include
annual observances, such as Thanksgiving, Memorial
Day, and the Fourth of July. The Christmas
celebration of the birth of Jesus is much more
ambiguous. Jesus is revered in Islam as a prophet
and as a model of the spiritual life, but insofar
as Christmas celebrates the Incarnation, it is for
Muslims unacceptable. Christmas is observed, but
usually without exchanging presents.

Ismailis

Nizari Ismaili Muslims, followers of a distinct
religious orientation within the Islamic
tradition, have arrived in North America primarily
since the mid-1970s. About half of the American
Ismaili population derives from India and Pakistan, while the other half originated in Europe
and Africa with a few from Syria, Iran, and central Asia. A significant number, perhaps 5,000
Ismailis (Nanji 1983, pp. 156-57), eventually
landed in Canada and the United States after being
expelled from Uganda in 1972. Thus they represent
a variety of cultural and ethnic backgrounds. In
1987 an informed interviewee estimated that there
were 15,000 Ismailis in America and 40,000 in
Canada. The Ismaili population in Atlanta, estimated at about 450 people in late 1985, was
believed to number about 1,000 persons in the
summer of 1987.

Muslims in the Shi'ah tradition emphasize the
importance of the _imam_ (spiritual leader, teacher,
and guide) who through his inspiration illumines
the esoteric or spiritual (_batin_) depths of the
true worship of God below the exoteric surface of
Qur'anic revelation and of traditional religious
practice. While some knowledge of God is accessible through reason, and while the human in-
tellect can grasp aspects of the revelation in the
Qur'an, the Shi'ah believe that reason is limited

and requires completion through the divinely in-
spired authoritative teaching (<u>ta'lim</u>) of the
living imam issued from time to time in promulga-
tions called <u>firman</u>.

Shi'ah Muslims are "partisans" of Ali, the
son-in-law of the Prophet Muhammad, and believe
that Ali was chosen by God (and so designated by
the Prophet before his death) to be the spiritual
leader and continuing channel of spiritual interpretation.   Ali, in turn, designated his son and
so on through a continuing line of spiritual
guides. Almost all Shi'ah Muslims are in agreement
concerning the identity of the first six imams.
Ismailis diverge from the numerically larger
Twelver Shi'ah tradition (predominant in Iran) in
recognizing Isma'il (eighth century C.E.) as the
designated seventh imam. Nizari Ismaili differ
from another branch of Ismailis in affirming the
succession through Nizar, son of the Fatimid
Caliph al-Mustansir in Egypt in the eleventh century. Ismailis affirm that there has always been
a living imam to guide the faithful up to the
present time when the forty-ninth imam (since
1957) is His Highness Shah Karim al-Husayni, Aga
Khan IV.   The first Aga Khan left Persia for
northwestern India in the first part of the nineteenth century to live among followers who converted to Ismaili Islam centuries earlier. One of
the core ethnic components of Indian followers of
the Aga Khan is a Gujarati speaking group known as
Khojas.

Nizari Ismaili Muslims understand themselves
to be true Muslims rather than a sect of Islam or
a heresy. In contrast to the emphasis Sunni Muslims sometimes place on the unchanging character
of Islam as "the straight path," Ismailis understand Islam to be one faith of submission to God,
which takes a variety of institutional forms from
one cultural context to another and in different
time periods. Rather than emphasizing the concrete details of cultural Islam as it developed in
Arabia in the first and second Islamic centuries (
seventh and eighth centuries C.E.), Ismaili tradition has evolved (as have all of the Islamic
traditions), first in one form and then another.
Islam is not monolithic. In India Ismaili Islam
developed in an Indian rather than a primarily
Arabic form, and currently, in America, Ismaili

faith is evolving in an American form. Islamic
faith is, according to Ismaili interpretation,
continuous, yet changing; primordial, yet pro-
gressive and adaptive to changing circumstances.
The office of the imam is crucial to this understanding, for he is the channel of inspiration and
the guide to the true inner nature of submission
to God rather than merely to the cultural forms of
religious tradition.

In accordance with this spirit of continuity
of faith preserved through change, religious
praxis in Ismaili tradition has been modified at
various times and in different contexts. Ismailis
normally pray three times each day (rather than
five)--at dawn and twice in the evening. While
the prayers are said in Arabic language and begin
with the Fateha (the first Sura of the Qur'an) as
in Sunni Islam, they have been abbreviated and can
be recited in three to five minutes. Prayer, like
all Ismaili praxis, has an outer form of words and
intellectual content plus an inner spirituality
as conversation with God and as connection to the
imam. Prayer is as much a matter of attitude and
intent as outward form. One may pray while
working, for example--in fact, work is itself
understood to be a kind of prayer as the material
working-out of an inward faith.

While the daily ritual prayer (du'a) may be
said while one is alone, prayer with a group of
people engaged in prayer is believed to be much
more efficacious. It is the established custom
for Ismailis to gather to recite the prayers every
day before dawn and at sunset. According to Ismaili informants about half of the community in
Atlanta attends prayer at the jamaat khana
(meeting hall of the people) at least once each
day. On Fridays about 90 percent of the community
attend prayer in the evening (see Chapter Four).

The inwardness of faith emphasized by Ismailis
is not reflected in any sort of withdrawal from
the world or asceticism. Ismaili faith is very
much oriented toward participation in God's creation. Material work is emphasized as a virtue
and is part of the interest in the welfare, education, and economic improvement of the Ismaili
community as a whole. It is one's duty to work and
to produce economic gain. The zakat is paid by
Ismailis directly to the imam, who in turn uses

the funds collected for the welfare of the community (people outside the Ismaili faith have also been beneficiaries).

At some point in childhood individuals make their personal commitment to the imam. At least once in their lifetime Ismailis should make their silent commitment to the imam in his physical presence. The current Aga Khan, Karim, visited New York City in November 1986 in part to make it possible for Ismailis in America to take bay'a (allegiance) and for darshan (seeing and being seen). Large numbers attended from Atlanta and from all across America. Hajj or pilgrimage to Mecca is not an obligation for Ismailis, but pilgrimage at least once to the imam is an obligation.

The Muslim daylight fast during the month of Ramadan is observed by Ismailis only in abbreviated fashion, primarily for two days--the twenty-first and twenty-third days of the lunar month. The Ismaili emphasis is on the inward meaning and the intent rather than the details of ritual customs.

CHRISTIANS

Legend, especially the account of Thomas Christians, has it that the Christian tradition was initially brought to India by St. Thomas the apostle in the first century. Historians dispute this claim, but the consensus points to the presence of the Christian church in India from at least the fourth century. Some pre-Reformation Christian traditions in India have institutional connections to Roman Catholics, but others recognize Syrian Orthodox patriarchs. The latter retained Syriac as the language for their worship and Mesopotamia as the source of the authority of its bishops. One group transferred to Rome during the sixteenth century, but a portion of these broke away in the following century to form the Malankara Syrian Orthodox Church. Protestant Christian groups date primarily from the eighteenth and nineteenth centuries. Christians made up less than 3 percent of the population of India in the early 1980s (Thundy 1983, pp. 42-48).

Well over half of the Christians from India in

America hail from the southern state of Kerala. In 1987 they numbered between 100 and 150 families in Atlanta. A great variety of Christian denominations is represented. There are Christians from mainline Protestant denominations, some of whose denominations joined either the Church of South India or the Church of North India following Indian independence; and there is a variety of other Protestants, Catholics, and Orthodox.

The personal religious praxis and consumption habits of Indian Christians have apparently changed very little in America. Most Christians were raised according to strict standards of religious observance and general behavior, and almost all were raised in theologically conservative settings. Because of this Indian background, Protestants, and even some Catholics and Orthodox, often prefer conservative Protestant churches over others. Many, like this father, testify to regular, frequent worship:

> We regularly pray every day, read the Bible, and pray at home. Today, if I pray, next night, my wife. Then the oldest boy and girl, then the next boy. Every moment counts.

There were fourteen Christians in the Atlanta questionnaire population. This sample is not statistically significant, but it does tend to confirm reasonably high rates of religious praxis among Indian Christians. The rate for daily individual worship was 57 percent and for at least once a week, 21 percent. About 21 percent felt that they were more religious and about the same percentage felt that they were less religious since coming to the United States. Approximately 67 percent attend group worship at least once every two weeks, and another 8 percent attend at least once a month.

Indian Christians in Atlanta are attending established Christian churches and tend to blend into the individual and family worship patterns of the churches they join. Native languages and musical styles similar to bhajans are still used for hymns within the family; but otherwise, particularly as the children grow up and use English predominantly, little distinctively Indian Christian practice is apparent, except on the rare occasions when local Indian Christians congregate together (for example, at Christmas).

Some Indian Christians have testified that their being Christians probably gives them easier access to American culture. They feel more identity with American society because of shared beliefs and, in certain cases, practices. They can meld right in to existing churches. But others, like this man, saw no advantage in it:

> No.   That did not make any difference,
> for me at least. They don't know from
> looking at my face whether I'm Hindu or
> Christian or somebody else. They just
> know that I'm an Indian, that's all.
> . . . Being a Christian, I'll be a
> little more comfortable mentally in a
> church rather than a temple, and the
> Hindu will be uncomfortable in a church.
> And he will not be able to have
> fellowship.

Some Christians have noted definite advantages for social relations to other Indians in America that were not available in India, as one testified:

> And one thing is, we are inferiors
> there.   We   are   untouchables   as
> Christians in India, OK? We always
> carry that in our mind. Today, I go to
> Dr.____'s house. . . . I go and eat on
> his table and he comes to me and eats on
> my table. But in India I'll not be able
> to go to his home and eat. And he will
> not be able to come to my home and eat
> because the area in which I live . . .
> is a separate place [from the rest of
> the town].

Some Indian Christians indicated that they did not identify strongly with India, but one stated that he felt a religious obligation to be active in the Indian community and to contribute money for the center:

> Definitely I will contribute. Yes, I

will,   because I don't want to   be
separated from them.   If I want to
witness, I must be one among them. So I
don't see anything wrong in that to
contribute $100 or $500 or whatever it
is.

Because of their belief system, some Indian
Christians deliberately avoid being present and or
taking part in Hindu worship because it involves
images and polytheism. But others maintain contact and draw lines of religious distinction elsewhere. One man explained his personal practice
when he attends puja:

> I do go to them [Hindu pujas]. I don't
> want to be aloof. I want to be one
> among them [Indian Hindus].   Otherwise,
> it's hard to. When they are able to
> come to Christmas party at my home, I
> should be open to go to their puja.   I
> mean, I did not sit there and do puja,
> but I came. . . . I did not attend any
> temple or puja in India. I was curious
> to know how they celebrated, and there
> is nothing wrong in learning something.
> . . . No, we don't take [prasad, food
> that has been offered to the deity].
> But we don't tell them that we don't
> take. . . . We avoid that. . . . We, as
> Christians, whether Indian or American,
> will show our love and affection in the
> way Christ taught. They will   know
> [about Christian faith].

But some Indian Christians, like this man, participate in Hindu worship without any sense of re-
striction, including eating the prasad:

> Q: Do you eat the prasad?
> A: Yes, but it has no significance for
> us. But I can go through every motion
> of every religion.

NOTES

1. The neo-Hindu Indian practices religion at the individual worship level in some spiritual sense that is clearly of Hindu origin but does not identify himself or herself as Hindu and takes part in group religious activities less often than acknowledged Hindus.

2. A much older version of this same general type of theology of religious origins may be traced back to early Christian theologians and probably to Philo of Alexandria (de Vries 1967, pp. 13-18). The neo-Hindu theology of religions is pervasive among immigrant Hindus and influences their perceptions of all other religious traditions, as well as of the American religious situation: In so far as there is something good in other religious traditions, it must be basically the same as true spirituality in Hinduism. Thus, for example, the Christian Incarnation is just another example of a Hindu avatar (descent form of God). Muhammad, the Muslim Messenger of God, is also just another avatar. What both Jesus and Muhammad revealed is in total agreement with true Hindu spirituality.

While this evaluation of other religious traditions may serve theological needs of Hindus among themselves, this reading is more than likely to be judged to be descriptively inaccurate and theologically condescending by most Christians and most Muslims. The well-known Hindu religious tolerance for other religious traditions often turns out to be functionally equivalent to the paternalism toward other religious traditions so often evidenced by Christians and Muslims respectively: "Your religious tradition's beliefs are true to the extent that they agree with mine."

Neo-Orthodox Protestant Christian theologians in the first half of the twentieth century had affinities with these neo-Hindu notions at several points. Neo-Orthodoxy tended to talk about religion as something human beings make up to try to save themselves or to take advantage of other people. Religion is traditional, riddled with superstitions, often immoral, and typically corrupted by the passage of time. Faith, however, is concerned with true revelation. Faith is the human relationship to divine reality. For some of the

neo-Orthodox theologians faith is the human relationship to Reason or the Logos. This parallels
the neo-Hindu emphasis that faith is satya, Truth
or Reality.

3. The confusion involved in usage of the term
"Hindu" was made particularly obvious in 1985 when
the Ramakrishna Order, after almost a century of
calling themselves both Hindus and universalists,
got the Calcutta High Court to declare the Ramakrishna Order a non-Hindu minority religion (see
Swarap 1986).

4. Although there is no cognate for the word
"religion" (from Latin, religio) in any native
Indian language, there are Sanskrit terms that
correspond to the idea of religion reasonably
well. Among these words are dharma, which is
often translated "duty." But the word refers
more basically to people's aligning themselves in
their particular niches in the universe to the way
things really are, that is, to Reality. The notion dharma may include within its scope law,
moral obligation, teaching, meditation, and ritual
practices. Other Sanskrit terms, such as sasana
or sampradaya, denote a spiritual "dispensation"
or "teaching tradition" that has been handed down.
A sadhana is the path or discipline one may follow
toward enlightenment or liberation. Darshana
denotes the approach or viewpoint one employs to
realize Reality or behold God. Hindu Sanskrit
terminology has had considerable influence on all
of the indigeneous religious traditions of India.
And since most Indian immigrants to the United
States have had long acquaintance with and are
fluent in English, the words "religion" and "religious," as they apply to their traditions, are
clear enough that they know what is being said
when they are asked, "Do you consider yourself
religious?"

3
Religious and Cultural Institutions

The frequencies with which Indians engage in worship as individuals by themselves or in the context of their immediate families do not always correspond to the patterns of their participation in group worship. How often an individual takes part in group forms of worship depends in part on the ideology of group worship in the religious tradition of that person. The congregational character of some of the Indian religious traditions is pronounced, while in others it is muted. The sincerity and seriousness of a purported Christian who <u>never</u> attended church would be questioned by many Christians because Christian commitment generally entails commitment to the church in some form. Daily devotions as part of a congregation are also the norm within the Ismaili tradition, as is Friday noon prayer for Sunni Muslim men. But regular attendance at group worship is, in many cases, less central for Jains and Hindus than is typical in Christian and Muslim traditions.

In America, at least initially, differences in the ideology of group worship among the various religious traditions are reflected in differences in the rates of development of and participation in group-worship. People in religious traditions with strong group worship ideologies tend to organize earlier and to have higher rates of participation in group worship than do adherents of religious traditions with less emphasis on communal worship. Muslims, Sikhs, and Christians, for example, organize and participate in group worship at an earlier stage and at a higher rate than Jains and Hindus.

The survey was done at a certain stage of development. Rates of participation in group worship should increase greatly in future years as the number of children grows, as the total number of Indians increases, and as organizations become more developed. Low rates of participation in group worship for some Indian groupings (for example, South Indians) are to some extent due to meager institutionalization at the time of the survey. When the Sri Venkateshwara Temple is finished, participation should increase.

However, lags in development or participation in religious institutions by Hindus and Jains should be temporary (unless the local Jain population does not grow beyond the current small numbers). In order to survive in America, immigrant religious traditions have to develop stable voluntary associations to build the social structures of an ethnic community, to preserve a sense of cultural identity, and to facilitate the transmission of religious tradition to the next generation.

PARTICIPATION IN GROUP RELIGIOUS ACTIVITIES

Since the intervals at which worship activities for the various Indian groups in Atlanta are scheduled varies from several times each week to once each month, figures from the Atlanta survey for rates of attendance at least once every two weeks should be combined with results for participation at least once a month to provide a meaningful basis of comparison in Table 6. Using this method, the average attendance figure for the whole Indian population for at least once a month comes to 47 percent. The average rate of monthly attendance for women ran almost 15 percent higher than that of men. But the rate for Indian respondents who never take part in group worship (16 percent) is about the same for women and men. (Clothey's 1978 survey [1983, p. 168] of the

Pittsburgh population showed attendance at a temple or religious institutions at least once a week by 23 percent of respondents and less than twice a month by 77 percent.)

As expected for religious traditions with strong communal worship ideologies, average monthly rates of participation for Sikhs (93 percent), Muslims (89 percent), and Christians (75 percent) ran higher than for other respondents by a substantial margin. The lower rates of participation in group worship for Jains (44 percent) and traditional Hindus (60 percent) do not necessarily indicate a lower level of religiosity since the rates of daily or weekly individual worship for traditional Hindus and Jains were similar to those for Sikhs, Muslims, and Christians. When Hindu or Jain religious communities do develop religious institutions in America, social and communal/institutional reasons for participation in group forms of worship are as important and perhaps more important than religious motivations (see the discussion of Table 7 that follows).

Table 6 lists rates of participation in group worship for adherents of the various religious traditions from the highest rates of monthly participation to the lowest. The first horizontal line of Table 6 gives the rates of group worship for all respondents (N = 279). However, rates for adherents of the particular Indian religious traditions represented in the sample depend on correlation with a separate question in the questionnaire with a slightly smaller base number (N = 269). (The one Ismaili Muslim respondent was combined with Sunni Muslim respondents in the tabulated results.)

Respondents who identified themselves with a specific religious tradition participated in group worship at significantly higher rates than those people who did not do so. Neo-Hindus and Cultural Hindus had substantially lower rates of group worship participation (monthly rates were 35 and 22.6 percent, respectively). Lower rates of participation in group worship were also recorded for persons who indicated that they were not religious, people who were in the United States on temporary visas, and Indians who had no children. Low participation by people in the last two categories points to the communal/social character of

Table 6

Participation in Group Worship

	Number of persons	At least Once in 2 weeks	At least Once a month	At least Once a year	Never
		percentages			
All respondents	279	20.8	26.2	37.3	15.8
Sikh	14	14.3	78.6	7.1	.0
Muslim	9	66.7	22.2	11.1	.0
Christian	12	66.7	8.3	8.3	16.7
Traditional Hindu	70	28.6	31.4	34.3	5.7
Jain	9	11.1	33.3	55.6	.0
Neo-Hindu	102	12.8	12.5	49.0	15.7
Cultural Hindu	53	5.6	17.0	35.9	41.5

group worship. New arrivals and people without children tend to be less involved in community affairs. Participation in group worship in fact increases significantly with increased years in the United States.

Table 7 exhibits the relative strength of the motivations for taking part in group worship in the survey population. The first two vertical columns in each set of Table 7 list the percentage of respondents who ranked a particular reason for attending group worship as primary or secondary. The third vertical column lists the percentage of respondents for whom a particular reason played no role in whether or not they attended group worship.[1] The number of respondents represented in Table 7 is less than 291 because thirty persons did not answer the question and thirty-three persons checked their reasons for attending group worship rather than ranking them (thus making it impossible to gauge the relative strength of different reasons for participating). The first horizontal line of tabulations for each reason represented in Table 7 is therefore based on a population of 228 persons. Due to additional missing values in the questionnaire results, responses for adherents of the different religious traditions are based on the slightly smaller population of 218.

The importance of a "religious" motive for group worship varied considerably within the Indian population. On the one hand, religion was the most important motivation for attending group worship by a large margin. "Religious" was ranked as the primary reason for attending group worship by 46.1 percent and as the primary or secondary reason by 54.3 percent of the respondents. But on the other hand, religion played no role at all in the motivation for attending group worship for almost one third (31.7 percent) of the population. Sex was not a significant factor in the relative importance of a religious motive for group worship.

These survey results can be clarified by arranging the respondents into three groups. One group (over 45 percent) attends group worship primarily (but not exclusively) for religious reasons. A second group attends for a mix of religious and nonreligious reasons. The third

Table 7

Reasons for Participating in Group Worship

	Primary reason	Secondary reason	Not a reason
	percentages		
RELIGIOUS REASON			
All respondents [228]	46.1	9.2	31.6
Muslims [9]	100.0	.0	.0
Jains [4]	75.0	25.0	.0
Sikhs [13]	69.2	7.7	7.7
Christians [10]	60.0	10.0	30.0
Traditional Hindus [56]	55.4	17.9	17.9
Neo-Hindus [79]	48.1	6.3	31.7
Cultural Hindus [47]	10.6	6.4	63.8
[218]			

Table 7 (Continued)

	Primary reason	Secondary reason	Not a reason
	percentages		
FOR SOCIAL CONTACT			
All respondents	15.8	17.1	40.8
Muslims	.0	11.1	44.4
Jains	.0	50.0	.0
Sikh	23.1	30.8	7.7
Christians	.0	20.0	70.0
Traditional Hindus	19.6	16.1	32.1
Neo-Hindus	11.4	21.5	39.2
Cultural Hindus	23.4	6.4	59.6
TO PRESERVE TRADITION			
All respondents	11.4	17.5	43.9
Muslims	.0	.0	33.3
Jains	.0	25.0	25.0
Sikhs	23.1	38.5	.0
Christians	.0	10.0	80.0
Traditional Hindus	14.3	19.6	35.7
Neo-Hindus	12.7	21.5	39.2
Cultural Hindus	10.6	4.3	66.0

Table 7 (Continued)

	Primary reason	Secondary reason	Not a reason
	percentages		
TO CELEBRATE HOME CULTURE			
All respondents	8.3	11.4	51.3
Muslims	.0	11.1	44.4
Jains	25.0	.0	25.0
Sikhs	.0	15.4	23.1
Christians	.0	.0	100.0
Traditional Hindus	7.1	21.4	44.6
Neo-Hindus	10.1	8.9	45.6
Cultural Hindus	10.6	6.4	68.1
TO STRENGTHEN LOCAL COMMUNITY			
All respondents	3.1	7.0	55.7
Muslims	.0	22.2	33.3
Jains	.0	.0	25.0
Sikhs	.0	7.7	25.0
Christians	10.0	.0	80.0
Traditional Hindus	3.6	3.6	51.8
Neo-Hindus	2.5	7.6	51.9
Cultural Hindus	.0	10.6	74.5

Table 7 (Continued)

	Primary reason	Secondary reason	Not a reason
	percentages		
FOR FUN			
All respondents	2.2	1.8	73.2
Muslims	.0	.0	88.9
Jains	.0	.0	50.0
Sikhs	.0	7.7	46.2
Christians	.0	.0	100.0
Traditional Hindus	5.4	3.6	62.5
Neo-Hindus	.0	1.3	70.9
Cultural Hindus	2.1	.0	87.2
TO SPEAK THE LANGUAGE			
All respondents	1.3	5.3	59.2
Muslims	.0	22.2	55.6
Jains	.0	.0	25.0
Sikhs	.0	23.1	30.8
Christians	.0	.0	100.0
Traditional Hindus	1.8	5.4	50.0
Neo-Hindus	1.3	.0	58.2
Cultural Hindus	.0	8.5	72.3

Table 7 (Continued)

	Primary reason	Secondary reason	Not a reason
	percentages		
FOR APPROVAL OF OTHER INDIANS			
All respondents	.9	.9	73.7
Muslims	.0	.0	66.7
Jains	.0	.0	50.0
Sikhs	.0	.0	46.2
Christians	.0	.0	100.0
Traditional Hindus	1.8	1.8	73.2
Neo-Hindus	.0	1.3	69.6
Cultural Hindus	.0	.0	85.1

group (just under one third) attends (although much less frequently) predominantly for nonreligious reasons. Table 7 makes clear that religion is a strong reason for attendance for people who identify with specific religious traditions, including those who identify themselves as Hindus. The neo-Hindus are in the middle, both with regard to the rate at which they participate and the mixture of religious with nonreligious reasons for participating. Almost all of the people in the sample for whom "religious" is not a reason for attending group worship are cultural Hindus.

Taking part in group worship because of a religious reason was stronger with women than for men. Motivation to "preserve tradition" and to "celebrate home culture" are about the same strength for men and women. Attendance for "social contact" is a stronger reason for men.

Clothey's survey of a population sample from

the metropolitan area of Pittsburgh, Pennsylvania, conducted in 1978 shows broadly comparable results. Women and persons from Brahman families attended group worship at the Pittsburgh temple more often than other Hindus. Nearly a third of the nonreligious went to the temple at least once a month, and 45 percent of all respondents indicated that cultural, family solidarity, and social reasons were just as important as religious reasons for attending temple worship.

ETHNICITY AND RELIGION

Religious and ethnic factors reinforce and influence each other. Ethnic similarities sometimes override religious differences, but religious differences sometimes create sharp divisions within ethnic groups.

For the Indian population as represented in the survey, "religious" as the primary reason for taking part in group worship was more than three times stronger than the next strongest primary reason, "social contact," and it was more than four times stronger than any of the other primary reasons for attending group worship. It is, however, likely that the options offered in the questionnaire such as "preserve tradition" (11.4 percent) and "celebrate home culture" (8.3 percent), are not completely <u>discrete</u> reasons (although they are clearly not identical) and that they should be combined. "Celebrate home culture" and "preserve tradition" would run 19.7 percent, which would be stronger than the "social contact" motivation alone (15.8 percent) and more than two-fifths the strength of the "religious" reason. The <u>"religious"</u> reason would still be more than <u>twice</u> as strong as these two reasons combined. "Religious" would also be the strongest reason for attending group worship with first and second ranked reasons consolidated, but by only a small margin. For all respondents other ethnic factors, such as "strengthen local community," "speak own language," "approval of other Indians," "for fun," and "other," were very weak motivations, and for over half of the population they were not motivations at all.

Religious and ethnic/social reasons for attending group worship were of almost equal strength. While "religious" was the strongest reason Indians attend group worship, <u>ethnic</u> reasons ("social contact," "preserve tradition," "celebrate home culture") were almost as strong secondary reasons for the population as a whole. With respect to group worship, the Indian population was, however, polarized. Ethnic/social reasons were the strongest motivations for participating in group worship for just under one third of the population. Yet these ethnic reasons did not function as motivations at all for more than 40 percent of the Indian population.[2] Since half of the Indian population has been resident in America only since 1975, it may well be that the importance of ethnic factors will increase in a few years.

There is no general agreement in the scholarly literature about the meaning of "ethnic group." If fact, some would argue that the use of the two terms is redundant (Petersen 1980, pp. 1-5). Whatever the labels chosen, the intent is to point to a sense of peoplehood with which people can identify, whether the source of that identity be fictive, actual, or some mixture of both. Definition cannot be very precise because the boundaries of our identities continually shift with circumstances, with our distinction from whoever at the moment is not "us." Like other people, Indians have multiple identities, perceiving themselves according to one setting and circumstance as Indians, according to another as members of regional-linguistic and/or sectarian subcultures, and relative to other situations as Africans, Britishers, or Americans. It would be extremely difficult to give a satisfactory description of Indian culture by specifying the elements of culture that are shared by <u>all</u> Indians; but in some circumstances, nevertheless, Asian Indians in America constitute a single ethnic group, a people. Unaware as they usually are of "subtle" internal cultural differences, native Americans are perhaps the people most likely to perceive Indians as an homogeneous ethnic group. In other respects Indian regional or sectarian subcultures seem to many Indians to be the component ethnic groups. Bengali Muslims and Bengali Hindus, for example, share a great deal of common culture with a common language

being only the foundation.   In many important
respects a Bengali Muslim has more in common with
Bengali Hindus than with Pakistani Muslims.   But
there are nevertheless circumstances in which
shared religious identity can outweigh regional
cultural identity.

The largest Indian regional organization in
Atlanta is the Gujarati Samaj of Atlanta with over
1,000 members (Gujarat is in northwestern India).
The purpose of the Samaj is the celebration and
perpetuation of common regional language and culture.   Gujaratis meet frequently for classical and
popular entertainment programs, excursions and
longer trips, and for the celebration of annual
festivals important in Gujarati culture.   New
Gujarati immigrants are also sometimes offered
assistance, and families in distress are given
aid.   While the Gujarati Samaj is in principle,
like other regional organizations, open to all
Indians, the conduct of its events in Gujarati
language effectively limits participation.

There are also the much smaller regional
groups of thirty to fifty families, such as the
Georgia Tamil Sangam, Nrupatunga Kannada Koota,
Bengali Association of Greater Atlanta, the Telegu
Association of Metro Atlanta, the Sindhi Group,
the Kashmiri Overseas Group, the Maharashtra Mandal, and the Malayali Association. The Sikh Study
Circle (Punjabi) and the Durga Puja Society (Bengali) are both regional and religious organizations simultaneously.

A Bengali woman offered this explanation of
the tendency of Indian immigrants to organize on a
regional basis:

> It is common culture, language, yes.
> . . . The people from other states more
> or less have common food habits. We eat
> fish.   And I don't think the Punjabis or
> the Gujaratis, they really like fish.
> . . . Now people have different ideas.
> Previously, if you found a Bengali girl
> married to a Gujarati or a Marathi or
> Punjabi, people wouldn't hear of that.
> But now it doesn't really matter.   I
> have a cousin who is married to a Syrian
> Christian, and she is accepted in the
> family. So I think the more we get rid

of these ideas the better we are.

A South Indian explained why the Telegu Association, which meets about once a month for
dinner, movies, plays, picnics, or calendar celebrations, is needed:

> Q: What is the attraction [of a regional
> organization]?
> A: The language and the culture, food.
> . . . The language is most important to
> gather as a group. . . . See, if there
> is a Telegu Association, if any Telegu
> newly come comes here, and if they know
> that there are some Telegus, and they
> will feel so happy. And they want to
> join to it, and they want to talk to
> them,   and they will find out whether
> they know anybody whom they know, and
> they will feel some comfort that they
> know some Telegu family here in Atlanta.

In agreement, another South Indian male said:

> Caste to us does not mean anything in
> this country really. Amongst the Indian
> community   the--what brings people
> together is more, first, they are
> Indian; second, the language spoken.

One South Indian suggested that a common background of experience is more important in regional
associations than common language:

> It is strange that language should make
> that big of a difference because we find
> that 70 percent of the conversations
> go on in English. The extent to which
> the actual language that brings
> people together is usually rather small.
> But I guess the closeness comes from
> more common background and common
> experiences. "You are from Madras, I am
> from Madras. Do you know such and such a
> road? I used to live in Mylapore?"
> That brings people together.

Like the other regional associations, the

Tamil Sangam (South Indian) uses mailing lists to
contact compatriots for social gatherings every
six to eight weeks. Activities may include picnics, motion pictures in their own language,
classical music and dance programs, skits and
dramas, and the celebration of annual festivals,
such as Divali and Ponkal (Tamil New Year's Day).
Dinner is usually included. Rarely, there are
also programs of religious ritual. Some members
hope also to teach children Tamil language in the
future.

Perhaps the majority of Indian immigrants in
Atlanta agree that regional interests should be
kept within the bounds of the interests of the
overall Indian population. A Gujarati observed
about his own regional association:

> Personally, I was opposed [in 1983] to
> the idea of a new Gujarati Samaj. . . .
> We left those regional differences
> behind, and then we have come 10,000
> miles away. We don't want to revive
> that. . . . So I've done my duty, again
> sort of a stoop-to-conquer kind of
> situation. . . . I say, "Let us move in
> such a way that whenever there is an
> all-India function, we have plenty of
> support to work with and that we
> recognize ourselves as first, Indians,
> and then as Gujaratis." . . . I really
> hope that we create a situation in which
> all measure of Gujarati Samaj actually
> helps IACA [India American Cultural
> Association] instead of hurting it.

Some, such as this immigrant from Kerala,
admit the close cultural affinity within the region, even across religious lines, but are reluctant to form associations based on regional origin
at all:

> I don't really want to organize a
> Malayalee [Kerala] association. I
> believe we are citizens of the United
> States and that we have to open up our
> minds and see just a little bit more
> than the Malayalee association or small
> organization like that. I don't even

believe in an Indian association. I'd
like to have an Indian American cultural
association.

Regional ethnicity continues in the language
spoken at home among the first generation and to
some extent with the children, in close friendship
circles, in social circles, and in regional organizations and gatherings. Local regionalism is
reinforced by mobility: contacts with regionals
in other North American cities, especially cities
with large Indian populations where regional ethnicity is much more pronounced and where pan-
Indian ethnicity is for many purposes more difficult to mobilize, and local participation in
national regional organizations, such as, for
example, the Telegu Association of North America.
In January 1984, for example, basically the same
celebration, Sankranti (New Year), was celebrated
on the same day by three different South Indian
regional organizations.

A prominent Indian organization with mostly
Muslim membership is the Aligahr Alumni Association (a national and international association of
alumni of Aligarh Muslim University in Agra,
India). The association has monthly meetings,
celebrates the Eids, and organizes an annual
Mushaira (an Urdu poetry recital) with participants both local and from across North America, as
well as some from India and Pakistan. The roughly
500 Indian Muslims in the Atlanta area in 1988
have a social (but not religious) organization of
their own.

HINDU RELIGIOUS GROUPS

The survey conducted in Atlanta during 1984
and 1985 provided a profile of Hindu involvement
in group worship. Participation of group worship
shows a configuration that is different from the
worship of individuals.

Attendance and Reasons for Attendance at Group
Religious Activities

Traditional Hindus attend group worship much
more often, for a wider variety of reasons, and

for stronger reasons than neo-Hindus or cultural
Hindus.   They attend group worship at least once
in two weeks at almost twice the rate for neo-
Hindus and almost two and a half times their
monthly rate (See Tables 6 and 7 at the beginning
of this chapter). Traditional Hindus attend five
times more often than cultural Hindus every two
weeks and more than two and a half times more
often monthly. "Never" rates of traditional Hindus
are also significantly different from both neo-
Hindus (just over one third as many) and cultural
Hindus (less than one seventh as many).

The "religious" motive is the primary reason
for attending group worship for more than one half
of the traditional Hindus, and it is either primary or secondary for just under three quarters of
them. The rate at which the "religious" reason
does not figure in motivations for attending group
worship is much lower than for neo-Hindus and
cultural Hindus.

People who attend group worship often have
stronger reasons and more of them than people who
do not attend often. Ethnic and social factors
are ranked first by traditional Hindus at rates
close to those of neo-Hindus and cultural Hindus
and nonreligious motives are not a reason for
traditional Hindus at about the same rates as for
neo-Hindus.

When first- and second-rank reasons are combined, "social contact" and "support the local
community" are of similar weight for the three
groups of Hindus. To "preserve tradition" was
more important for traditional Hindus and neo-
Hindus than for cultural Hindus.   "Celebrating
home culture" was more important for traditional
Hindus than for either of the other two groups.

The second group of Hindus, neo-Hindus, are
similar to traditional Hindus on rates of individual worship, but only one half as many attend
group worship as do traditional Hindus, and three
times as many never attend group worship.   For
just under one half of the neo-Hindus the "religious" reason is first rank, but "religious" is
not a reason for twice as many as traditional
Hindus.   (neo-Hindus are less group-worship-
oriented, but they are not less religious than
traditional Hindus). Other reasons for attending
are also weaker than for traditional Hindus with

relative strength for neo-Hindus being "preserve tradition" first (12.7 percent), then "social contact" (11.4 percent), and "celebrate home culture" (10.1 percent). There were 15.7 percent who did not participate. <u>When they attend, the reasons neo-Hindus attend group worship are quite similar to the reasons traditional Hindus attend</u>, but the reasons are not as strong and the "religious" reason is less often a motive. Nevertheless, the strongest single reason for taking part in group worship among neo-Hindus is religious.

Cultural Hindus have much lower individual and group worship rates than the other two groups of Hindus, and almost one half do not take part in group worship at all. For a high percentage of cultural Hindus religion is not a reason for attendance, and for all cultural Hindus "religious" is a weak reason to attend. Cultural Hindus attend group worship primarily for "social contact," but all reasons for attending are weak--largely because the attendance rate is so low. Even for cultural Hindus who do individual worship daily, "social contact" is the primary reason for attendance.

The "religious" reason for attending group worship was five times stronger for traditional Hindus than for cultural Hindus and it was more than four times stronger when primary and secondary reasons were combined. The percentage of cultural Hindus for whom the "religious" was not a reason is three and a half times the traditional Hindu and twice the neo-Hindu. "Strengthen local community," "Speak the language," "approval of other Indians," "fun," and "other" are not reasons for attendance at all for more than one half of all respondents.[3]

Attitudes toward ritual forms among persons from Hindu background vary considerably. For many who are not themselves religious or traditional it seems nevertheless a matter not of mere approval, but of positive desire, that the rituals be performed as authentically as is possible in the "emergency" conditions of America. Rather than accommodating to social change in America, the unchanged character of ritual provides a sense of identity and continuity (as far as possible here). Even persons who pay no attention want the ritual to be done properly.

Opinions vary also concerning whether or not individuals have to pay attention to rituals to derive benefit from them. As one ad hoc priest explained, individuals present at a puja can absorb something as if they were present at a sauna bath--they will get hot and perspire whether or not they are paying attention. But one should in addition follow the action and harmonize with the puja by concentration, attuning to it. Silence is importance for this. One person complained, "Many have forgotten or do not know how to behave at puja." But there are others who express their increasing impatience with long, elaborate, obscure rituals. Some of the people functioning as ritualists simplify, shorten, explain, and justify the puja ritual as they do it.

Groups with Regular Meetings

Voluntary religious associations have developed rapidly, mostly since 1975. No religious group attracts all Indians or even all Hindus.

Vedanta Society

Encouraged by his popular success at the 1893 Congress of World Religions held in conjunction with the World's Fair in Chicago, Swami Vivekananda (1863-1902), spiritual heir to the Bengali saint, Sri Ramakrishna (1836-1886), lectured in America for several years and organized local chapters of his Vedanta Society before his return to India. The Vedanta Society was the earliest sustained Asian religious organization active in America, and its basic approach was for generations an influential model for the propagation of "export Hinduism" in America. Through its Vedanta Press in Hollywood, California, the Vedanta Society had a virtual American monopoly of English language publications concerning Hindu religious traditions until the 1960s.

The Vedanta Society's "modern" form of Hindu tradition purports to be the original, universal form of spirituality--the true heart of all religious traditions. Truth is One, all religions are acceptable, and individuals can join the Vedanta Society without leaving their religious traditions. The goal of the spiritual life is the realization of the fundamental nonduality of Reality, a realization that can be catalyzed by correct teaching, by meditation, by the presence and impact of a teacher who has already realized the highest truth, and by selfless service in the world. Many members of the Vedanta Society regard Sri Ramakrishna as the avatar in which the Brahman was manifested in this era for our enlightenment.

Although it has not become a large, popular movement either in Atlanta or elsewhere in the United States, the Vedanta Society has appealed to a broad spectrum of middle-class, educated Americans, to educated Asian Indians from various parts of India, and to people from other cultures as well. There are fifteen Vedanta centers in the United States under the supervision of the Ramakrishna Math and Ramakrishna Mission in Calcutta, India. The core membership is monastic, but lay members are very active in the local societies' affairs. Some of the monastics become swamis (self-mastered persons or teachers) after at least nine years of training (Carey 1987). Most swamis in America are Indians, but there are about twenty American male swamis, and about a dozen American women have become monastics.

The Vedanta Society in Atlanta is a satellite of the Vivekananda Vedanta Society of Chicago rather than a regular center with a permanent community of monastics. Governing responsibilities are carried by a lay Board of Directors (which includes Indians and non-Indians, males and females). A small group of Indians and Americans interested in Vedanta met in private homes for about six years before the first swami, Swami Yogeshananda, (an American) became a resident from late 1981 to spring 1985. A second monastic, Swami Atmavratananda, (also American) rotated into the position from late 1985 to summer 1987.

Programs of the Vedanta Society appeal to different types of religiously inclined people. For the philosophical there are Sunday morning lectures and discussions, weeknight study groups, meditation instruction, and occasional outside visiting lecturers, such as Swami Bhashyananda, president of the Chicago Vedanta Center, or John Dobson, a former Ramakrishna Mission monk, who lectures on the relationship between science and religion. A shrine room has also been available in the swami's residence, and there have been seasonal retreats to the Georgia mountains. For persons with a more devotional bent there are Sanskrit pujas, especially for religious calendar occasions, such as the birthdays of founding figures of the tradition, of popular Hindu deities such as Krishna, and even of Jesus (regarded as an avatar). Ritual and other occasions include hymn singing (bhajans) and the offering of fire (arati usually, but sometimes the older Vedic havan ritual), and dinner. Society members have also presented religious dramas occasionally.

The Vedanta Society in Atlanta will probably continue to appeal to persons of philosophical, passive nonparticipatory orientation who also appreciate occasional priest-performance rituals. Basic membership (loosely defined) is about forty persons with average Sunday morning attendance about twenty. Its present slow rate of growth will probably continue with new members coming primarily from adults among new Indian immigrants with previous connections to the Vedanta Society and among native Americans. Although weekly youth classes have been offered for short periods, little of real substance is being done to interest second-generation Indian children or teenagers, even though, in my judgment, a philosophical form of neo-Hinduism is much more likely to be attractive to them than more traditional religious forms.

The future of the Atlanta Vedanta Society is heavily dependent on the stable presence of a resident swami (or swamis) and the generation of steady, generous financial support and participation locally. The Indian leadership of the Vedanta Society has limited western experience and is very conservative. Only two new centers have been authorized in the last twenty-five years. As far as Atlanta is concerned, the Indian leadership considers it irregular to have a Ramakrishna monk living alone who is not in a center. There is also a great demand for swamis, especially in Bengal, India, where half of the mission's work is located.

Atlanta Hindu Puja Society

Originally begun in 1970 by a few, mostly Punjabi, families who were among the early immigrants to America, the Atlanta Hindu Puja Society grew to about twenty-five families from different parts of India. Worship once or twice a month usually attracts about thirty persons and is held in private homes. Sunday morning worship continues to rotate from one home to another despite the availability of space in the India Cultural and Religious Center available since the summer of 1984. The number of participants is thus limited by the ability of the various homes to accommodate the congregation.

The ideology of the society is somewhat eclectic, but the general tone is liberal neo-Hindu. Some of its worship format derives from the Arya Samaj (a neo-Hindu movement centered in the Punjab), but ideological and liturgical contributions from participating individuals are added as desired. Worship mixes Hindi, Sanskrit, and English language with bhajans (hymns) in Hindi.

Whatever images members wish to bring are used in worship, but the presence of deities is not formally invoked as would be normal in a traditional puja. The images (murti) used in worship do not imply the "real presence" of the deities but are there to help direct attention toward God. Portable altar material and images for puja are set up in each home for the duration of worship. Images supplied by members include representations of Krishna; the Trimurti (triad of forms) of Brahma, Shiva, and Vishnu; the family of Shiva, Parvati, and Ganesh; and the couple Rama and Sita.

The worship leader for specific occasions is often the host. Worship follows a standard printed form but varies for special ritual calendar events such as the birthday of Lord Rama (Rama Navami) when the Hindi version of the Ramayana by Tulsidas is read nonstop in relays over a roughly twenty-four-hour period, or such as Kali Puja (the worship of the Mother Goddess in late autumn) when the Devi Mahatmya (700 stanzas) is read.

The standard worship format, which takes about an hour, is sometimes preceded by havan, a Vedic ritual revived under Arya Samaj influence in which burning camphor is offered. Worship usually

begins with the reading of about ten stanzas of
the Vaidika Sandhya (a salutation to the Lord God
who ensouls the universe) from the <u>Rigveda
Samhita</u>, first in Sanskrit by all present, and
subsequently in English translation by one of the
children. Other Sanskrit stanzas (such as the
Gayatri mantra, also given in English) are read or
recited. Then there may be a brief commentary by
a member or a guest speaker or a reading from a
commentarial text. Group singing of bhajans in
Hindi is then led by various individuals accompanied by children ringing bells and sometimes by
a <u>tabla</u> (drum). Flowers, food, money, and light
are offered during arati. Hands are extended to
the flame and carried to the forehead as the
flames are carried among the congregation. Finally, the <u>prasad</u> (a sweet farina-type mixture)
that has been offered to God is consumed by the
worshippers. A vegetarian meal follows. One
member of the group affirmed that all celebrants
share the merit of worship equally:

> All those who are participating, if they
> are concentrating and doing puja, all
> will get the same fruit. It is not that
> I am the host and I will get more
> exalted. . . . If all are attentive,
> then all have equal right to get that.

In accordance with the generally neo-Hindu outlook
of this congregation, all religions are considered
good:

> No religions I have ever heard so far
> teaches you to go and steal things or go
> and abuse people or go and do something
> wrong. All religions are good. Just
> like if you have to reach to, say,
> Peachtree Plaza from here. I can reach
> there from many ways. . . . All these
> religions are good and their all
> objective is to reach God. So I cannot
> blame any road as bad. Some are longer,
> some shorter. I don't know. But all
> are good--which way you follow. But <u>do</u>
> follow.

Vishwa Hindu Parishad

Vishwa Hindu Parishad (pan-Hindu association) was organized in Bombay, India, in 1965 to unify Hindus for their common interests. The association stresses the common spiritual basis of all Indian religions. What the movement means by "Hindus" is not very specific. Indian religious tradition in general and Indian culture as a whole are what are important--not specific religious traditions or regional languages and cultures. Formally, the Vishwa Hindu Parishad regards all religious traditions originating in Bharat (India) as Hindu. Thus, Sikhs, Jains, and Buddhists are included. Although Christians, Jews, and Muslims are not Hindu, people of these traditions should be treated with respect insofar as they share and live up to some of the high aspirations and practices common to Hindu faiths. As a local leader put it:

> We define "Hindu" for our own purpose as all the people who follow the philosophy which originated in India and which have some common theme like love, and following that definition, extremely arbitrary, we consider the Parsees [Zoroastrians] as Hindus. . . . We try to unite all Hindus wherever they are. . . . Our goals are to promote an identity for our future generations.

Or as another active Atlanta supporter saw it:

> Our primary emphasis is unity among Hindus. We believe that only if the Hindu community is strong, it can survive. . . . We say that we should respect and recognize all religions that have a pretty much a good following like Christianity, Islam. But there are some religions--you cannot call them "religions," maybe "sects"--that even within Islam and Christianity, that don't follow the teachings of Christ. . . . If we see they have religious discipline, then we respect them. And we don't convert any of the

non-Hindus.   We believe that by giving
exposure to Hindu literature they can be
better Muslims and Christians.

In common with other neo-Hindu movements, the
Vishwa Hindu Parishad tends to view itself as not
religious, or at least not religious "in the bad
sense."   Hindu teaching is regarded as simply
true.   As the following witness explained, Hindu
teaching is scientific and appeals to reason:

> It is not dogma. It's more like a
> philosophy.   Everybody can propagate a
> philosophy. . . . "Darshan" means "to
> see the truth." That is why we call our
> philosophy "darshan"--because it seeks
> the truth.   Once it becomes [a question
> of] the pursuit of truth, you are going
> to listen to anybody. . . . All of the
> Hindus, for example, it doesn't matter
> which religious teacher comes in, they
> are going to listen to him very
> respectfully.

In the United States the organization aims to
unite and to perpetuate the various strands of the
Hindu religious tradition, especially for the
benefit of the second immigrant generation. Vishwa
Hindu Parishad publications cite authorities from
the whole spectrum of native Indian scriptures,
and they present ideas and arrange live presentations from a wide range of contemporary neo-Hindu
teachers.   Swami Chinmayananda of the Chinmaya
Mission is one of the best-known gurus influential
in the movement.
Since its introduction among Indian immigrants in the United States about 1970, the organization has held ten national conferences, with
the last in July 1985 at Madison Square Garden in
New York City, attracting 5,000 delegates from all
over the world. Two southeastern conferences have
also been staged since 1983.
The organization also defends the Hindu tradition against what it perceives to be threats to
Indian culture from outside. Some people, as in
the following testimony, suspect that Muslims and
Christians are trying to convert all Hindus:

And from outside, the Christians and
Muslims are trying to do whatever they
can to convert all the Hindus. . . . In
India what happens when a person is
converted to Islam, he changes his name
right away. He totally associates
himself with the Arab countries. So you
have literally destroyed this person.
You have taken his whole background away
from him. He is totally transplanted.
This person is not only not a good
Hindu, he is out of India because his
loyalty is to the Islamic world--which
is very unfortunate. . . . And also we
are very much upset by their attitude
created mostly by foreign influence from
Islamic countries and also from the
West--Germany and the United States.
. . . But they believe that not only
should an Indian be Christian, but he
also should be western, democratic,
capitalistic.

It has also been suggested that the Indian
government is too soft on religious minorities,
giving them greater protection and privilege than
their relative numerical strength in India war-
rants. There is some apprehension that the minorities will take over. Minorities have also been
blamed for instigating communal riots. The conflict with Islam is currently focused by a dispute
between Hindus and Muslims over a site in the city
of Ayodhya (east of Lucknow) on which a Muslim
mosque (Babari Masjid) has stood for centuries,
but which Hindus claim was originally a temple to
consecrate the birthplace of Lord Rama (Ram
Janmabhoomi Temple).
Locally, in Atlanta, Vishwa Hindu Parishad
meets weekly on Sunday mornings in the India Cultural and Religious Center. A one-hour modernized
version of puja, in some respects reminiscent of
Protestant Christian worship, is also conducted
once a month on Sunday mornings. Scriptural
chants are followed by a lecture and discussion
before hymns are sung and food and fire is
offered. Food that has been consecrated is consumed by participants at the end of worship.
Nonritualistic and nonsectarian neo-Hinduism is

the ideal--as a contributor to an organizational magazine forthrightly states:

> Ritualism is like a Kindergarten of Hindu Dharma. The advanced form of Hindu Dharma deals with Yoga and Vedanta. . . . The process of freeing Hindu Dharma from the clutches of orthodoxy has been going on [for decades] (Nanda 1985, p. 41).

Vishwa Hindu Parishad is very much concerned about the religious and cultural education of children. Indian youngsters in America not only do not have the opportunity to "breathe in the values of Hindu life" from a dominant Hindu culture, but also are exposed to cultural value systems "not congenial to the Hindu way of life." The Sunday children's program (Bal Vihar), which runs concurrently with the adult program, teaches elementary yoga postures and exercises, scriptural stanzas, religious stories, and Indian history.

Sunday Vishwa Hindu Parishad meetings in Atlanta usually attract twenty to thirty adults plus children. Participation increases when popular outside speakers are scheduled. As one participant suggested, "They bring brilliant speakers to talk about religion and philosophy and things like that." Other local Indian organizations and individuals with no institutional connection to the Parishad regularly cooperate to mount educational programs for the children. Over 500 persons attended the 1985 southeastern regional conference, which featured speakers from Rajarajeshwari Peetham in Pennsylvania and popular swamis from the Vedanta Society. The Atlanta 1986 week-long summer camp with sixty volunteer leaders enrolled sixty-five campers from four states. In all, five youth camps were held nationwide in 1986 with 900 participants.

Swadhyaya Group and Bala Sanskar Kendra

Several Atlanta families began meeting in private homes on Sunday mornings in 1980 to provide religious training for preschool and elementary children. The group, which is based on the teachings of Shri Pandurang Vaijanath Athavale, called Pujya Dada or Dadaji (revered older brother) or Pujya Shastriji (revered teacher), has gradually grown to about sixty adults in addition to their children.

Dadaji's "Vedic philosophy" is based on the idea that religion should be material and cultural, as well as spiritual. While various standard Hindu scriptures are employed as authorities, the basic appeal is to satya (truth, reason). God pervades all human beings. All good things are viewed as gifts that have been given to us by God as a parent provides for its children. As God has given to us, so we should return all wealth to God. Wealth should then be redistributed to those in need as to fellow siblings. The true incentive for work is not money or goods, but bhakti, the devoted love and service to God that we as children of God owe to our Parent and to our fellow human beings. The aim is neither communist nor capitalist, but equality among people who generate a "we-feeling" as children of God who return gifts to God and then share them as family members.

The central discipline of the movement is swadhyaya, or introspection, the regular study of one's inner self, and its basic praxis is karma yoga, work done as a sacrifice to God. Swadhyaya leads a listener to see God in a speaker and leads a speaker to recognize God in a listener so that the two together can come to share a common goal of self-development. A technique called bhakti pheri is used to recall God's gifts so that we want to return them to God and thus to other persons. Eventually, people come to treat each other as children of God and attain unity and equality.

True renunciation is not retiring from the world as monk or nun, but selfless service within the world for other members of the human family. One active follower explained karma yoga as follows:

> You know basically you have to attend to your daily requirements and your responsibility to your family along with doing some of God's work. Otherwise, people, you know, when they get tired of doing these day-to-day chores and these responsibilities, say, you know, "Forget

it" and "Let me just be a <u>sadhu</u>" [monk
or nun]. . . . But you are not really
fulfilling your responsibility.

Good works are supposed to be done incognito.
Government and large institutional support are
refused, and donations are not acknowledged pub-
lically.

Athavale's religious and economic movement is
based in and around Bombay where a school for
spiritual knowledge (Tatva Gyana Vidyapith) was
founded in 1956. Followers who have been trained
in the school have, since 1958, been donating
various periods of time (usually two to three
weeks a year) to apply the teachings and practices
in villages, primarily in the state of Gujarat,
but also in other areas of northwest India. Followers state that the program has freed many
villages from hunger, poverty, and crime by converting whole villages into huge joint families.

The program has been applied in Indian villages in various ways. In one village land is
cultivated in common and the crops are distributed as <u>prasad</u> (food offered to God and then shared
among worshippers). Other examples are communal ownership of fishing boats with agreement to
donate part of everyone's catch to God so that it
can be redistributed to any persons who had no
catch on a particular day. In some villages hut
temples for all creeds have been established where
social and economic inequalities are banished in
the presence of God. Collections are treated as
prasad and distributed to the poor.

Dadaji's "great revolution" in Atlanta is
still in the early stages of development (in contrast to that of Chicago, which is well
developed). No service programs are yet
operational because only about eight families are
strongly committed. Gradually, parents who
brought their children for religious training have
themselves become interested. The group currently meets in the India Cultural and Religious
Center on Sunday mornings. Followers are enjoined
to recite twelve Sanskrit prayer stanzas a day, at
morning, noon or evening, and bedtime--a regimen
that is comparatively easy to follow since only a
few minutes are necessary. In addition to face to
face techniques employed by Atlanta followers,

there are print and videotape versions of Dadaji's discourses.

A children's school, called Bala Sanskar Kendra, meets on Sunday mornings at the same time as the parents' meeting. Children are taught the Sanskrit stanzas used in prayer, hymns, stories intended to develop good character qualities, and gratitude toward God and toward one's parents and elders.

Smaller Hindu Groups

The small Hindu religious groups in Atlanta are based either on regional Indian traditions or they consist of local groups of devotees of Hindu gurus.

Durga Puja Society

The worship of the Goddess Durga by publicly subscribed (sarvajanin, "all the people") sponsorship in the fall of the year has become extremely popular in northeast India over the last century (Preston 1983; Sarma 1969). Bengalis, who first staged the puja for Durga in Atlanta in 1980 in the garage of a private home, were enacting Bengali ethnicity at the same time that they were celebrating a religious event. Since more than 150 people from the southeastern United States attended, the puja was held in rented halls in subsequent years and in the India Cultural and Religious Center after it opened in 1984. Saraswati puja is also performed in February. A Brahman engineer learned the ritual expressly to perform it for the local community. In 1986 the relatively small Bengali community (about forty families) split over personal issues, and two separate celebrations of Durga puja are currently held.

Durga puja in India is performed with a clay image, which is immersed in water and destroyed after the ceremony. In Atlanta the image is made of a material resembling Styrofoam and is not destroyed. Changes in ritual customs are justified in the American situation, as the officiant explained in 1981:

With the face and everything, it costs

us about $1 ,200. So, we thought, "We
will keep it, and we will use it until
it is damaged or something." . . . It is
a change, but as in our land we say, you
know, when you are sick or when you are
outside your country, there are certain
things you can change according to the
situation. So, we do it. . . . He [the
priest] gives life to the image. And
after that [the ritual] he does certain
things, and then we just wrap it up.
. . . We keep it in an airtight box for
the rest of the year. . . . It's the
same thing as sarvajanin puja [in
Bengal].

Festival Groups

Annual festivals are also staged by several
other state or regional groups. The Gujarati
Samaj, for example, holds celebrations of Lakshmi
puja (for success at the start of a new year), the
traditional Garbha dance accompanied by a puja for
the Goddess Amba, the nine nights of Navaratri,
and the festival of lights, Divali. The Tamil
Sangam, the Kannada Koota, and the Telegu Association celebrate New Year (Ponkal, Sankranti)
separately. The Kannada Koota also sponsors
Ganesh puja. The Kerala people, including Christians, celebrate their ethnic holiday, Onam.
These annual festivals are primarily of regional
interest, and they are held for entertainment as
well as for social and religious reasons. For
some participants, like this woman, the nonreligious reasons for attending are uppermost:

Navaratri. That is a Gujarati festival.
. . . We get about 300 to 400 people.
And people come from, everybody comes.
Gujaratis are there. Punjabis are
there. South Indians are there. Why
they are there? Because it's fun more
than anything else. It's a good get-
together. I don't think it is being
done from a religious point of view.

Swaminarayan

Several dozen Atlanta Indian families support the exclusively Gujarati Swaminarayan religious tradition. The two branches of Swaminarayan in America both stem from the founder, Sahajanand Swami (1781-1830), who is worshipped as the avatar of God/Krishna and as the human manifestation of the highest reality.

The Akshar Purushottam Swaminarayan Mandal branch of Swaminarayan has been active in the United States longer and has grown more rapidly. The Akshar Mandal was founded in 1971 and built its first temple in Flushing, New York, in 1977. The guru/avatar of this branch, Shastri Narayan-swarupdas Swami (Pramukh Swami Maharaj), has toured the United States, visiting temples and followers in 1974, 1977, 1980, 1984, and 1985. He visited Atlanta briefly during the last two tours. Pramukh Swami gives detailed spiritual and mundane advice to followers, which is arguably of positive assistance in their adjustment to the demands of life in America (Williams 1986a). The organization possibly has between 10,000 and 20,000 followers in America among immigrants from central and south Gujarat. The fifteen to twenty core families who meet regularly in private homes for sabha (congregation) in Atlanta are currently seeking a church building to purchase to convert for their use as a temple. Centers for regular meetings are set up in thirty cities (Williams 1984, pp. 196-8). Besides New York City, the Akshar Purushottam has temples in Chicago, Los Angeles, and Houston.

The second branch of Swaminarayan, the International Swaminarayan Satsang Organization, U.S.A., was chartered in New York State in 1980. A devotee from Atlanta served as one of the Satsang's five trustees and is its president in 1988. A temple was inaugurated in Weekawken, New Jersey, in 1987, and additional temples are in the planning stage for Los Angeles and Chicago. This branch is a smaller movement in America because fewer of its Gujarati followers have immigrated to America (Williams 1986b). The guru of this tradition, Tejendra Prasad Ji Maharaj, has made tours of America four times during the 1970s and 1980s and on each occasion has made brief stopovers in

Atlanta.   The local following is only five families who assemble for worship monthly.   The number
of adherents in Atlanta is small primarily because
few persons from north central Gujarat have
settled here.

Sathya Sai Baba

Eight to ten North Indian families have been
meeting on Sunday mornings with a Sathya Sai Baba
group in Atlanta since 1980.   Sai Baba claims to
be the reincarnation of Sai Baba of Shirdi (who
died in 1918) and the incarnation of the universal
God. He is acclaimed for the performance of mira-
cles.   His devotee groups, which emphasize devotion to him and service, have spread from India to
the countries settled by Indians overseas (cf.
Taylor 1987).

Hindu Gurus

A wide variety of Hindu gurus and swamis
travel through Atlanta and other areas of the
United States from time to time, some establishing
only peripheral contacts, others returning for
fairly frequent visits, and others forming lasting
links with individuals and families who become
their disciples. Swami Chinmayananda is undoubtedly the best known among the many itinerant
religious professionals who teach in Atlanta occasionally.   Another member of the Chinmaya
Mission, Brahmacharini Pavitra, lectures in Atlanta more frequently and has participated in summer
youth camps and a southeast regional Vishwa Hindu
Parishad meeting. Saraswati Devyashram of the
Rajarajeshwari Peetham in Pennsylvania has visited
Atlanta several times. Yoga teachers and other
spiritual guides also lecture locally from time to
time.

Some Hindus take initiation (<u>diksha</u>) as disciples and maintain long-distance relationships with
gurus in India, who may or may not visit the
United States on occasion. Often enough, gurus
are chosen who have been related to the family in
some way for some time. Taking initiation
(<u>diksha</u>) is generally a major responsibility that
sometimes requires a transformation in life-style,
as well as a transfer of religious loyalty.   A

guru is to his pupil (<u>sishya</u>) like a second
father. A husband and wife explained why the wife
decided to be initiated by her guru and what the
relationship is:

> Husband: He is the guru of my mother.
> . . . He is surrounded by many devotees.
> . . . When he visited . . . she just
> came to me and asked, "Do you have any
> objection if I get initiated?" I said,
> "No, go ahead and do it." So she did.
> . . . And one day suddenly I might be
> initiated [also]. But one thing is
> there, that I really believe--that this
> realization of things comes from within
> yourself. Nobody can impose [it upon
> you]. Even if somebody imposes, it will
> be very temporary. . . .
> Wife: From a long time I had a very
> earnest desire in my heart that I should
> be initiated from him. And my mother
> also was initiated from him since a long
> time. And in India it is very difficult
> to get him. . . . He is so popular, and
> he is surrounded by so many people that
> you can't touch his feet either. So I
> was looking, really looking, for the day
> when I can contact him directly. So
> year before last year he came just 200
> miles away from here. . . . But when I
> reached there, and when I saw him, I
> couldn't move from there. And I stayed
> there for that same night and the day
> after that day. It was something in my
> heart [that indicated to me] that this
> time I couldn't go without getting
> initiated from him. So I asked him.
> . . . And I have a really, a very great
> respect for him. So whatever he will
> tell, I will do.

SIKHS

The Sikh Study Circle has met in private homes
for <u>satsang</u> ("congregation of truth", that is,
group worship) every four to six weeks on Sunday
mornings since it organized in the mid-1970s.

Attendance at satsang varies from thirty-five to fifty adults plus their children. In 1987 there were about fifty-five Sikh families in the Atlanta area. For the celebration of special annual events, such as the birthday of the founding guru, Nanak, halls are sometimes rented and attendance may swell to 150 to 200 persons (including Sikhs from other regions in the southeastern United States). Sikhs observe many North Indian festivals in common with Hindus, as well as the specifically Sikh birthdays of major gurus, the martyrdoms of Gurus Arjun and Tegh Bahadur, and the anniversary of the foundation of the Khalsa. From the small sample (fourteen people) of Sikhs who took part in the Atlanta survey in 1984 and 1985, 79 percent responded that they attended group worship at least once each month.

Although Sikh worship technically could be done at home, Sikhs are scattered over the Atlanta metro area, and group worship is the primary occasion for association. A Sikh woman summarized her reasons for attending satsang as follows: to meet Sikhs beyond one's circle of friends, to give support to the religious group, to let the children (boys, especially) see other little boys with little turbans, for sharing one's feelings with others, to act out a sense of belonging to a group and a people, to give an opportunity of worship before the Granth for people who do not have one at home or who do not know how to conduct the worship, and for sheer enjoyment.

Satsang normally lasts about three hours. The Guru Granth Sahib is given the place of honor on a low table that serves as an altar in a room of a private home, which has been cleared out for the occasion (sometimes the living room is used; sometimes the garage). The Granth is treated as though it were a living guru present in the room. Everyone who enters the presence of the Granth has already removed shoes and has the head covered to show respect. Women use the end of their saris or a shawl; men have their turbans or, if they are shorn, another cloth (a handkerchief, if nothing else is available). Each person prostrates before the Granth and makes a small offering of money.

Group worship begins with readings from the Guru Granth Sahib, often led by women, but occasionally by men, which continues for more than one

hour.   In India it was the custom for women to
lead prayer in the home and for granthis (professional readers) to do it in the temple. Sikh men
are thus not accustomed to leading prayer and
women. Next, hymns are sung (shabad or kirtan) for
approximately one hour with various individuals
leading. Some hymns are solos; others include the
congregation's response with refrains. Women lead
most of the singing also. A woman opined that
some of the men are too self-conscious to sing:

> I'll do it, because I enjoy it and it
> doesn't matter. You know, in the
> satsang, to me, I lose the shame of my
> voice or something. But I think men are
> more conscious about that.

People arrive at various times during the
first two hours of worship. During both the
reading and the singing, the congregation is at-
tentive, and many of them meditate on the presence
of God, often with the eyes closed. Sikh devotion
has a strong mystical emphasis, but generally this
is practiced within a group rather than alone.
There is no ascetic, monastic, or fasting tradition in Sikh religion.
The hymns are followed by a lecture.   In
Atlanta this discourse is usually devoted to
teaching Sikh history and doctrine, but sometimes,
especially during the traumatic events of 1984 in
India, it may also have political content.   Then
there are more readings from the Granth, prayer,
and a reading in common recalling the founding of
the khalsa as prasad is stirred with a sword and
then distributed to all present. A common meal
(langar) follows, which is offered to everyone
regardless of caste, race, or social distinction
and which also celebrates the solidarity of the
Sikh community.
In 1988 there was no gurudwara ("gateway or
access point to the Guru, or God") in Atlanta,
although land for a gurudwara on the eastern side
of the metropolitan area (on the opposite side
from the location of the India Cultural and Religious Center) was given to the Sikh Study Circle
by a donor from another state in 1983.   Construction of a building awaits funding and the con-
certed action of the local Sikh community.   Sikh

communities have a practical need for temples in
the American situation to be able to sustain the
community and transmit the tradition to the next
generation. A gurudwara is a permanent place of
worship that centers symbolically upon a copy of
the Sikh scriptures (the <u>Adi Granth Sahib</u>) as the
presence of the revelation of God. Gurudwaras are
run and financed by their members.

Until late 1983 there were tentative plans to
set a room aside in the India Cultural and Religious Center (see Chapter 3) to serve as a gurudwara, but for a variety of reasons this did not
work out. Then, as several Sikhs remarked, the
fund-raising campaign changed to include a Hindu-
Jain temple in order to attract greater Hindu
financial backing. A church building was purchased to serve both purposes. But it became
apparent that it would be extremely difficult,
and perhaps not at all feasible, to set aside two
separate large rooms for a gurudwara, on the one
hand, and a Hindu-Jain temple on the other, in
addition to using the old church sanctuary for
general meetings. A gurudwara must be in a room
that is not used for any other purpose. Many
Sikhs also preferred not to have their place of
worship in the same building with the images for
Hindu deities, and most Sikhs, in fact, preferred
to build their own separate gurudwara if at all
possible. So, it was decided that the building
would be renovated for a Hindu-Jain temple only.
There was then no other appropriate space to de-
vote to the gurudwara.

A Sikh woman argued that while the privacy of
American homes has its attractions, it is also
lonely, and changing from one place to another
gives one a certain sense of rootlessness. Having
a gurudwara in Atlanta would help to preserve the
religious tradition by undergirding the discipline
of devotion, and because of that, it would deepen
the sense of spirituality. With a gurudwara, it
would also be easier to teach the beliefs and
ethics of the tradition, to maintain the behavior
patterns, to transmit the tradition to the second
generation, and to foster family closeness.

There are also no granthis in Atlanta except
for visitors who come from other Sikh centers for
special occasions, such as Guru Nanak's birthday.
There are no official priests in Sikh tradition,

but the role of the granthi (traditionally, a caretaker for the gurudwara and a reader/singer) is, in America outside Atlanta, being extended to more pastoral functions, such as officiating at weddings and funerals. Granthis are unofficial specialists who make a living in these roles in India and overseas.

There has been some disunity within the local Sikh community over the immensely disturbing events in the Punjab and north India since the summer of 1984, about relations to the government of India and to the India American Cultural Association, and concerning some local issues. Sikh participation in IACA almost stopped completely in the summer of 1984 because of the Indian government assault on the Golden Temple at Amritsar (and the participation of the Indian embassy at the inauguration of the new India center in July 1984) and because of the assassination of Prime Minister Indira Gandhi in October 1984 and the subsequent riots in which large numbers of Sikhs in India were murdered. One section of the Sikh population supported the IACA goal of maintaining an umbrella pan-Indian Atlanta organization that would coordinate and facilitate the functions of smaller regional and religious associations. Other Sikhs confined their activities primarily to Sikh community interests for an extended period, but many were beginning to recommence activities in conjunction with the India Atlanta Cultural Association in 1987.

The largest concentration of gurudwaras in America is in California, where the American Sikh population is also by far the greatest. According to Kapany (1979, p. 208), there were three gurudwaras in Los Angeles, two in San Francisco, and one each in Yuba City, Stockton, and El Centro in 1979. Kapany also listed two in New York City, two in Washington, D.C., and one each in Detroit, Cleveland, Chicago, and Houston. There are two others in New Jersey and a gurudwara in Durham, North Carolina. There is also a large Sikh population in Canada, concentrated primarily in Vancouver and Toronto.

OTHERS

Smaller Indian religious groups include Christians, Jains, Jews, and Zoroastrians.

Christians

Indian Christians in Atlanta tend to search out existing Christian churches to attend that they perceive to be similar to the churches they knew in India. As one affirmed: "Being a Christian not only opens the door to getting to know more people, but it also is a bond. You are a family in Christ in some way, and you really utilize that." Protestants tend to choose more conservative churches because these churches have greater resemblance to the churches they knew in India. Since Indian Christians in Atlanta join churches according to their individual or family preferences, they participate in a variety of different Christian institutions and have arranged their uniquely Indian Christian gatherings as occasional additions to their normal worship schedules.

As is also true for the rest of the United States, more than half of the Indian Christians in Atlanta emigrated from the southern Indian state of Kerala. The list of Indian denominations represented in the United States in <u>Keralites in America</u> (Andrews 1983, pp. 289-93) indicates the great diversity among Indian Christians who have enough people and who have chosen to organize separate Indian churches in other parts of the United States. Churches listed include the Church of God, the Indian Orthodox Church, the Indian Pentecostal Church, the Mar Thoma Church, the St. Thomas Orthodox Church, the Syrian Orthodox Church, the Malankara Orthodox Church, the India Catholic Church, the Jacobite Syrian Orthodox Church, the Church of South India, the South India Assembly of God, the Assembly of God, the Knanaya Church, and the Knanaya Catholic Church. The Mar Thoma Syrian Church of Malabar had fourteen priests and twenty-four parishes, and the Malankara Orthodox Diocese in America had thirty-five parishes and forty priests in 1986 (Williams 1986c). Where local populations are large enough to support it, for example, in Houston, Kerala

Christians have organized their own churches.

Reliable estimates[4] indicate that the 1988 Indian Christian population in Atlanta would total between 300 and 350 persons. About 80 to 100 are from Baptist backgrounds; 40 to 50 are Methodist, 40 to 50 are Roman Catholic and Orthodox; 30 to 40 are Presbyterian, 35 to 45 come from Church of God families, and 50 to 70 have a Mar Thoma heritage. There are also some Jacobites. Mar Thoma Christians, who speak Malayalam, the Kerala regional language, attend different churches regularly but have arranged monthly gatherings with guest ministers from Mar Thoma congregations in the northeastern United States. Malayalam speaking Church of God Pentecostals have also arranged their own gatherings for prayers every two weeks in private homes, and they are hoping to organize their own church at some time in the future. There is also a very recent Indian Christian Association, which has occasional meetings for Christians from different regions and language groups.

Kerala Christians began congregating twice each year about 1982, first, for the traditional Kerala regional festival of Onam in August, and second, for Christmas. Onam is a New Year harvest festival that celebrates the Kerala Hindu tradition that King Mahabali defeated a demon on that day. Christians also participate because the festival has become an expression of regional ethnicity. The Malayalam Christmas observance in 1986 swelled to about 400 persons, even though the local Kerala Christian population was estimated to be only about forty-five families. Since 1985, Christmas celebrations for Christians and for the Indian community generally have been held at the India Cultural and Religious Center. The 1986 program attracted an audience of about 150 persons. Some Indians regret the absence of Indian churches in Atlanta. This man explains why:

> Whenever I go to the _____ church or the _____ church, I am not so free as I am in an Indian Christian Church. People feel that we don't know English, and we'll not be able to speak American and things like that. And I want to be really active in the church. . . . But it is a little hard, being a foreigner,

to take an active part in the church.
So we are there. Someday, if the Lord
wants to use us, he'll use.

But the lack of a common language also makes it
difficult for Indian Christians to organize among
themselves, and worship in English would lose much
of the Indian character of Christian worship:

> The most difficult part of it is, we
> speak different languages. The Malayala
> speak Malayalam. Mysoreans speak
> Kanarese, and Tamilians speak Tamil. We
> speak Telegu. And there is no way we'll
> be able to get together and have a
> Christian fellowship.
> Q: It would not work in English?
> A: It would, but they would rather have
> their own prayer meeting. But it takes
> a little time and effort. But it is
> possible, and we will do it.

There have been a few meetings intended to organize Indian Christians from time to time, but none
have produced a long-term organization with regular meetings.

Because of the paucity of religious ties to
other Indians, some Christians have only restricted contacts with Indians and with Indian organizations:

> The Indian Christians here don't feel a
> social need to depend on other Indians
> at all. There is no social need. . . . I
> have such an active life with all kinds
> of people that I don't feel a need for
> it. . . . For religious, when they have,
> like festival activities and functions
> and things like that, for that we don't
> have any particular need because we
> don't celebrate them all.

Immigrant Hindus are tolerant, and they are
often mildly interested in learning to appreciate
the spiritual message of the Bible. But there is
little interest in conversion to Christianity, and
mission work among Indian immigrants by Indian
Christians has had only limited success.

Jains

The thirty or so Jain families in Atlanta were
unorganized and not in contact with each other
when the early fall birthday anniversary of Guru
Mahavira (Mahavir Jayanti) was first celebrated in
a private home in 1982. Although the number of
Jain families has more than doubled since then,
they are still scattered widely over the metropolitan area, and in early 1988, they were still
not well organized. Mahavir Jayanti has been
observed irregularly by an informal Jain Society
that involves only a portion of the Jain population.

There are no Jain temples in Atlanta, and
there are not likely to be any that are exclusively Jain unless settlement patterns alter drastically. Jains do participate in the Atlanta
India Cultural and Religious Center temple (discussed in Chapter 4) that was inaugurated in the
fall of 1986. An image of Mahavira shares the
altar area in the temple with eight Hindu images.
While no one I consulted was aware of similar
arrangements in India, there are American precedents, for example, in the Hindu and Jain temple
in Monroeville, Pennsylvania (metropolitan Pittsburgh).

A Jain puja is held every first Sunday of the
month by families who volunteer to perform it, and
in 1988 this worship averaged an attendance of
twenty-five to thirty persons. The puja is much
abbreviated compared to the elaborate puja of
several hours duration that would be routine in
India.

Beginning in 1986 Mahavir Jayanti has been
celebrated with a <u>snatra</u> puja (bathing ritual) at
the India center in addition to the celebration in
a private home. About 150 people have been taking
part (Some from outside Georgia; some are non-
Jains). Presumably, the two observances will
combine if Jains become better organized.

The prospect is that the Jain population here
will remain too small to operate separately and
that they will not feel it necessary to have their
own exclusive religious arrangements. Jains are
considerably attuned to Hindu religious sensibilities and they willingly cooperate in religious
matters. Some Jains are active in the Vishwa

Hindu Parishad because of common religious and cultural interests. Educational programs for the children's cultural and religious nurture are especially attractive to them. Sentiments expressed to me by several Jains resembled neo-Hindu religious ideology.

The Federation of Jain Associations in North America (FJANA), founded in 1981, claimed that half of the 25,000 Jains in the United States belonged to the association in 1987 (as noted in Chapter 1, this figure is probably twice the actual Jain population). They also stated that 41 percent of the Jains in America came from Gujarat, 37 percent from Maharashtra, and almost all hailed from North India. Nearly 40 percent of all Jains in North America live now in the states of New York, California, and New Jersey ("Ohio Jain Federation" 1987).

There are Jain temples in New York City; Boston; Chicago; Cleveland, Ohio; Allentown, Pennsylvania; and in several California locations. Some Jains follow the teaching and guidance of distant teachers, such as Swami Chitrabhanu in Boston, who combines Jain and Yoga practice and publishes books and pamphlets. There are also a small number of Jain monks domiciled in New Jersey, but local informants say that they are "modern." (Traditional monks can travel only where they can walk. So they are effectively confined to India.)

Jews and Zoroastrians

The North American Zoroastrian Association is located in Chicago with local associations on the West Coast, the upper Midwest, Toronto and Ottawa, Canada, and northeastern American cities. Lopate (1986, p. 84) estimated 7,000 Parsees in North America. Parsee students pass through Atlanta temporarily, but the only Zoroastrian family in Atlanta converted to Christianity some years ago. The Parsee (so called because they came to India from Persia) population is shrinking because most groups do not accept converts and recognize only the children of Parsee fathers.

The several hundred Jews from India living in America are clustered in New York and Chicago. None live in Atlanta.

INDIANS AND "EXPORT" INDIAN RELIGIONS

The terminology "export religions" refers to indigenous Indian religious traditions (Hindu, Jain, Sikh, Muslim) "packaged" primarily for and attracting primarily westerners. Indian participation in most forms of Indian export religion in America is minimal, and the impact of "export religions" has been confined primarily to native Americans. There are exceptions, such as the Vedanta Society--which one might classify as "export religion" since it attracts many non Indians and stresses its more than Indian, more than Hindu character. Nevertheless, the Vedanta Society has a base in the Indian population in India, which many of the export religions do not have; at least half of the Atlanta congregation is Indian; and for fund drives, presentation of programs, and the like, a large section of the Atlanta Indian community is forthcoming with support. In contrast to the clearly "export" traditions, Vedanta Society uses the facilities of the India Cultural and Religious Center frequently and often cosponsors events with other Indian groups.

The International Society for Krishna Consciousness

Among export Indian religions active in Atlanta is the International Society for Krishna Consciousness (ISKCON). ISKCON is both traditional and export. It stems from a sixteenth century Vaishnava movement in Bengal associated with Chaitanya. It is a "new" form of monotheistic Krishna devotion the particular theological and praxis format of which seems largely to have originated with the founder, Bhaktivedanta Swami. Its theological, institutional, and devotional content is clearly derived from Hindu Vaisnava tradition, but the packaging is, for the most part, for non-Indians. Indians sometimes attend and provide lay support, including financial support. But they are very seldom involved as practitioners of the life-style and almost never involved as monks (brahmacharis). ISKCON monks have earned a positive reputation in India. ISKCON representatives did attend the inauguration of the India Cultural and Religious Center in 1984.

ISKCON now attracts large numbers of Indians in some cities, although only two Indian families attended consistently in Atlanta until about 1985. Many others came for special events in the liturgical year, such as Krishna's birthday. A number of native American blacks in Atlanta have also joined ISKCON, both as lay people (from all age groups including the elderly) and as celibate monks, and several blacks are in local leadership positions.

From about 1970 until 1986 the ISKCON temple was the only Hindu temple in the city--a circumstance that has changed with the inauguration of the temple inside the India Cultural and Religious Center and will alter again when the Sri Venkateswara Temple in south Atlanta is completed. Some Indian Hindus were attracted by the temple, as this graduate student attested in 1981:

> We don't find any opportunity here to go to the temple, and that is the only temple we have, you know. . . . On some special occasions a lot of Indians do go there. But they don't go regularly. . . . You know the philosophy which they preach, we might differ because of the thing they call demigods we consider them as gods, OK. So, ideologically, there might be some difference. But after all, you know we are going to a temple, and it is God's place--so that all the difference which is there, I think, vanishes.

But other Indians, like this young man, have little interest in ISKCON:

> They are doing many things that are good, but their attitude is very much western. It's not Indian. It's not Hindu. That's why we don't associate with them that much as with other groups. . . . As far as the temple is concerned, if we go there . . . anybody can go there. So, as individuals, it's our choice.

One person who attends ISKCON worship regularly said that the chanting of <u>mantras</u> (stanzas), such as the famous Hare Krishna mantra, was a major reason he attended:

> The sound vibrations are very important. And when you hear these things, it automatically elevates you to some transcendental ideal, OK. . . . So I believe that if you hear these things continuously, then some changes must be there. And throughout the scriptures we found that you have to chant. . . . So chanting is very popular . . . <u>shabda</u>, sound vibration.

Some newcomers, like this graduate student, sometimes go because they are homesick:

> It's just that sometimes you feel like going and praying in the silence. Mostly that's the difference that you don't get everywhere, that you can't get at home. There is a priest there and sometimes you feel like it. . . . It is sometimes when you are away from home, and sometimes you don't have anybody in this country, or if you are bored, you definitely get some kind of consolation there. At least I do.

From about 1985 Atlanta Indian participation in ISKCON increased to ten to fifteen families who come to worship with regularity and who give regular financial support. Several dozen more Indians often celebrate the major holidays at the ISKCON temple.

One woman consulted who began attending with her family in the last three years suggested that the ISKCON priests are better informed about the ritual and the general Vaishnava (Vishnu) tradition than ritualists functioning elsewhere in Atlanta, that liturgical year celebrations are held on the correct days instead of being transposed to the more convenient weekends, and that the religious program as a whole is better run for the whole family than any other in Atlanta. She expected to continue worshipping at the ISKCON temple even after the Sri Venkateswara Temple is completed, in part because she is not from South India.

Other Indian devotees also cited the erudition and dedication of the ISKCON priests and teachers, in ritual, in theological matters, and in Sanskrit language, as a major attraction and contrasted how much the Hare Krishna teachers know compared to other Hindus available locally. Several devotees contacted began to attend ISKCON worship more than ten years ago in cities where no other forms of Hindu worship were available, and they have simply continued their participation in Atlanta. They also felt that the ISKCON temple was still the only real Hindu temple in Atlanta. An increase in the Indian population in Atlanta in the last two years was also suggested as a reason for the increase in Indian devotees. The new Indian participants are mostly North Indians, and they include Gujaratis, Punjabis, and Bengalis.

Radha Soami Satsang, Beas

Radha Soami Satsang, the True Association (Satsang) of the Lord (Soami) of the Soul (Radha), was founded in 1861 by Guru Shiv Dayal Singh (also called Soami Maharaj) in Agra in north central India. Radha Soami's world view and spiritual path have features in common with aspects of the Sikh, Hindu, and Muslim mystical traditions, as well as with Neo-Platonic tradition. Radha Soami Satsang, Beas (Beas is a town in the Punjab near Amritsar), traces the true succession from Masters Jaimal Singh to the current Master (since 1951), Charan Singh.

The Atlanta sangat (association), which began in the late 1970s, has four Indian families and has grown to about fifty people who meet on Sundays in private homes. Satsangis practice surat shabda yoga--a spiritual discipline (yoga) that returns the soul (surat) to its true home in the highest realm of the Supreme Spirit by means of the audible sound stream (shabda) which flows from the material world to the Spirit.

A true Master who provides the key to liberation is crucial to the spiritual path. Testimony indicates that the presence of the Master is vividly felt:

We feel that he has already done it
[related to us]. . . . So he is in a
position to tell us exactly what to do,
where to go. He gives us assurance that
he is going to guide us, that he is
there inside waiting for you. We very
strongly believe in his presence inside
of us. . . . There is an inner peace, a
calmness about him. . . . You have to
feel you are in a divine presence. . . .
This person--what really comes across is
the deep sense of peace. It is very
peculiar, but the world does not seem
important. . . . You have this feeling
that he has risen above the concerns of
the earth.

Healthy, Happy, Holy

The Atlanta Sikh Study Circle welcomed native
American converts to Healthy, Happy, Holy (3HO), a
neo-Sikh movement in America, to satsang, but the
American Sikhs came into conflict with Indian
Sikhs on practical and theological issues (cf. La
Brack 1979, p. 142) and stopped participating. The
Americans complained that Indians allowed people
to worship with them who did not observe the five
k's, they allowed non-Sikhs into the fellowship,
they served meat and beer at langar (a communal
meal), and in the Americans' judgment, Indians
emphasized the social character of the event more
than the religious. Although many Sikhs in Atlanta eat meat and drink alcohol at home, neither has
been served in the langar since about 1980. At any
given satsang, up to one third of persons in attendance are not Sikhs. (Hindu Punjabis worship
with Sikhs with some regularity.)
Local Indian Sikhs consider the American 3HO
people to be more strictly observant, but they
also regard them as too fanatic and too political.
Questions have also been raised about whether or
not they are following a living guru (which is
against the mainline Sikh tradition) and whether
the Kundalini Yoga taught in 3HO has any organic
connection to Sikh religion. The 3HO organization
in Atlanta usually involves less than a dozen

people.

Other export Indian religious traditions represented in Atlanta that attract only a very few Indian immigrant followers include Transcendental Meditation (SIMS), Siddha Yoga Dham, Meher Baba Lovers, the Theosophical Society, and Sufism Reoriented. Quite probably, more Indians have tried Transcendental Meditation than the others. Neither Sunni nor Ismaili Muslims have much interest in the various forms of Sufi meditation available from time to time in Atlanta.

INTER-GROUP RELATIONS

Relations among Indian organizations in Atlanta have changed with increased population and the passage of time (cf. Bowen 1987, p. 15). The initial period when the local Indian population was only a few hundred persons was marked by a high degree of cooperation. Cultural and religious events were staged with little formal organization and included anyone who was interested, regardless of origin in India or overseas. A Punjabi woman recalled:

> When we first came here, like twelve years ago, [1969] it absolutely didn't matter which part of the country you were from as long as you were from India. . . . Some of our friends were performing [for a Gujarati program], so we just went there even though --and sat through more than half of it, you know-- even though we did not understand what was going on, what they were talking about, for example. You know, they had a skit. We couldn't understand the words, but we sat there and enjoyed it anyway.

The pan-Indian inclusiveness that was characteristic of the initial phase of immigration can continue for an extended period in a small local Indian population. But the Indian population had increased to about 1,000 persons in Atlanta by 1975 , and regional and religious groups began to organize separate social functions. Indian reli-

gious and regional voluntary associations func-
tioned autonomously, with little competition, but
also with little direct cooperation. One Indian
group seldom considered the convenience of
another. Events were often scheduled at the same
times in locations scattered over the metropolitan
area. Information about Indian social and religious events was not widely or systematically
disseminated.

The development of regionalistic tendencies
seems to be an inevitable result of the increased
size of the local population. Like many other
informants, a South Indian stated in 1983 that

> the smaller the town, the less the
> number of families belonging to one
> particular language group, the more the
> people come together on the basis that
> we are Indian. And then, it sort of
> segments itself. South Indians . . .
> they tend to stick together, and the
> North tends to generally separate itself
> from the South. I guess there are
> really strong differences in terms of
> outlook and way of life and things like
> that between the North and South. And
> you find that. It is not that the
> differences are large. It is just that
> some of them are there.

A male graduate student from the South
regretted the persistence of regionalistic divisions in America:

> Indians, I think wrongly, tend to be
> regionalistic. It's not very helpful as
> far as I can see. . . . If you go and
> talk to a South Indian and tell them,
> hey, why don't you go and talk to the
> North Indian, the South Indian is going
> to sit there and say, "Why should I go
> there?" And if you go to the North
> Indian, he is going to say, "We are the
> majority anyway, and we don't care if
> you come or not. And if that guy wants
> to come, let him come." It's a kind of
> stalemate.

Very few immigrant organizations are newly invented for America, and organizational boundaries common in India tend to carry over. Indians tend to split into factions, and the social basis for religious groups tends to be small. Group organizers are sometimes suspected of forming cliques to enhance their social prestige and power. Although none of the religious groups is in principle exclusive, de facto they all fail to reach out to and to attract the Indian population at large. Each Hindu-related Indian group (that is, Hindu, Jains, Sikhs) has its own flavor of religious practice with appeal to different groups of Indians. Each religious group appeals to a relatively small number of Indians on a regular, sustaining basis.

The drive to create an overarching Indian organization began to develop during the same period that subculture groups organized. The India American Cultural Association (IACA), which became the umbrella organization for a large section of the Indian population by the mid-1980s, launched the funding drive for an India Cultural and Religious Center in 1975. After the India Cultural and Religious Center was opened nine years later, regional groups and religious voluntary associations began to operate to a considerable extent from the center. The number of community events staged by both large and small Indian groups also increased, and schedules conflicted much less often (primarily because the same space was being used). Even fairly small regional groups, such as Kashmiris and Sindhis, organized formally to be able to reserve space in the center. For the Krishna Janmastami (Krishna's birthday) celebration one month after the center opened, for example, seven Indian Hindu organizations, in addition to the IACA, cosponsored the event. Thus, in the most recent period (from 1984 to 1987) subgroup activities have increased in frequency at the same time that there is much greater consolidation of community activities and cooperation among the smaller Indian groups.

PAN-INDIAN INSTITUTIONS

The development of permanent, self-sustaining

Indian institutions signals a change from the
mind-set of migrants or sojourners (who intend to
return home eventually) to that of immigrants who
plan to remain in their adopted country permanently. A change in attitude has become evident in a
gradually growing segment of the Indian population
since 1975, when the drive to raise funds to obtain a building to use as a cultural center was
launched.

The India American Cultural Association

The India American Cultural Association was
incorporated in 1970 as a nonprofit organization
specifically to gather money and supplies for the
Indian Red Cross to be used for Bangladesh relief.
IACA was reactivated in March, 1975, and was more
formally organized to promote pan-Indian culture
and to improve relations between Asian Indians and
Americans.

Most of the functions organized by IACA have
been aimed to broaden support for the association
and to generate funding for the center. IACA
activities and programs since 1975 include amateur
and professional entertainments, dinners, food
booths in the Arts Festival of Atlanta and the
DeKalb International Festival of the Arts, popular
and classical music and dance performances using
both local and imported talent, floats in annual
Atlanta Fourth of July parades, poetry readings,
sports contests, motion picture showings, group
trips and outings, celebrations (melas) of national holidays (Independence Day, Diwali, and Repub-
lic Day), and lectures by visiting religious
leaders. A newsletter/magazine, Voice of India,
has been published quarterly since 1976, and general membership meetings of IACA have been con-
vened since 1980. From time to time, even before
the Indian center opened, there have been programs
for children, such as instruction in Indian classical dance and short courses on Indian history
and religions.

The linguistic, geographic, political, ethnic,
and religious differences among Asian Indian immigrants to America are considerable. But as was
the case with earlier American immigrants, such as
the Italians, the importance of some social boundaries separating Indians from one another will

decrease over the next generation or two as shared
characteristics begin to take precedence.

The first characteristic shared by immigrants
is the most obvious, namely, that Asian Indians
originate from a single country, which has func-
tioned as a political unit since 1948. The
logo of the India American Cultural Association
consists of an outline map of India superimposed
on an outline map of the United States. No local
organization has been designed to serve all South
Asians (Indians, Pakistanis, Bangladeshis, Sri
Lankans, Nepalis), but IACA is the only organization that comes close to serving all of the immigrants derived from India. The 1984 Atlanta survey indicated that 88 percent of the respondents
immigrated directly from India rather than from
some other country. Persons who resided before
the partition in what is now Pakistan identify
themselves readily as Indians, but identification
with India and participation in IACA is sometimes
weaker for people whose forebears left India
several generations ago, such as Indians from
Trinidad, Guyana, or East Africa.

The sense of Indian national identity is not
always strong. One canvasser was told by a couple
that they were reluctant to join IACA because of
their experience with a similar association in
another American city--a history of bickering and
fighting. They were apprehensive that the course
of events would be similar in Atlanta.

Many Indians interviewed emphasized the importance of Indian identity. This Hindu woman's
concern over divisiveness within the Indian population was common:

> We should really work cohesively
> together. We can have subgroups. There
> could be different satellites within the
> umbrella organization. We could all
> work a little more united, with a
> little more strength. . . But typically
> wherever Indians have gone anywhere all
> over the world, they have their own
> Indian organizations, and then they have
> their ethnic organizations. . . . There
> is nothing wrong for our children to
> know our language [Bengali]. I would
> promote it. They ought to know. But we

don't have to get together and invite
only our subculture groups to do that.
This is the very thing that has kept
India so much divided for many, many
years. . . . And me, for one, having
whatever national spirit I have, I like
to be only an Indian.

Especially among persons from some of the numerically smaller immigrant groups, such as this
South Indian man, there was a strong emphasis that
IACA should appeal to the greater Indian unity--a
unity that would in some respects be a new cultural creation, an advance over anything that has
pre-existed among Indians in India:

People have felt that the IACA is being
sort of snobbish, aloof. . . . They
don't worry about, you know, reaching
all others or getting all the groups
together. . . . IACA has never gone out
to bring the various groups that we are
talking about together. That should be
the first objective of any Indian
organization, anywhere in the world, to
bring all Indians together first. Then
you have achieved one independence,
another independence.

Prior to the opening of the cultural center a
Gujarati woman believed that separate regional and
religious groups could be combined under an overarching Pan-Indian organization:

I feel that it is for everybody. If
everybody joins it, it will be the best
thing with all under one umbrella. I
feel that . . . still you would have the
Hindu Society. We would still have
Swamiji [resident monastic for the
Vedanta Society]. You'd still have the
Sikh society. Everybody could grow
under it. . . . I really feel that if
IACA could do that it would be a
tremendous achievement for Atlanta's
Indian community. . . . But it takes a
lot. Because some people have been
brainwashed that IACA belongs to this or

> that [faction]. Some people are so traditional, in the sense, communal for the language purpose, that they wouldn't understand that if they help us out, we could still carry our tenets under the auspices of IACA. We could still hold the Gujarati Samaj under the auspices of the IACA. . . . I believe in different language groups. But I don't want any parochial interests. That gets so narrow-bound that they lose the larger, the greater interest of the community.

A second, more pervasive unifying force of much greater duration that immigrants share is their background in the culture and history of South Asia. The content of the Indian culture to which immigrants sometimes make an appeal is often unspecified, and in fact, is rather amorphous. Most Indian languages are linguistically related, and most employ a large vocabulary of Sanskrit-derived terminology, for example, but Indian dialects are still not sufficiently similar to make regional languages mutually intelligible. Nevertheless, traditional classical culture (in art, architecture, music, literature, and dancing, for instance) has common themes. Classical-style Urdu poetry readings held two years in a row by the Aligahr Alumni Association have attracted North Indians generally, not just Muslims, as audience and as performers. Contemporary popular culture, such as Bombay motion pictures and film music, is also pan-Indian. Telephone calls to the Friday evening Indian music programs on FM radio come from all sections of the South Asian population. Even second-generation Indian immigrants call in and, by their remarks, evidence their knowledge about the genre. The turnout for major Indian media stars on tour (for example, the popular playback singer, Manna Dey) is also general for the South Asian population. But when the content of common Indian culture becomes more specific, it also tends to become both sectarian and regional.

A common Indian spiritual heritage is often claimed by some Indians as a third basis for Indian unity. While Indian culture no doubt permeates all Indian religious traditions, and while there are undoubtedly shared religious themes and structures, "Indian spirituality" tends to be interpreted differently by the Hindu majority than by the religious minorities. The Hindu majority affirms the reality of Indian culture, tolerance of other religious traditions, and maintains an officially evenhanded policy. The sense of Indian spirituality is much stronger for Hindus, Sikhs, and Jains than for other Indians.

A young Muslim man felt that Indian unity was possible only if religious concerns were excluded: "I would definitely love to do it [The proposed cultural hall] if it is, doesn't have anything Hindu, Muslim, or anything. . . . No religion at all." Another simply believed that few non-Hindus were interested: "So five hundred, maybe a thousand, people are there [at the IACA]. So another thousand are not interested." The neo-Hindu idea that all true spirituality is really the same has little cash value when it comes to uniting or to promoting cooperation among the various Indian religious traditions in Atlanta or America generally. No Indian religious minority would regard itself as merely a subvariation of Hindu spirituality or Hindu culture. And there are times when those outside the Hindu majority become for those within the majority "those people" (that is, outsiders). The Hindu majority, both in India and in America, is in a position comparable to that of the WASP majority in America--which plays the ambiguity of white Judeo-Christian tradition as common or distinct as occasion and advantage demand.

Minority religious groups often have a perception of Indian culture that is more explicitly pluralistic than that of the Hindu majority. As perceived by Indian religious minorities, what majority Hindus mean by Indian culture is largely Hindu culture. The minorities resist assimilation under Hindu spirituality or absorption by the Hindu tradition and are frequently suspicious of the motives and actions of the Hindu majority. Jains in Atlanta cooperate with Hindus, and Sikhs have also, at times, cooperated fairly closely. Christians, Jews, and Muslims tend to emphasize international or American contacts rather than Indian relations. Sunni and Ismaili Muslims are only peripherally involved in pan-Indian activities.

A fourth unifying factor among Indian immigrants is the real and the imagined differences of
Indians from other Americans. Indians sometimes
perceive Americans to be very different from
Indians, not only culturally, but also morally.
Some Indians would prefer their children to marry
almost any Indian rather than an American because
of their projected notions that Americans are
prone to divorce and have a weak sense of family
obligation.   Immigrant nostalgia for the "ideal
India" left behind also contributes to a pan-
Indian cultural image that is opposed to
"decadent" American culture.

Americans also perceive Indians to be different from native Americans but have little
awareness of differences among Indians that are
important to Indians. The perception of Indians
as a single homogeneous group by the overwhelmingly much larger non-Indian American population
may reinforce the sense of commonality among Indians. For the second immigrant generation the way
Indians are perceived by the larger society will
be even more important.

A fifth factor undergirding Indian immigrant
unity is the minority status of Indians in
America. Even in metropolitan areas, such as New
York City where Indians are numerous, they are
still numerically overwhelmed by the non-Indian
American population. Indian immmigrants have
mutual interests that will be represented only if
Indians represent themselves. IACA quite consciously expends a portion of its energies to improving relations with the larger non-Indian
American public. Since about 1985, Indian involvement in the American political process has
considerably increased--even for Indians who are
not U.S. citizens. The Indian American Forum for
Political Education, which is concerned with such
Indian issues as immigration regulations, discrimination, and U.S. relations with India, has
local organizations in over thirty states and an
annual national meeting. President Ronald Reagan
appointed Joy Cherian from this organization and
from the Asian Voters Coalition to the Equal Opportunities Commission in 1987. (Cherian was also
an invited speaker at the 1987 Atlanta IACA annual
banquet.) The National Association of Americans
of Asian Indian Descent (NAAAID) is occupied with

similar issues. There have also been national conventions of Asian Indians in North America.

Annual and semiannual banquets staged in Atlanta by IACA have regularly invited political office holders, such as Atlanta Mayor Andrew Young, Georgia Congressman Newt Gingrich, and New York Congressman Steven Solarz (chair of the U.S. House of Representatives Asian and Pacific Affairs Committee), to make speeches. Congressman Solarz has been particularly responsive to the interests of Indian Americans. Representatives of the Indian government, such as the ambassador of India to the United States, have also spoken at gatherings of the Indian community. IACA also cooperates with other immigrant groups in Atlanta, such as the Asian/Pacific American Council, Inc., which includes Chinese, Filipinos, Koreans, and Vietnamese.

The need to cooperate in a small Indian population is an extra minority incentive in a location like Atlanta, where pan-Indian cooperation is necessary to get large-scale activities done. In cities with large Indian populations groups can often operate on their own without depending on the whole Indian population. The importance of population size is clear in a comparison of Atlanta with Pittsburgh, for example, which has three temples and corresponding Indian population divisions. The New York metropolitan area also has a very large, highly segmented Indian population. By contrast, the Indian population of several hundred persons in Augusta, Georgia, maintains an "ecumenical" form of Hindu worship twice each month, which is supported by most Augusta Indians.

Gujaratis are numerically predominant in the constituency of IACA, but care has been taken to insure regional representativeness in leadership roles. Women are represented in the governing structure, although male domination is a continuing cultural habit even when women occupy offices of authority. Membership is overwhelmingly Hindu or Hindu background, but a few individuals make efforts to include the religious minorities.

Despite high mobility, traveling distance and convenience do play some role in Indian institutions in Atlanta. Indians in the northeast beyond the perimeter highway (in Gwinnett County)

have organized biweekly Hindu gatherings because
the Indian center in the northeast beyond the
perimeter (Cobb County) is too far away (see Chapter 4).

The IACA is a voluntary association with
all of the problems that go along with that kind
of institution: inefficiency, unreliability,
shifting personnel, incomplete effort, and contacts developed by acquaintance rather than by
systematic design. Some Indians think Indians
are, in general, poor organizers:

> One thing about Indian organizations.
> They don't know how to organize. So you
> can see a group coming up and going
> down. It all depends whether one person
> leaves here and moves to another town or
> there are some conflicts between two
> persons or some financial troubles or
> whatever.

Dedication by larger numbers of volunteers and
efficiency improved greatly during the fund drive
and especially after the dedication of the cultural center. But profit-making Indian businesses
in Atlanta still claim to have much more comprehensive mailing lists than IACA.

Until the last few years IACA has concentrated
its canvassing efforts among Indians of higher
income (as is evident from the contrast in incomes
for the 1984 Atlanta questionnaire respondents as
compared to the 1980 U.S. Census figures for
Georgia). It is the more prosperous Indians who
get involved in community centers, and people
running the centers are naturally more interested
in new participants who can pay their way. Ticket
prices for annual IACA banquets began at $15 in
1982 but by 1987 had risen to $50 per person.
Manual and service workers, recent immigrants with
low income, and people who work weekends take part
in IACA activities only sporadically. Two South
Indians indicated that in their opinion the IACA
does not reach the whole Indian community because
they are mostly North Indians and mostly professionals who do not know how to relate to
nonprofessionals. One complained that they aren't
interested in you unless you have money to pay
operating costs of the Indian center.

The India Cultural and Religious Center

The facility purchased for the India Cultural and Religious Center (ICRC) is a former Pentecostal church in the town of Smyrna in northwestern metropolitan Atlanta, just outside the perimeter highway. The 16,000-square-foot building on three acres was acquired in 1984 for $240,500 with a $120,000 mortgage. The retirement of the mortgage was celebrated in just over three years at an annual banquet in November 1987. The amount of money raised and the size of the operating budget of the ICRC testifies to the affluence of its supporters. The altar and baptismal font in the church sanctuary were replaced by a large stage, and two rooms and a hallway upstairs have been renovated to serve as a temple room. Other rooms are utilized as office, library, nursery, kitchen, dining room, and classrooms. A fairly complete list of activities staged regularly at the ICRC two years after the commencement of its operations includes a variety of annual festivals, some religious, some "ethnic," and some national, observed by regional groups, religious groups, and/or the whole community; meetings of the India American Cultural Association, music, drama and dance programs; presentations by representatives of the government of India, of Indian state governments, of American local, state, and national government; weekly religious worship and education programs for children and adults; weekly Hindi language classes; India Youth of Atlanta meetings, parties, and debates; daily and weekly Hindu and Jain puja in the temple of the center; programs for the birthday anniversary of M. K. Gandhi; memorial services for the deceased; and weddings.

The fund drive to establish a center for Indian community programs began in 1975 shortly after the reorganization of the IACA. The original idea was to purchase a building, probably in north central metropolitan Atlanta conveniently located for most of the Indian population, where a variety of cultural programs would be held and which would serve as a physical base that would help to promote Indian unity. The original IACA funding drive was for an Indian cultural center that would also provide for temporary worship areas for all Indian religious groups (actually only Sikhs, Jains, and Hindus could have reasonably been expected to participate) and as a place for weddings, and so forth. But religious aspects of the plan were played down until the funding campaign got into high gear in 1983.

The fund-raising campaign initially moved very slowly and did not achieve its $50,000 goal by 1980. But subsequently canvassing became more vigorous and involvement more general. Momentum had increased so much by 1983 that it was clear that a property would be acquired in the very near future. How the center was to be used became an issue that required concrete and detailed decision making on the part of its supporters.

A general body meeting in September 1983 raised fundamental questions about the purpose of an Indian cultural center in Atlanta for first generation immigrants and their children. One point of view maintained the originally disseminated view that the India center should be primarily cultural. According to this "secular" approach, it should be all right to have incidental religious functions in the building, but the center should not contain a temple, mosque, or church. A second, contrary, "pluralistic" point of view that ultimately prevailed contended that at least for Indians, religion and culture cannot be separated. Almost any Indian cultural program one could think of, it was argued, would have religious content--whether it was dance, drama, literature, or cultural festivals like Diwali. A third approach argued the significantly different view that the distinction of "Hindu" religion and "Hindu" culture from Indian religion and culture is made solely by <u>foreigners</u>. "India" and "Hindu" are interchangeable--there is really no problem in combining religious and cultural functions in the Indian center.

The September meeting (and a subsequent general meeting in October 1983) agreed that the name of the center would be the India Cultural and Religious Center. In name and fact the second point of view just summarized prevailed--that Indian religion and culture are inseparable. The official stance of the center is <u>pluralistic</u>, even though almost all religious activities at the center are Hindu. The proposal of a temple to be included in the center proved to be a great boost to the fund-raising campaign. There were potential donors of Hindu background who would generously support a religious center who had less interest in a merely cultural center. The fund drive was strengthened, but some Indian religious minorities were alienated. Indian Muslims are now less willing to participate in center events because of the Hindu shrine in the building. Some Sikhs also feel that they were not allowed to construct a shrine. More than one non-Hindu would have agreed with the chagrin manifest in this opinion: "I am apprehensive about the new emphasis on religion for the [ICRC] building. Religion among Indians tends to divide."

There is now a temple/shrine area in the center that is primarily Hindu but which also contains a Jaina image of Mahavira. (See discussion in Chapter 4.) The India center is supported by the first generation of immigrants for both cultural and religious reasons, and the schedule of explicitly religious events at the center since the opening has been heavy.

A second, very important motivation for supporting the India center was the belief among people in the first generation that the center would make it possible to transmit Indian culture and religion to the second generation. One parent expressed a widely shared view at a 1984 general meeting:

> I am deeply distressed at the division occurring in this community. There should be no divisions in this community. We are 11,000 miles from home. We came here to make money, and we have made it. The issue is the second generation. I could go back to R_____ and make a place for myself. But the point is the young people. The Indian community is very much divided.

In an interview a North Indian couple affirmed that the children were the most important factor in their support for the India center:

> Husband: I was against it, but then I have come around.

> Wife: I think that change in me was
> brought about mainly because of our
> child. . . . Until then, I did not think
> that it was really necessary to have it
> because you could have your functions
> anywhere. You could always rent a
> place. . . . I think it's more for the
> benefit of the children because they can
> associate themselves with--well, we are
> Indians and this is our center and . . .
> As the community grows, those things
> [weddings, funerals] are going to be,
> you know, more and more. All those
> things. You need a place of your own.

Another person argued that the center would help
provide an Indian identity for the children:

> There   is an identity crisis.   The
> children are Americans. So we need a
> religious center for their identity.
> How have other minorities survived in
> America?   Muslims, for example, have a
> weekly school. We need a place to do it
> [teach religion].

But, although most parents agreed that providing Indian culture for the children was of
primary importance, a segment of the population
expressed skepticism that the availability of an
Indian center would make much difference.   Some
even went so far as to suggest that second-
generation Indians would not even use the center.
They projected that by the time the first generation became old, the center would fall into
disuse and would have to be sold, perhaps even at
a financial loss.

However, those who were more optimistic about
the long-range, multigenerational importance of
the India center prevailed. In fact, the age of
the children was apparently an important factor in
generating financial support and subsequent participation. The oldest child of 70.1 percent of the
respondents to the 1984 questionnaire in Atlanta
with children was fifteen years of age or younger,
and the oldest child of almost half of the respondents was six years of age or younger. The time
was ripe for a cultural center if it was to help

transmit Indian culture and religion to the children.

The number of contributors listed in the inauguration issue of <u>Voice of India</u> was 323. The
Atlanta Hindu Society and the Sikh Study Circle
were early organizational supporters and financial
contributors to ICRC fund. At the time of the
inauguration support for the center was predominantly Hindu and North Indian. Support among
immigrants from other parts of India has become
much stronger in the three years since 1984.

Inauguration ceremonies for the center took
place in July 1984 with participation representative of the Indian government from the Indian
embassy in Washington, D.C. All but a few Sikhs
boycotted the event in protest of participation by
the government of India because of the Indian army
assault on the Golden Temple at Amritsar just the
previous month. Sikh support for the center
varies and has increased to some extent since
1986. A fund drive for a separate Sikh gurudwara
(temple) has been underway for several years (see
discussion on pages 140-42.)

Individuals and groups previously skeptical
began to participate and to schedule events once
the ICRC began operations. Many people who were
organizationally involved before the center opened
are now working very hard and regularly as volunteers. Use is now close to capacity on the weekends. Cosponsorship of religious and cultural
events by the smaller religious and regional
groups and by IACA has increased considerably.
The IACA aspires to be the umbrella organization
for the Indian immigrant population in Atlanta,
but use of the center and participation in IACA by
Muslims and Sikhs continues to be limited.

Student Organizations

According to reports ("Number of Foreign Students" 1986), there were 16,070 students from
India in America in 1985 and 1986. In Atlanta
there are usually fifty to seventy Indians on
student visas. Almost all are male graduate students (some masters degree candidates, but mostly
Ph.D. students), and the great majority are enrolled at the Georgia Institute of Technology.

Since over 90 percent of the students are single,
their contact with Indian families and thus with
the larger Indian immigrant community is usually
quite limited. Families from the same region of
India sometimes invite new students into their
homes in the fall to get fresh contacts from home
and to discover who has cultural talents useful in
the local community.

Most graduate students work about two years
after receiving their graduate degrees before
returning to India, but many also manage to change
to permanent immigrant visas. Students usually
marry after completing the degree, but do so before completing their studies. Married students
with wives present tend to become involved in
Indian community affairs more than single students
do. But in general, temporary sojourners get much
less involved in Indian immigrant affairs than
permanent residents. A few students are involved
in the Vishwa Hindu Parishad, the Vedanta Society,
and the Sikh Study Circle.

The (student) India Club of Georgia Tech is
the oldest Indian organization in Atlanta. The
club gives assistance to newly arrived students,
helping them to get settled and find apartments.
As one student testified, the India Club has often
been the only resource when they first arrive:

> The newcomer is a student, or even as
> anybody else may even come here as an
> immigrant to work--the first few months
> are very, very difficult. And the best
> thing anybody can do is help you during
> that initial period. I see that as one
> of the things any group can do. . . . I
> don't think the IACA has been doing
> anything along those lines.

The club also arranges programs for students.
Indian motion pictures were shown for several
years (until rendered obsolete by video cassettes
of Indian movies), visiting speakers (often of a
religious sort, such as Swami Chinmayananda) have
been scheduled, and student-acted Indian-language
dramas have been staged. Abhinay, a Hindi and
Sanskrit drama group with a graduate student core,
has staged at least five productions. Dance and
other music programs have also been scheduled, and

there is an annual picnic in the summer when officers are elected.

In principle pan-Indian, the India Club is in fact almost entirely Hindu. A very few Muslims and Sikhs have at times been involved in the club. Most non-Hindus came at an earlier period primarily to see movies that were screened. Pakistanis usually do not participate in the club's activities. As a student organization, the India Club gets some financial support and free use of facilities from the Georgia Institute of Technology. There is also an India Club at the University of Georgia in Athens.

The Pakistani Student Organization is the major Pakistani organization in Atlanta. It was originally a student organization about fifteen years ago, but the majority of its members are at present former students.

In 1986 a Muslim Student Association chapter of the Muslim Student Association (MSA) of North America was established at Emory University. Some Indian Muslim students are included among the members of this international organization initially founded in the United States at the University of Illinois, Urbana in 1963. MSA now has 130 chapters and publishes religious literature, including two magazines, through its Islamic Press. MSA coordinates Muslim undergraduate and graduate student activities on campuses across the United States and Canada. Most of these students are foreign students completing their education in North America, but many will remain to work after receiving their degrees. The Muslim Student Association spearheaded the formation of the Islamic Society of North America in 1982 in the hope of creating an umbrella Muslim organization for all or most Muslim institutions in North America.

NOTES

1. "Reasons for attending group worship" listed in the questionnaire were compiled from more than fifty interviews with people from various sectors of the Indian immigrant population. (Only 1.8 percent of the respondents ranked "other" reasons primary or secondary.)

2. It could be argued that too much emphasis on religion as the source of Indian ethnic identity would in fact be divisive because religious diversity is so great and the local Indian population is so small. The local population is also sufficiently affluent to provide many nonreligious sources of identity, and Indians in fact need a "secular" identity (as India does) to maintain their precarious cohesiveness.

3. In interviews the opinion was often offered (especially by the second generation) that the first generation attends group worship primarily for social reasons. The role of social contact in the perception of others is stronger than in self-perceptions of the first generation in interviews, but the importance of social contact is clearly evidenced in the questionnaire responses of the first generation.

4. Thanks to Ms. Norma Charles for her generous assistance.

4

Temples and Mosques

Immigrants take an important step toward community formation when they invest in a building and dedicate it for the purpose of group worship. Establishing such a place marks the beginning of their transformation from the short-term attitudes of temporary sojourners to the long-range expectations of permanent residents. More than a decade passed before it became obvious to immigrants of the late 1960s and early 1970s that they were becoming permanent immigrants, not just visitors who work in America for an extended period. Large numbers of children were born to the immigrants both in India and in America during that decade. The children identified increasingly with American culture while their cultural and religious ties to India remained largely at secondhand. As adult first-generation immigrants began to realize that they were unlikely to return to India, many became concerned that their children might lose touch with their heritage.

The need for ethnic cultural regeneration and preservation also became unmistakable when the first small wave of immigrant children reached the age of majority having acquired only rudiments of Indian culture and religion. The children entered public and private American elementary schools to facilitate their advancement in American society, but typically at the cost of never

becoming   conversant with their   Indian   religious
and   cultural backgrounds.   When it appeared   that
the second, much larger wave of Asian Indian children born in America was likely to suffer the same
fate unless something was done to prevent it, many
of   the   older immigrants got involved   in   establishing Indian cultural and religious centers.

The   early 1980s were also years in which   the
older immigrants became acutely aware that so many
of   the second generation are between the ages   of
one   and   fifteen years.   Replies to   the   Atlanta
questionnaire   administered   in 1984, for   example,
show   24   percent of respondents with   the   oldest
child age six or less and 46 percent with children
ages seven years to fifteen years.   Thus, 70   percent   of   the children were fifteen years   old   or
less.   Early immigrants did not spend a great deal
of time worrying about the future for their   children.   Eventually, they came to realize that their
children   are going to stay in America   and   that,
consequently,   they   are going to   be   in   America
permanently   also. Not all adult   immigrants   were
convinced that either a cultural center or a   temple would really help to perpetuate Indian culture
among   the second generation. As did many   others,
one   felt that the responsibility lay elsewhere:

> I think that if the culture is going   to
> survive, it's going to be in the family,
> not   in   any   hall.   Even   individual
> worship   couldn't   help   it. . . . the
> parents   are   the best ones   to   educate
> their children in culture.

"Secular"   cultural centers help to provide   a
sense   of   ethnic identity and of belonging   to   a
group for both the first and the second   immigrant
generation.   Because so many different   religious
traditions   are   represented, it could   be   argued
that   Indian immigrants could cooperate with   each
other only on a nonreligious or pluralistic basis.
In some respects ethnic similarity is more   important   for Indian immigrants than shared   religious
characteristics (see   Chapter 5).   But   for   most
Indians   a secular cultural center is not, by   it-
self, adequate to provide a sense of <u>being</u> <u>at</u> <u>home</u>
in a universe that is ordered.

For   <u>most</u> Indian immigrants, the   exercise   of

religion in groups and the dedication of a place
for group worship are necessary ingredients in the
process of becoming at home (having a _desh_ or
place where one belongs) on the foreign soil of
America. Whether it is a mosque the _qibla_ (niche)
of which points toward Mecca, a temple fixed in
place upon the "sea of chaos," or a gurudwara
where the guru is honored, a religious sanctuary
locates people in a cosmic order; it constitutes a
point through which access to sacred reality is
possible; and it makes transcendent meaning and
value accessible.

Building temples, mosques, and gurudwaras
became possible for Indian immigrants in the early
1980s in many American urban centers because of
their relative affluence and because of a much
larger population after 1975. In fact, they began
to establish religious centers almost as soon as
it was feasible to do so. Places for worship are
set up when there are enough persons of similar
religious conviction who have the financial and
other means necessary and when they commit to
finance and to maintain a place of worship.

Indian immigrants have often established temples and mosques primarily with their own
resources. But in many cases there has been
assistance from outside the local immigrant com-
munity--from other parts of the United States,
Canada, India , and other countries. The type of
worship place established varies. Some have been
temporary and makeshift; others are permanent, but
not ritually dedicated; while still others are
consecrated temples, mosques, or gurudwaras. Some
places of worship have been newly built for the
purpose; others are reconstructed from existing
buildings.

HINDU TEMPLES

Although temples are not absolutely necessary,
they nevertheless serve as important supporting
institutions for the practice of Hindu religion.
There are also religious needs, some of which are
felt more acutely by Hindus outside India, which
only temples can fulfill. As Narayanan (1984) has
argued, the installation of a Hindu temple and the
invocation of God into its central image makes _God_

present in that place and the land becomes holy.
The land becomes karma-bhumi (a land where actions
have their fruits, that is, where human deeds are
significant). Before the ritual, the site is
symbolically formless ocean ("without form and
void" as in Genesis, Chapter 1). Bhumi-puja
(ground breaking or dedication of the land) symbolically creates a temple site with a solid
foundation, and by extension, it brings the land
in which it is located into existence, thus induc-
ting a local area of America into God's universe.
At the same time the space is purified and given
form as a locus the worshippers can occupy.

When the deity responds to the rite of invocation and consents to dwell in its image (murti)
in the holy place (garbhagriha) of the temple, God
becomes locally accessible for human worship. A
point of access, a fording place (tirtha), is
established between immanent and transcendent
reality. That is to say, God who is everywhere,
who is universal, and who is in all things and all
spaces nevertheless consents to become present, to
become incarnate, in the temple in a special way--
even here in this strange land so far from home.

Clothey (1983, pp. 194-200) disclosed additional implications of building a temple in America. Beyond its symbolizing the divine presence,
the ritual (pratistha and kumbhabhisekham) by
which the Sri Venkateswara Temple in Pittsburgh
was dedicated embodied the cosmos for its devotees. Further, the dedication process literally
includes the implantation of various kinds of
seeds and plants, which transplant and implant the
temple from India to American soil. Germination of
the seeds gives symbolic assurance that the new
location is acceptable. By symbolic extension the
worshipping community is also transplanted with
its god to its new home. The installation of the
deity's image and the invocation of the deity,
Clothey maintained, follows the ritual structure
of a royal coronation. The ritual enactment of
the kingship of God is simultaneously a bringing
of the subjects of the divine king into being, and
it is an affirmation of their peoplehood,

> thereby legitimating for all time the
> immigration process. Hindu immigrants
> are a people, whose "god-king", like

themselves, while deeply rooted in the
Indian tradition, has now become a
permanent part of the American landscape
(Clothey 1983, p. 195).

In summary, Clothey suggested that a Hindu temple
founds a world, making a public statement that
this country is now also an Indian American land;
it expresses the transition of the immigration
process both by the betwixt and between symbolism
of its being the house of God and by the adjustments and adaptations that have been necessary to
build, maintain, and operate a Hindu temple in
America; and finally, it gives the worshippers
roots in American soil deep enough to connect to
the nutrients of the Indian cultural heritage.

The first Hindu temple constructed in America
(in Pittsburgh) was modeled after the most popular
Hindu temple in South India, the Sri Venkateswara
Temple at Tirupathi at the southern extreme of
Andhra Pradesh state. That temple is now primarily devoted to the worship of God as Visnu, but it
also has earlier associations with the worship of
Siva, and some ritual elements of the Siva tradition still survive. The temple, which is the
abode of Visnu Narayana as Lord (Isvara) of
Venkata Hill (one of the seven hills where the
temple is located), has an impressive reputation
for hearing the prayers and granting the requests
of the more than 30,000 devotees, on the average,
who make pilgrimage there daily. Donations make
the temple foundation the wealthiest in South
India. In the last generation or so, satellite
temples of the Sri Venkateswara Temple have been
built in other locations in India where there are
large numbers of South Indians, and it has also
become popular among overseas Indians to dedicate
temples to Sri Venkateswara. Devotion to Sri
Venkateswara continues to be strong in America,
and several temples for this deity have been built
or planned in Indian population centers in the
United States.

The Pittsburgh temple, the first Sri
Venkateswara Temple in America, was dedicated in
1977 (before construction was completed). Financial support was sought and obtained from Indians
scattered across the country. Help in drawing up
architectural plans, in providing skilled Indian

artisans, and commissioning the temple images   and
some   of its symbolic decorations was provided   on
an exchange basis (for medical supplies and scientific equipment) by the Tirumala Tirupathi Devas-
thanam (the Sri Venkateswara Temple foundation) in
India.

As far as possible in America, the Pittsburgh
temple is intended to reproduce the original Indian temple and its worship (Clothey 1983).   The
image of Sri Venkateswara (Balaji, Visnu) in the
central sanctuary is flanked by the images of the
goddesses Sri Padmavathi (Lakshmi or Sreedevi) and
Sri Andal (Bhuma Devi).

However, some Hindu immigrants in America
doubt that it is really possible to establish
genuine Hindu temples outside India. Objectors
usually express doubt that ritual requirements can
be met in America. Some argue that genuine Vedic
rituals require spatial and temporal coordination
by reference to specific rivers nearby that are
mentioned in Hindu scriptures before puja (ritual)
can begin. All of these rivers are in India.   In
strict interpretation, according to these commen-
tators, substitution of American rivers and other
coordinates is not possible. But there is apparently room within the orthoprax (astika) tradition
for disagreement on this issue. I observed a puja
performed by a traditional priest in Chicago in
1966 that was explicitly oriented to the Chicago
River and other local streams. Pujas in Atlanta
routinely orient by the Chattahoochee River and
other local rivers that are symbolically substitu-
ted for Indian streams. And substitutions for
unavailable materials have in fact been made in
Hindu rituals for more than 2,000 years.

A second objection is that ritual purity requirements are not met and cannot be met in America. Purity regulations certainly are difficult to
enforce here. Compromises have been necessary and
arrangements have been made in ways that would not
be done in India. Building plans, for example,
must be modified to fit financial limitations of
the supporting community, to utilize building
materials that are available, and to comply with
local building codes. Temple buildings are often
constructed for multipurpose uses, which result
in the central sanctuary's being placed over lower
floors used for nonritual purposes. Toilets must

in most cases be available for public use within
the temple area. Temples are generally open to
the public, including non-Hindus unfamiliar with
purity requirements, and food is served to worship
participants that may not have been prepared by
brahmans (Clothey 1983, p. 199). Time schedules
are also frequently shifted to the weekend for
convenience and to promote larger attendance, even
when traditional timetables call for ritual performances during the week.

The fact that temple building has been pro-
ceeding apace indicates that objections of this
sort are being overcome. Acceptance of innova-
tions in America is not limited to nontradition-
alist Hindus, although it may be that "modernists"
have less difficulty making adjustments. For many
Hindus it is very important that ritual, and especially temple ritual, preserve the authentic
Indian form as much as possible. Deviation in
ritual duty is felt by some traditionalists to be
of a piece with deviation in other duties, especially the adoption of undesirable aspects of
American culture. But for others the "American
emergency" is a set of new local conditions that
call for new measures. Thus, social, political,
and economic necessities assume as much importance
as ritual niceties, and the temple comes to serve
broad community needs rather than narrow, possibly
sectarian interests. Some less traditional Hindus
suggest that because India is halfway around the
world, Indian rules need not apply here. And for
some liberal Hindus America represents a fresh
start for a more universal and more spiritual
(neo-Hindu) form of the Hindu tradition.

Resolution of conflicts within local Hindu
communities attempting to construct a temple has
not always been possible. Hindus in Pittsburgh
split into two groups, one group composed primarily of North Indians who favored a "modern" temple
with images of many deities, the other supported
predominantly by South Indians who wanted a temple
devoted to one primary deity and constructed in
traditional South Indian architectural style.

Pittsburgh Indians began in 1973 to worship
in a renovated Baptist church that contained temporary shrines for the use of Hindus, Sikhs, and
Jains. This group negotiated with the Tirumala
Tirupathi Devasthanum, the foundation associated

with the Sri Venkateswara Temple in South India, for their aid in drawing up the plans for a Sri Venkateswara Temple in Pittsburgh and for supplying materials and skilled labor for the construction process. After the ground-breaking ceremony had taken place in the spring of 1975, a deep division concerning the ideology of the proposed temple among Indian supporters became obvious. Basically, one faction wanted to broaden the scope of the temple by increasing the number of deity images contained in the temple and to avoid dedicating the temple to any single primary deity (Clothey 1983, pp. 176-80). When the group as a whole agreed to make this change, the Indian temple foundation withdrew its offer of support. Subsequently, one section of the Indian population withdrew to incorporate the Sri Venkateswara Temple of Pittsburgh, Inc. This association purchased a new site and dedicated their Sri Venkateswara Temple in June 1977. The other group continued to meet in temporary quarters until the Hindu Temple of Pittsburgh (in Monroeville, Pennsylvania) was completed. Ground breaking occurred there in October 1980.

The division that developed within the Pittsburgh Hindu community expresses ideological divergence and the survival of Indian regionalism. The Monroeville temple is understood by its patrons to be modern or neo-Hindu. Its eclectic accommodation of many deities is intended to represent the devotion of the Hindus in Pittsburgh from many different sectarian traditions--to include as much diversity as possible with its "unity in diversity" approach. Increasing the number of images is, from one immigrant Hindu point of view, a "pluralistic" solution to the problem of sectarian diversity. Despite the "polytheistic" connotation an increase in the number of images in the temple may have for native American Christians or Jews, the emphasis on many deities underscores the monotheistic focus of Hindu religion for insiders, namely, that since all gods are the same, it does not matter which are imaged in the temple. In fact, the diversity of images evinces the universality and the rich depth of Hindu spirituality. The ritual forms and the architecture of the Monroeville temple are also less traditional and less orthoprax than the Sri Venkateswara Temple. The variety of images in the Gita Temple in Elmhurst, New York, also expresses what Williams (1986b) calls "ecumenical Hinduism."

Divisiveness among Indian immigrants in Pittsburgh also is due to the continuation of regional bases for congregating. The ideological or symbolic differences in the two temples partially correspond to differences in the sensibilities of North and South Indians. Clothey's (1983, p. 176) survey of attendance patterns shows a clear trend toward regionalistic patronage. No South Indians in his survey attended the Monroeville Temple exclusively, but 40 percent attended the Penn Hills (Sri Venkateswara) Temple exclusively. In contrast, 24 percent of the North Indians attended only the Monroeville Temple. The division within the Indian Hindu population is not absolute, however, for 45 to 50 percent of respondents in the survey attended both temples.

Temples are also important for the religious life of Hindus who reside at considerable distances away. The older, established temples advertise in Indian immigrant newspapers for various kinds of pujas to be performed at the temple for a fee by qualified priests when the sponsors are not present. Prasad is mailed back to the sponsor in dry form (for example, fruit or nuts) so that it may be consumed. Some Atlanta Hindu families, for example, sponsor pujas at temples in Pittsburgh or New York for important life-cycle milestones, such as a child's birthday. A mother explained:

> Like on birthdays, there is a thing called sahasranamarchana, the name of the Lord, thousand names. . . . That archana you can do for your son's birthday by mail, $11. And you give your son's name and the birth star. That will be done, and they send you the prasad. Then there is kalyanam utsavam you can do by mail. You can send them money, and they will do the wedding festival of Lord Venkateswara.

The pace of Hindu temple building in America is increasing. The first Pittsburgh temple was followed in short order by the Mahaganapati Temple

(Hindu Temple Society of North America) in Flushing, New York, in 1978 and the Sri Meenakshi Temple in Peerland (Houston), Texas, in 1982. By the mid-1980s temples were in various stages of planning or construction in most metropolitan areas where the Indian populations number more than a few thousand. Temples are listed in Indian media where the Indian population is even smaller (such as Augusta, Georgia, or Huntsville, Alabama).

Announcements or advertisements in Indian immigrant media sometimes list temples that are only in the planning stages. Accurate numbers are thus not available. The January 1988 issue of <u>Hinduism Today</u> ("Temple Services" 1988) lists forty-six immigrant Indian Hindu temples for the continental United States (excluding export Hinduism temples). Of this total, seventeen are in metropolitan areas in the northeastern and middle Atlantic states, nine in the southern states, twelve in the upper midwestern states, eight in California, and one in Colorado. (There are also ten Hindu temples listed in Canada and a few in Hawaii.) Melton (1987a, pp. 1006-9) listed four additional temples and there are no doubt others, depending in part upon what qualifies as a temple.

Traditionally, a permanently dedicated temple usually requires the full-time services of a professional priest. But some of the temples listed do not employ permanent, full time priests to perform rituals several times every day as do the Pittsburgh and New York temples mentioned. There is considerable local variation, in part due to financial limitations, in part because of differing sensibilities about temple rituals, and also in part because of the scarcity of professional priests in America. Except for export Hindu traditions, such as ISKCON, there are, so far, no training facilities for Hindu priests in America. Professional Hindu priests in America are imported directly from India, and sometimes this has been difficult to manage (cf. Pattabhiran 1986). Tradition-minded priests are often reluctant to leave India. Typically, professional priests do not qualify for high-priority immigration categories, and professional certification for them as priests is sometimes difficult to document. Priests at established American

temples often help interested communities to start
temples by helping with the architectural and
renovation plans, officiating at dedications, and
by giving assistance in obtaining priests. Each
of the Pittsburgh temples assisted local Indians
to set up temples in Atlanta.

In America Hindu temples tend to become like
other American voluntary associations, and in time
they will begin to resemble American synagogues
and churches. Even the layout for Hindu temples
in America is much more suited for congregational
worship than is so often the case in India. Lay
leadership is strong in Hindu temples as it is in
Protestant churches and as in American religious
organizations generally. Financing is broad-
based, and major donors receive public recognition
by having their names displayed on plaques. Gov-
ernance tends to be broad-based also. Cultural
halls encourage nonreligious activities, as in
ethnic churches and synagogues. Priests perform a
variety of functions not normal in India--
junketing around the country to perform weddings,
to do pujas, to teach children's schools, and so
forth. Visiting, "circuit-riding" gurus do much
the same and already function to some extent like
pastoral counselors.

The first generation of Hindu immigrants rein-
forces its own motivations for temple building by
its expectations of what the religious and cultural needs of the second generation will be. The
irony of Hindu temple-building activity in America
is that it emphasizes that aspect of Hindu religion that so far has the least meaning and that is
most opaque to second-generation Indian immigrants. It is quite possible that traditional
temples and traditional rituals are the least
likely aspect of Hindu tradition to be perpetuated
in America in the long run. Most second-generation Hindus have little notion of what is going on
in the ritual except to pick up the cues for its
termination and to know when it is time to eat
prasad. There is little understanding or interest
in the rich symbolism of puja. Teaching immigrant
Hindu children to appreciate and to participate in
temple ritual may be a task of monumental propor-
tions. The responsibility for sustaining temple
Hinduism may fall almost entirely on the shoulders
of new immigrants from India.

The India Cultural and Religious Center Temple

The original conception of the Atlanta India center included some kind of arrangements for religious activities from the beginning of the drive in 1975, but the intentions were not very specific. People I interviewed in the early 1980s expressed various opinions about how religious activities should be handled, but their most frequently articulated expectation was that there would be temporary altars set up for specific occasions for any Indian religious groups who desired it, in a building that would be primarily a cultural center. Side rooms could be set up for religious occasions, and of course, weddings could be held there. The arrangements to be made for a Sikh gurudwara were more vaguely conceived since, to serve as a gurudwara, there must be a permanently dedicated and separate room for the Granth Sahib. Even Muslims and Christians were supportive of the India center, provided that it were primarily a cultural rather than a religious one.

When the fund drive for the center really began to get underway, solicitors discovered that many people were willing to give money for a religious center that included a temple but were not interested in giving money otherwise. The religious emphasis for the center that had been present in some form from the beginning then became much more pronounced. The plan to put a temple inside the center was consciously adopted in 1983. Thus, the India center became the India Cultural and Religious Center, and people began to designate gifts for the ICRC temple.

A temple committee drew up renovation plans shortly after the former church, which became the India center, was occupied. The second-floor temple was located directly over the first-floor kitchen and dining area of the building, an arrangement that would in all likelihood not have been condoned in India. The initial cost to convert two upstairs rooms, a kitchen, and a hallway for the temple area was $75,000. Two thirds of this amount had been collected by early 1987.

While renovations were in process, priests invited from the Monroeville, Pennsylvania, temple conducted puja for Krishna Janmashtami and Diwali in 1985 and advised the temple committee con-

cerning renovations. Swamiji Dharmanand Saraswati,
who has a connection to the Monroeville temple and
who is director of Parmarth Ashram in Hardwar,
India, also gave a lecture. While renovations
were underway (and even afterwards), annual religious festivals were sometimes celebrated in the
rooms to be used as a temple, and at other times
they were held in the former church sanctuary
downstairs in the center. In 1986 these observances included four Hindu festivals (Maha
Shivratri, Sri Rama Navami, Krishna Janmashtami,
and Deepavali) and one Christian festival (Christmas).

The renovated space, which can seat 100 to 150
persons on the floor, was inaugurated as a temple
with temporary images and mandapam (a canopied
platform) on October 25, 1986, by priests from the
Hindu Temple of Monroeville. Permanent images are
being carved in white marble in North India and
are expected to arrive in Atlanta during the summer of 1988. Preparation of the images is spon-
sored by the Birla Trust (in India) on behalf of
the Vishwa Hindu Parishad.

The nine images (murti) being prepared are,
from left to right facing the platform: Siva,
Durga, Venkateswara, Ganesh, Radha-Krishna, Rama-
Sita, Mahavira, Nandi, and Hanuman. The temple
will eventually be served by a full-time priest.
But in the meantime a regular daily worship
schedule is maintained by families on a voluntary
basis and using a locally standardized book of
rubrics. Arati is offered at 6 P.M. daily.
Bhajans are sung at 6 P.M. every fourth Sunday,
and Satyanarayan puja is conducted at 4:30 P.M.
every second Sunday.

Bylaws drawn up as part of the constitution of
the India American Cultural Association state that
the India Cultural and Religious Center may be
used by anyone in the Indian community and their
friends for religious, cultural, and educational
activities and that the center is the location for
the religious institutions of the Indian community
of Atlanta. But it is difficult to envision how
all Atlanta Indians could locate their religious
institutions in the ICRC given the religious and
cultural diversity within the Indian immigrant
population. It would be difficult or impossible,
for example, for Muslims to worship in a building

where there is a temple dedicated to multiple deities. The difficulties of the situation were recognized and formulated as a challenge to the Indian community in an editorial in the Voice of India:

> How can this be the place for all our religions? What "Indian" culture shall I encounter in the precincts of this center? Does it enrich or pollute the sacred traditions? Let these profound questions trouble our minds. We are not looking for a harvest of lazy, sleeping, unreasoning, indifferent minds. This shall be the battleground of our intellect. The sharp edges of our creative minds shall meet here to discover a new synthesis (Rao 1984).

The appeal of the ICRC temple is intended to be broad and pluralistic (and thus more "modern") like the temple in Monroeville, Pennsylvania, and not as traditional and "sectarian" as the Sri Venkateswara Temple in Pittsburgh or the Sri Venkateswara Temple to be constructed in Atlanta. Also like the Monroeville temple, the India center shrine has greater appeal to North Indians while the Sri Venkateswara Temple in Atlanta is primarily of interest to Telegus, Tamils, and Karnatakas (South Indians). Eventual competition for support between the two temples is a possibility. However, the India American Cultural Association provides a unifying structure in Atlanta that is apparently absent in Pittsburgh. There is less regional polarization in the Atlanta Indian population than there is in Pittsburgh, and the Indian population is also smaller than that of Pittsburgh. Even though they are outnumbered by North Indians, South Indians participate in significant numbers in IACA, and their allegiance can be expected to continue even after the Sri Venkateswara Temple begins operations.

The Atlanta Hindu Society along with other interested individuals played a major role in developing plans and in seeking donations for the ICRC temple. The Monroeville Hindu Temple priests gave advice and assistance.

Eight of the images in the temple are Hindu.

An image of Mahavira has also been installed, and
Jains volunteer to offer puja on a regular
schedule. But Jains also continue to hold major
annual pujas, such as the birthday of Mahavira, in
private homes. When asked about this temple arrangement, one Jain commented that it did not
matter to him whether the image was Jain or Hindu:

> I am happy with that because, to me, God
> is God. And it could be unified under
> all umbrellas. [It is good] to have one
> place to actually go ahead and worship.
> I have no problems with it.

There is no distinct provision for Sikh worship because arrangements for a separate gurudwara
could not be worked out and because Atlanta Sikhs
are hoping to build a separate gurudwara on the
eastern side of Atlanta. Sikhs have, however,
observed some major annual festivals, such as the
birthday of Guru Nanak, in the downstairs former
church sanctuary.

Prior to its opening, support for the India
Cultural and Religious Center in the Indian population was uneven, especially among Bengalis,
South Indians, Christians, and Muslims. Since
operations began, use of the center has been
heavy, and support among Hindus from areas other
than North and Northwest India has greatly increased. Indian Christians also use the center.
Christmas programs, for example, attract several
hundred Indian Christians. Muslim involvement is
still meager or occasional, and nonreligious, and
group participation typically occurs only by
special invitation.

But even among the more directly involved
Hindus and Jains, controversy about the temple was
not completely avoidable. One source of conten-
tion had been whether the consumption of meat and
alcohol would be permitted within the India center
building. An initial compromise was incorporated
into the bylaws prohibiting the consumption of
meat and alcohol on the second floor "where dedicated facilities for religious ceremonies are
located." This prohibition was felt by some Jains
and Hindus to be required to maintain the purity
of the temple. But whereas many center supporters
wanted to be able to use the downstairs portion

for secular-cultural purposes that might include serving meat and alcohol for dinners, parties, or receptions, some Hindus wanted to be able to offer meat actually or symbolically during worship in the temple. The resolution embodied in the by-laws was contested by some IACA members in a motion raised at the January 1988 general body meeting to prohibit meat and alcohol on the entire premises. In discussion at the meeting, which at times was quite heated, some people objected primarily to the consumption of alcohol on the premises. But an attempt to separate the question concerning alcohol from the meat issue was unsuccessful. Possibly the most telling argument of the majority in 1988 was that the people who made donations for the center had done so on the basis of the compromise laid down in the bylaws and that it would be unfair to change the arrangements four years later. Several people who spoke at the meeting were clearly more concerned with maintaining the unity of the Indian community than with taking a side on the issue. In a general and remarkable degree of agreement, the previous arrangement allowing meat and alcohol consumption downstairs in the center was upheld by a ratio of almost five to one.

The Hindu Temple of Atlanta

The possibility of building a Hindu temple in Atlanta was raised before a group of about thirty Indians meeting at Emory University by a visiting official from the Tirumala Tirupathi Devasthanum in April 1978. Everyone present was aware of the recent dedication of Hindu temples in Pittsburgh and New York City , and there was considerable interest in the proposal. But no local preparation or planning had been done before the meeting, and this interest did not result in any action. Further, the funding drive for the India American Cultural Center was already underway at that time, and that project was supposed to include provision for some sort of temporary religious shines for Hindus, Jains, Sikhs, and other interested Indians.

Five physicians from South India began separate discussions in the late 1970s about constructing a Sri Venkateswara Temple in Atlanta. In 1983 the group expanded to about fifteen supporters who then began a fund-raising drive. Broader community support was obtained and a five acre plot was purchased in Riverdale in the south central metropolitan area.

Total cost for the Lord Venkateswara (Balaji) Temple of Atlanta is expected to exceed $1 million. Construction will occur in stages. First, the shell of the temple will be built. The outer walls, temple towers, and entrance will follow as funding permits. Out of $450,000 pledged toward temple construction, $235,000 had been donated by April 1987. Ground breaking (bhumi-puja) for the Atlanta temple took place in June 1986 officiated by a priest from the Rajarajeshwari Peetham in Stroudsburg, Pennsylvania. A second (Satyanarayana) puja was performed at the site in April 1987.

Lists of donors that have been distributed indicate that financial support for the Sri Venkateswara Temple is about 90 percent South Indian and primarily Telegu. Many patrons are physicians, a few of whom were trained at the Venkateswara University medical school. About 90 percent of the backing is from persons living in Georgia, but some donors are listed from neighboring southeastern states, as well as from Illinois and New York. But North Indians have also contributed funds, and some Atlanta Indians have contributed to both the Sri Venkateswara Temple and to the India Cultural and Religious Center temple.

The Atlanta building committee visited the Sri Venkateswara Temple in Pittsburgh, the Rama temple in Chicago, and other temples before approving plans for construction. The temple will have a South Indian temple architectural style that resembles that of the Tirupati temple. The primary deity image will be of Sri Venkateswara. There will also be images of Sri Lakshmi on his right and Sri Boodevi on his left. The central deity will also be referred to as Balaji, a name North Indians are said to use for the deity Venkateswara (especially Bengalis). The intent is to universalize it, that is, to make the temple more attractive to North Indians. A shrine for the goddess Durga will be located to the left of the entrance of the main hall, in part for the same reason, but also because one of the major patrons is a Durga devotee. In front of the entrance, shrines for Ganesh and the Navagrahas (nine deities or nine planets) will be installed. After the temple is completed, deities have been installed, and a permanent priest has been secured, a Sansrit traditional ritual will be conducted daily and for special occasions. Local supporters hope that Hindus across the southeast will then worship at the Atlanta Sri Venkateswara temple because it is so much closer than Pittsburgh. In early 1988 a date for the start of construction had not yet been set.

The Greater Atlanta Vedic Temple

A group of Hindus led by a child psychiatrist under the auspices of Vishwa Hindu Parishad began to meet in December 1986 for a bal vihar (children's school) to teach Hindu religion and culture to the children. These biweekly meetings terminated when the doctor left for half a year but were restarted in the summer of 1987 at the request of parents who wanted this type of education in religion and culture to continue. The meetings expanded to a range of programs for the whole family led by various volunteers in the group as teachers of religion, Hindu culture, Hindi and Sanskrit, traditional music, yoga meditation, storytelling, and ritual. Programs strive to present religion in a practical way with emphasis on ethics and proper behavior and with an attempt to present religious beliefs in logical or rational forms.

In early 1988 there were twenty-five to thirty families who attended regularly, and participation was increasing gradually. Participating families come in part for convenience. They are located in Gwinnett and DeKalb Counties (northeast and eastern metropolitan Atlanta) and for the most part are generally forty-five to sixty minutes driving time away from the India Cultural and Religious Center in Cobb County (northwest metropolitan Atlanta). Some participants prefer the flavor of their own group, which they view as primarily religious rather than social. Some question what they perceive as too much politics at the ICRC, and some are also perturbed that meat and alcohol are allowed in the lower floor of the India center. Cultural origin may also play a role, for about half of the families supporting the meetings are overseas Indians from Fiji, Guyana, and Trinidad rather than immigrants directly from India.

A standard form of worship has been worked out and put in booklet form using shlokas (stanzas) from the Vedas, religious stories for the children, bhajans (hymns), arati (offering of fire), and prasad (offering of food). While the group refers to itself as "Vedic," worship elements in fact derive from many different Indian regional and overseas cultures. Teaching of the children remains the primary focus. Special programs for the children are scheduled for annual festivals, such as a storytelling contest and traditional dress contest as part of the celebration of Holi in early March. Havan (a fire ritual) will also be celebrated at that time.

The meetings rotate in private homes and run one and a half hours plus lunch. Participation is already straining the capacity of private homes, and a location with a building that can be renovated or on which a building can be erected is currently being sought. There should then eventually be a building designated as the Greater Atlanta Vedic Temple. There is also the expectation that some sort of professional person will be hired as teacher and priest (<u>pujari</u>) to be in charge of the group's programs.

MOSQUES

Ideally, Islam calls for the unity of all individuals under God in a society and under a political state that is Islamic (submissive to God). The official separation of religion and state enshrined in American law and government gives ample opportunity for the practice of Islam, but it provides no direct support by the state. Muslims in India operate under a separate civil code of family law that incorporates the <u>shari'ah</u> (Muslim praxis and law), but in America all citizens, regardless of religious affiliation, are covered by the same state laws regulating families. State laws governing inheritance by women generally (and widows especially), divorce settlements for women, and custody of children in cases of divorce are in potential and sometimes actual conflict with Islamic regulations (Haddad and Lummis 1987, p. 110-12).

Muslims in India are also a minority without government support, but they constitute a very large minority; and, because Muslims and non-Muslims have lived side by side for centuries, various accommodations were worked out long ago. But in America the prevailing daily schedule and yearly calendar of the non-Muslim majority are almost completely indifferent to the timetables for Muslim group worship. However, Haddad and Lummis reported (1987, p. 77) that most Muslims who wish to do so can secure time off from work to attend Friday noon prayers. Muslims adjust to the American situation, as an Atlanta man described in 1984:

> That's an obligatory prayer on Friday. And people meet locally because, in this country, that's a working day. So it's not feasible to go in a similar way [as in a Muslim country]. But in many Muslim countries Friday is the off day for them--so that they could do that. That is the sabbath day. . . . Here we pray in somebody's house on Friday--six or seven people who are working in the plant [nearby].

Similarly, a Muslim teacher has been able to get his department head to cooperate:

> But in my teaching, if it is possible, I ask my bosses to set my routine so that I get two or three hours off around prayer time on Friday. This trimester I have off from 12:30 to 2 P.M.

Because they are apprehensive about native American attitudes toward Islam, Muslims generally maintain a low profile for their mosques and try to attract little attention to themselves. One man explained:

> Basically, this community doesn't want
> any sort of publicity in the sense of
> getting some name or fame. It [the
> Atlanta Mosque address] is just a
> listing [in the telephone book], and
> that way it gets out. It's fine. But
> not for any intention that it should
> have some publicity.

Lovell (1983, pp. 93-94), and Haddad and Lummis (1987, p. 3) estimated a total Muslim population between 2 and 3 million in the United States. Booth (1988, p. 726) suggested a figure of 3 million for Canada and the United States together. He also believes that nearly 85 percent of the Muslims in North America are of the Sunni tradition (the remainder would be Shi'ah). Approximately one half of the Muslim population is located in just six metropolitan centers. Haddad (1979, p. 2) suggested that roughly 2 million American Muslims were Bilalians[1] (black Muslim converts to Sunni Islam). Ghayur (1981, pp. 157-59) calculated that there were 40,000 Pakistani, 25,000 Indian, and 4,500 Bangladeshi Muslims in America in 1980. Despite their relatively large numbers, Muslims in America have so far achieved little political power, and few have been elected to public office (Abdul-Rauf 1983, p. 277).

The size of the Muslim community increases primarily through reproduction and continuing immigration rather than from direct programs of proselytization. There have been some conversions of native white Americans to Islam (most often they are women who marry Muslim professionals, according to Ghayur 1981, p. 151), but high-pressure missions and conversion programs are not part of the spirit of Islam. As one witness stated, "If it's forced upon [a person], it is not Islam." Another expanded at greater length:

> So far as conversion . . . is concerned
> . . . How do you do it? You do it by
> living a Muslim life, not by just
> calling somebody and forcing it. You
> have to live a Muslim life, which, if it
> looks [like] an exemplary life to your
> neighbor and other people, then they

will be interested. Then you call them
and tell them. . . . So there are people
who have problems, and they have been
solved by some of the Muslim community
people. So they get into it [Islam].
Then they get converted.

Immigrant Muslims in America derive from all
of the countries of the world where there are
Muslim cultures. There are major ethnic and linguistic differences among Muslims, and these distinctions tend to form the basis of association
among Muslims, as much as does their common religion. De facto, there are (unofficially) ethnic
mosques and ethnic-based Muslim organizations in
urban areas where Muslims are numerous enough to
make these organizations viable (Haddad and Lummis 1987, pp. 24-58). In Atlanta also, ethnic
divisions among Muslims were manifest especially
before the Atlanta al-Farooq Masjid was opened--as
this informant remarked:

[Muslims from other countries] have
their own community and own language.
. . . Only on the Eid Namaj festival
[marking the end of the Ramadan fast],
on the prayer, we all meet together.

Even among Indian Muslims regional ethnicity is
quite strong. As one spokesperson put it, "In
every Indian community I think language-wise they
are closer than religious-wise." Another remarked, "There is Islam, and then there are
Muslims."
National Muslim associations, such as the
older Federation of Islamic Associations, the
newer Islamic Society of North America (from
1982), and the Muslim Student Association (from
1963), attempt to bring Muslims together into one
ummah (house, family) based on religion despite
the divisive pulls of ethnic differences (Waugh
1983, p. 20). Two languages are typically used in
mosques, with one language always being English
(Lovell 1983, pp. 101-3). English transcends
ethnic insularity for general communication, as
Arabic transcends it for ritual prayer. The
Qur'an is typically used in a version with English
interpretation facing each page of Arabic text.

As a local Atlantan admitted, fluency in Arabic, the language of the Qur'an and of prayer, is often limited:

> But most of us read Arabic, but we don't understand that much compared to a person from the Middle East or [one] who has really, really learned it. There are a few people here from India and Pakistan that are very well-learned, well-versed in Arabic, and they know a lot about this religion.

Mosques are used regularly by many Muslims for weekly prayer. But according to Lovell (1983, p. 102), some American mosques have temporally displaced group prayers from Friday noon to Friday nights or even to Sundays. Mosques are very heavily used for observance of the two annual Eid celebrations (at the end of Ramadan and during the month of pilgrimage to Mecca). Other annual mosque observances drawing large numbers include the birthday of the Prophet Muhammad, and commemorations of the Prophet's journey to Jerusalem, the Prophet's ascension to heaven, the Battle of Badr, and the new year (Hijra) (Lovell 1983, p. 102). The mosque is also a place for daily prayer, for Saturday and Sunday classes for children and new converts, for lectures, for marriages, and sometimes for other social events. According to Waugh (1983, pp. 22-25) local mosques in North America have more local autonomy than they do in countries in which they are administered by the government. Regula and Saleem Qureshi (1983, p. 140) argued that mosques in America tend to develop local community structures to compensate partially for the loss of a predominantly Muslim culture and of extended family structures.

A mosque is not absolutely necessary for the practice of Islam. But especially in a country that is predominantly non-Muslim, Islam needs the institutional support of a mosque to prosper, and a trained imam (prayer leader) is a practical necessity (Abu-Laban 1983, p. 80). The imam is not a priest--the relationship between each person and God is direct, requiring no intermediary or mediator. But the professional imam may be the only person who really knows the Qur'an. He also

leads prayer for group worship, for the annual
calendar events, and for the rites of life transitions. In America the imam also tends to assume
functions similar to Christian ministers or Jewish
rabbis. He gives sermons, provides individual and
group counsel and advice, renders opinions concerning questions of religious belief and practice, teaches children, visits patients at hos-
pitals, and participates in mosque administration
and planning alongside relatively autonomous
mosque executive committees. (Since the local
congregation pays the mosque expenses, it usually
hires the imam and has greater control of its own
affairs than is the case in many Muslim cultures.)
He also provides by his life a role model for
Islamic values and serves as a spokesman for the
mosque to non-Muslim religious organizations and
to the larger society (Waugh 1983, pp. 23-25).
Almost all imams now serving in America were
trained in other cultures (Haddad and Lummis 1987,
p. 158). The American Islamic College in Chicago,
established in 1983, now provides studies in
Islam, Qur'an, and Arabic language, and it has
begun to train imams living in America to serve in
American mosques.

Mosques have been built in large numbers
across America and Canada. Lovell (1983, p. 101)
compiled a list of 266 mosques, clubs, and centers
in the United States, 156 of which were Bilalian.
The remaining 110 mosques and centers were situa-
ted in urban areas in twenty-nine states and the
District of Columbia.

The Al-Farooq Masjid of Atlanta

Of the nineteen Muslim organizations listed
for Georgia by Haddad and Lummis (1987, p. 4), two
are student organizations, five are mosques and
centers, and twelve are masjids (mosques) of the
American Muslim Mission. More recent information
indicates that there are now seven mosques in
Atlanta alone. Relations between international
Muslims and Bilalians are good, and direct cooperation is gradually increasing. Unconfirmed
estimates usually suggest an Atlanta population of
10,000 to 12,000 Sunni Muslims. Among these,
there were roughly 100 South Asian (mostly Paki-

stanis) Sunni families in 1982. Indian Sunni
Muslims had increased to about 500 persons in
early 1988.

After meeting in private homes, rented halls,
and university facilities for several years, Muslims from several different countries, with some
financial support from Arab governments and other
sources outside the United States, opened the
Atlanta Mosque near the Georgia Institute of Technology campus in 1983. The mosque, subsequently
renamed the Al-Farooq Masjid of Atlanta and Dar-
Alnoor School, attracts Muslims from India, Pakistan, Bangladesh, and many other countries. Most
worshippers are Sunni, but small numbers of Shi'ah
and of native American blacks (Bilalians) also
worship there. The two-story building has a
prayer room upstairs large enough for perhaps 500
men, a prayer room for women and children, another
room, and a kitchen downstairs. Shi'ah and Sunni
differences are deemphasized in mosque affairs and
do not generate significant conflict. Divisive
political and doctrinal discussions are quietly
avoided. One Muslim who worships at the mosque
frequently testified: "So far as Iranians are
concerned, it's nothing to do with Shi'ah or
Sunni. There are a few. They come [to the
mosque]. Very good Muslims. They cooperate."

The relatively small size of the international
Muslim population in Atlanta has so far retarded
tendencies to break up into ethnic groups. Group
worship is open to anyone. As an Indian
explained, English, by necessity, becomes the
common language of communication:

> Basically it [the language] becomes
> English. People from Kenya, Middle
> East, Saudi Arabia, Egypt--I have never
> seen any Islamic functions being done,
> either at home or outside, which are
> being restricted to only Indian Muslims
> or Indian and Pakistani Muslims.

The Atlanta mosque is open for salah (prayer)
daily (with men upstairs and women downstairs).
Friday noon and evening prayers during the month
of the Ramadan fast regularly attract 200 to 300
persons. Attendance is higher for major annual
religious events, such as the festival at the end

of Ramadan (Eid al-Fitr). There were 400 to 600 supporters in 1986.

Arabic language and <u>Qur'an</u> educational programs are conducted for children on Saturdays and Sundays. One person gave this account of the educational program:

> On a Saturday or a Sunday we would expect about twenty or twenty-five children. . . . Anyone who wants specialized training, since the imam is there, can receive it, especially in the evenings. If anyone wants to learn Arabic, he can do it here and learn Arabic. You know, any special need, the person is available. But the response to that has not been very encouraging except for the Sunday classes. And, you know, we are still in the development stage.

"Prayer places" have also been rented in northwest Atlanta near the Lockheed aircraft plant and in northeast metropolitan Atlanta to make group worship convenient, especially during the daytime, when a round trip from the workplace to the mosque downtown might require up to two hours. These places used for prayer are not proper mosques. Once a building has been bought and dedicated as a mosque, it cannot be sold again. Around 1984 a Muslim cemetery south of Atlanta was made available for burials (see Haddad and Lummis 1987, p. 156).

The number of Muslims participating in my Atlanta survey of 1984 was too small (eight persons) to be of statistical value. Yet rates of participation in group worship in the survey are commensurate with results from the statistically more reliable survey done by Haddad and Lummis (1987, pp. 27, 29). For a population of 343 respondents in their study, 51 percent indicated that they attend a prayer service or Islamic class at least once a week, 13 percent at least once a month, and 26 percent at least once a year. Living near a mosque was scored very important by 46 percent of respondents, quite important by 25 percent, somewhat important by 21 percent, and of little or no importance by 8 percent. In my sur-

vey Atlanta Muslims registered 63 percent for
attendance once in two weeks, 25 percent at least
once a month, and 12 percent at least once a year.
Responses to another Haddad and Lummis question
(p. 29) showed that 29 percent of respondents had
attended Friday prayer at a mosque or Islamic
center "often" in the past six months and 16 percent "sometimes" during the last six months.
Pakistanis (which included some Indian Muslims in
the Haddad and Lummis study) had a higher rate of
participation than the average for their survey
population (which included many Middle Eastern
Muslims). Haddad and Lummis (1987, p. 130) also
point out that women attend worship at American
mosques with greater frequency (although more
often on Sundays than on Fridays), and they assume
much more of the responsibility for educating
children than in most countries.

The Ismailia Cultural Center

Ismailis in America are united as much or more
by their faith than they are by common ethnicity.
Although it is true that many Ismailis have a
common background in northwestern Indian culture
(especially those from the Gujarati-speaking Khoja
ethnic group), some Ismailis in Atlanta have a
Syrian cultural background. And even Gujaratis
who immigrated to eastern Africa (the first as
early as the 1860s) have fairly weak cultural ties
to India. The Ismaili community is international,
and English has by necessity become its common
language.
    Although the unity of Ismaili community is its
faith in the living imam, Aga Khan IV, the group
activities of the faithful expand beyond the purely religious into social, educational, and economic interests. Individual and community, religious, social, and economic development are seen
as intertwined. This broad range of activity is
expressed in two partially parallel institutions
which function at the local level simultaneously:
the jamaat khana (meeting or congregation place)
and the Ismailia Cultural Association.
    The jamaat khana is the multifunctional educa-
tional, welfare, social, and economic community
center of the local congregation. Personal and

social activity in the faith is emphasized.
Prayer can be done while one is working, and work
is seen as a natural expression of faith and even
a kind of prayer. In fact, material work is
judged to be intrinsically good, and the goal of
improving the general welfare, including the economic resources, of the community as a whole is
included in the work of faith. The spiritual
quest requires action within the material world.
Work is the melding of external, exoteric materi-
ality with internal, esoteric spirituality, the
submission of life as a whole to God. Although
personal ostentation or extravangance is forbidden, when the wealth of the Ismaili community
increases, the imam is symbolically glorified
(Clarke 1978, pp. 75-76). No professional staff
is employed to run Ismaili centers. Since service
to the community is given high religious and
social value, all work for the center is voluntary
and unsalaried. Local leaders of the jamaat
khana, who rotate in office, are the <u>mukhi</u> or
steward and the <u>kamadia</u> or accountant.

Ismailia Cultural Associations handle religious affairs, including the conduct of worship,
religious education, the explication and preaching
of Islamic values, and the publication of literature. Ismailis emphasize that worship should be
carried out in a group context. Personal worship,
for example, is judged to be more effective when
it is performed in the physical presence of the
rest of the local community. The strong sense of
community identity through the shared religious
faith is reinforced by community participation in
daily worship at dawn and sunset and by the roughly 90 percent attendance rate on Friday evenings.
Worship includes the daily prayers (<u>du'a</u>) recited
in unison in Arabic, the communal recitation of
<u>ginan</u> (poetic hymns in Gujarati language) and
other forms of worship in English. Although Ismailis stress tolerance toward others, including
those, Muslim and otherwise, of differing faith
traditions, worship at the jamaat khana is closed
to outsiders.

Ismaili communities have considerable local
autonomy, but they also occupy a very definite
place in a centralized, corporate hierarchy, and
the imam's consent is in principle necessary for
all major decisions. Building plans for a new

center in Atlanta, for example, were submitted to
the imam for his approval. Ismaili government is
highly structured under regional, national, and
supernational councils. There is a written international constitution covering all Ismaili communities and there are also separate constitutions
for Ismailis in specific countries (Nanji 1983).
The American Ismaili constitution is included
within the bylaws of the local Atlanta community's
articles of incorporation as a nonprofit organization.

In Atlanta the Ismaili community currently
meets in a building conveniently located at the
junction of a principal uptown street and an
interstate highway. The present center, which can
accommodate just under 800 people, will be succeeded in mid-1988 by a much larger and more ver-
satile new building in northeast Atlanta. In 1988
the Ismaili population in Atlanta is estimated at
somewhat over 1,000 persons. Almost all of the
local Ismailis are Indians.

NOTES

1. Bilal was an Ethiopian early convert to
Islam who gave the call to prayer at the Medina
mosque during the lifetime of the Prophet
Muhammad.

5

The Second Generation

First-generation parents have less understanding of American culture, especially as it applies to children and teenagers, than do their children. Of course, native-born American parents also have difficulty understanding <u>their</u> children, but the native-born have at least experienced some of the repetitive aspects of the process of growing up in America. Indian parents in America experienced a very different process of maturation.

THE PARENTS' DILEMMA

The dilemma posed by their residence in America is the same for the parents as for their children: how to perpetuate their Indian culture while participating fully in American culture. One parent's question is typical of very many: "How can we expect them to live in America and yet follow our Indian way?"

Responses to the Atlanta survey, as well as questions posed during interviews, show that Indian immigrant parents are concerned about preserving their culture and perpetuating its most important values among the children. Preserving South Asian cultural values among themselves was given a rating of "very important" or "important" by 96 percent of the respondents (282 persons) to the Atlanta questionnaire survey conducted in 1984 and 1985. And 94 percent of the respondents who had children at the time of the survey (209 persons) rated preserving South Asian cultural values for their children "very important" or "important."

Responses to the survey question, "If it is important, which cultural values do you want to preserve in America?" showed a consensus about what was <u>most</u> important. Respondents were re-quested to rank their responses as "most impor-tant," "next most important," and so forth. Table 8 exhibits a tabulation of the responses for 219 persons. The left-hand column shows cultural values given the highest percentage of "most important" ranks, the middle column lists cultural values given the highest percentage of "next most important" ranks, and the right-hand column gives the percent of respondents for whom a particular cultural value was not listed as one of the cul-tural values to be preserved in America. "Family" was the runaway favorite. <u>"Family"</u> <u>was</u> <u>ranked</u> <u>most important</u> by 61 percent of the respondents. It was ranked first almost three times more often than any other <u>single</u> cultural value, and it was ranked first more often than <u>all</u> of the other listed cultural values combined.

The cultural importance of "family" did not vary significantly from one religious tradition to another. Only those respondents who were not married or who had been in the United States five years or less gave "family" a low ranking as a cultural value they desired to preserve. For cultural values ranked "most important," "Indian character (honesty, etc.)" ran a distant second, followed by "religion" in third place.

Table 8

Indian Cultural Values Most Desired to Preserve

	Most important	Next most important	Not listed as a cultural value
		percentages	
Family	61.2	15.1	12.3
Indian Character (honesty, etc.)	22.8	20.1	18.7
Religion	16.4	30.1	21.5
Cultural arts	10.0	14.6	23.3
Language and regional culture	6.4	17.4	24.2
Other	.5	.5	95.0

Indian parents are often not clear about what should be kept from Indian culture and what should be discarded, and in addition, they are not sure that they can determine what their children do. A Hindu father's remarks point up these ambiguities:

> My wife and I should like for the children not to date. It is not part of our tradition. But how can we expect them to live in America and yet follow our Indian way? It might be imposing too much on them, restricting them too much. Are we going to damage their mental development by imposing that "You

> must eat vegetarian food"? His friends
> at school will be eating hamburgers.

Some parents, who feel that they will in fact not
have much say, are prepared to give in to the
inevitable:

> If I don't allow it, he will still go
> and date. I don't want him to. So it
> would be better if I gave him
> permission. He will have a better
> parental feeling about me instead of
> doing it without having my permission.
> So, I will give him permission.

Other parents just don't know how things will turn
out:

> I think we will have some influence as
> to who they date or what their values
> should be like. But how much we will be
> able to influence them--we don't know
> that yet. For that, we have to wait and
> see.

Most parents want their children to succeed as
Americans, but at the same time to maintain close
ties with their families and with the Indian community. Parents are thus drawn in two different
directions, and they sometimes have difficulty
keeping their desires for their children as Indians and their aspirations for them as Americans
in balance.

Maintaining Indian Values

Parents are apprehensive about what they perceive to be corrupting aspects of American
culture, such as crime, violence, drug use, divorce, sexual promiscuity, and pornography.
Concern about threatening forces in American culture is perhaps strongest among Muslims, who often
feel American culture to be in direct competition
with a properly Muslim life-style. Muslim publications recount American "social disorders" with
alarm. The high percentage of one-parent
families, the high divorce rate, the number of
couples who live together without marriage, inten-

tional and accidental childbirth outside matrimony
(cf. Mukherjee 1985, pp. 57-73), sexual promiscuity among teenagers, adultery among married
persons, sexual abuse of children, alcohol and
drug addiction, and the prevalence of sexually
transmitted diseases are all attributed to the
collapse of family, the decline of parental
authority, and to an assault on traditional
values. Devout Muslims seek the remedy for these
ills in a society that lives according to the laws
of God, and they believe that Islamic principles
offer the only really effective means of correc-
ting these disorders (Qutub 1987).

The disturbing aspects of American culture
that Indians reject are, for the most part, judged
to be regrettable by native Americans also. Many
Indians recognize a common moral cause with most
Americans, but some feel a special kinship with
the moral aspirations and behavior patterns of
conservative Christians. Mormons, for instance,
are frequently mentioned as the kind of Americans
who have attitudes toward the family and behavioral habits similar to their own. Most Indians, like this Hindu father, do distinguish
between "good" and "bad" aspects of American culture:

> We have to dissociate from what is
> happening as an aberration of society,
> or the evil in the society, from the
> society itself. There is the divorce
> rate, or there is promiscuity. I don't
> think Americans think . . . that this is
> the right thing to do. . . . We can get
> our children from following the "bad
> side" of American society. I say that.
> And I don't say "American values."
> Because I do not mean they [Americans]
> don't have values. But I think we
> [Indians] get a little closer, because
> we know the value of family life.

A Christian father stated his belief that his
children will be able to make proper choices about
what is good and that they will reject what is
not:

> I'd like to show American people this,

that we are some sensible people who are, you know, smart enough to survive. And at the same time we want our kids to get an exposure in two cultures. We don't want them to throw away all of the Indian culture. We want them to take some of the good parts of Indian culture and then blend it in with the American. . . . It would involve our kids mostly, I guess . . . to have an education in Indian culture. You figure they don't know anything about Indian culture, right? . . . There are a lot of things in Indian culture that are valuable. I don't want them to lose that touch. . . . Within the family itself and by association with other families you are indirectly affected because they see that the other people are doing the same thing, so they feel comfortable.

Americanization of the Children

American education systems and peer groups thoroughly Americanize Indian youth. In many respects, Indian parents expect and accept this process. Discussions between Indian parents and their children have to bridge the same generation gap as any other parent-child conversations in America, and the internalization of parental values by children is no more guaranteed for Indian immigrants than it is for native Americans. Parental reservations most often surface when questions about dating and about the eventual marriage partners of their children are asked. A Christian father claimed that he talks with his children frequently:

I discuss certain things with my children. I don't want my children to Americanize yet--in the sense that I am not going out to dance, I am not going to clubs, I am not having girl friends, I'm not having fun outside my house. And I don't expect my children to be like that either. I don't want them to

be alcoholics. I don't want them to
have sex outside the family. And I
don't want them to behave as an American
teenager, period. . . . I did not date
when I was young, and I don't expect
them to be dating. . . . My country was
different. . . . I can't expect the same
thing today, and they are in a
different place, in a different
situation. . . . So, if they want to
have dating and all that, there is time
for that. Not now [the oldest child was
seventeen years of age]. First they
have to achieve their goal of education,
what they want to be.

A Christian woman, whose oldest daughter was about
seventeen, operated more permissively:

> Q: Are you allowing your older daughter
> to date?
> A: Yes. I have no problem. I don't
> control her. She's just like an
> American. She has been raised here, and
> I don't have any problem. When she does
> anything wrong, I tell her this is not
> right. But if it's not wrong, I don't
> control her. She's a good girl, and she
> understands. . . . For them they don't
> miss [Indian culture] that much. They're
> very here and they're like Americans.

The first wave of the second-generation Indians is college age or older, and some of the older
children have already married, but the far greater
proportion are age fifteen or less. The question
of marriage for the children, although a problem
for the somewhat distant future for many parents,
nevertheless occupies their minds, and they generally have opinions about what should happen. Only
a few parents expected to be able to arrange their
children's marriages without consulting them. For
most, a "mixed" or "partly arranged" marriage
seemed appropriate. In any case, parents from all
religious traditions wanted their children to
marry other Indians. This is evidenced, for example, by the following exchange with a Christian
mother:

Q: Do you prefer that your children
marry other Indians?
A: I very much prefer that. Yes.
Q: Do you think it's feasible?
A: It is with my children.   I have
confidence in them. They believe that
we parents did the best for them as well
as we could. . . . If they wanted to go
ahead and marry somebody whom they
wanted to, then I wish they will discuss
it with me. We will discuss thoroughly
the goods and the bads.

A Hindu mother had similar preferences:

I would like him to marry in the Indian
community--not necessarily an Iyyengar
[a jati or caste name] girl. I know in
my heart that this is a faint
possibility.   It is a thin thread I am
holding on to --that he will marry an
Indian girl. A very small possibility.
I know it's good that he picks a girl.
But in my heart, even at that time, I
will be praying that I wish he had
[picked an Indian].

A Hindu father listed some reasons Indian mates
are preferred:

I prefer that they should marry an
Indian. I prefer, for then only will
there be a continuation of the language
or they will have some attraction to go
to India for a visit. But once they
marry an American, he or she will have
no interest to go to India to
visit. . . . And particularly their
children are not interested at all in
it.   I think that maybe what will
happen is that there will be no links to
them in India.

A Christian father acknowledged that some parents
might be persuaded to change their minds by the
time the question really comes up:

> When we think about our daughter, we are
> really protective. I don't think that
> we want to let her marry someone else or
> anything like that, but we always
> feel. . . . I think for a lot of reasons
> my first preference will be for them to
> choose an Indian. But then, if that is
> not what they want, then we'll evaluate
> the situation at that time and see what
> happens. . . . We could change our
> attitudes.

I did not detect any differences in Hindu
attitudes toward sons and daughters. Technically,
Sunni Muslim men are permitted to marry women
outside the faith if they belong to a "religion of
the book" (Christianity, Judaism, Zoroastrianism).
But Sunni Muslim women are not permitted to marry
non-Muslims. In fact, American Muslims resist the
marriage of men outside Islam. Exogamy does occur
with some frequency, however, in the second and
third generations of other Muslim ethnic groups in
North America (Haddad and Lummis 1987, pp. 138-40;
Lovell 1983, pp. 116-17).

The fact that Indian and other Asian immigrant
children perform unusually well in school has
received considerable publicity (Gardner, Robey,
and Smith 1985, pp. 26-27). Indian parents give
the children strong encouragement, and they emphasize scholastic achievement, usually in technical and scientific fields that promise good employment and high social status. Yet Indian
parents feel that the situation for their children
is much easier than the way they themselves grew
up:

> We don't push our kids the way we do in
> India--with the whole family and the
> tribe. I still wake up in the night
> sometimes in a cold sweat thinking,
> "Tomorrow is exams!" . . . My children
> don't have that pressure. But yes, it's
> very important to us that they do well.

The children do not see their minority status as a
problem. They see no real difficulties ahead.
This mother suggested that they believe that they
can make the American Dream come true:

> These kids feel that there is no barrier
> like we of the first generation feel
> that there _is_ a barrier. The second
> generation does not feel so. . . . They
> have never encountered it. And they
> don't anticipate encountering it because
> they say, "Well, that's impossible."

The responses of two college students, the first
female and the second male, show that Indian young
people internalize the aspirations of their
parents:

> Q: Is the pressure from parents really
> to get good grades, or is it aimed for
> something farther down the line?
> First: Things like the American
> dream. . . . Your parents are like,
> well, "I want my children to have more
> and to be better off than I was." And
> so, education is primary. My father
> told me, he has said, "Well, you are a
> minority and it is important to do well.
> It is important that you try and do the
> best to succeed--especially in this
> country where you are in a minority."
> Second: There is a misperception of
> this concept of "pressure." I would
> rather label it as "strong encourage-
> ment." . . . What they want more than
> anything else is to see their kid become
> successful, become more successful than
> they have been, and to make sure they
> have a good life.

Some Indian students do _not_ make good grades in
school. For some of these, having failed to live
up to their parents' high expectations can be a
serious problem.

THE CHILDREN'S VIEWS

Indian children are, predictably, pulled between the American identity with which they have
grown up and the Indian identity of their parents,
which they share only fragmentarily. The children

are drawn between discovering their own way and
being dutiful children. They are looking for a
middle course between retaining their Indian character, their family ties, and their cultural heritage and becoming just like other Americans.   The
children know more about American culture than
they do about Indian culture and religion, and
they think they know America much better than
their parents.   Some think their parents are
prone to misconceptions because they generalize
incorrectly from their Indian backgrounds to this
unfamiliar situation.

I have not come across any second-generation
Indians who were unhappy with their ethnic identity.   Most are proud to be Indians and to be
Americans.   Except for some hassling to convert
from native American Christians, they are not
aware of any discrimination against themselves. A
male high school student reported:

> I don't get treated specially, and I
> don't get discriminated against either.
> I am more or less equal to everyone.
> I've never been discriminated against,
> and I seem to fit in with everything. I
> do a lot more stuff with American
> friends than I do with Indian friends.
> . . . It is just more positive than
> anything else.   I feel that I'm an
> American more than I am an Indian.   And
> I guess I act that way.

A college student also showed himself to be very
positive about his Indian identity in America:

> I was never ashamed of it [being Indian]
> and never wished I was anything else.
> The only thing I ever wished was that I
> had an easy name to pronounce. . . . I'm
> American, because now I'm an American
> citizen, and I've been raised in
> American culture. But for all practical
> purposes, I'm an American as far as
> culture is concerned, but I'm Indian as
> far as skin color and looks.   And you
> know, I was born in India in an Indian
> family, so much of Indian culture is
> still there. . . . Technically, I am

Caucasian. . . . When they ask for skin
color, I put "brown ." I always put
"brown." I mean, I'm not black and I'm
not white.

A woman college student was even exultant about
her identity: "I have always thought of us as
different. But it was only positive. . . . I have
always liked being different."

In a public debate at India Cultural and Reli-
gous Center over Indianization versus Americanization staged by the Indian Youth Organization in
1985, Indian youth took an "official" stance of
balancing the two processes. But their parents
were present and listening.

Beyond what they imbibe at home, very little
of the actual culture of Indian youth is Indian.
Even in the home some aspects of Indian culture,
such as Bombay motion pictures, are endured rather
than enjoyed. In fact, many lament their parents'
getting so addicted to videotaped nostalgic fan-
tasies, depictions of an Indian never-never land,
which, as far as the children can tell, is completely unreal.

Interest in classical Indian art, drama,
music, and dance is low among most Indian young
people, but it must be said there is not much
active fondness for western classical forms
either. In general, young Indians in America
have the same music and entertainment interests as
other young Americans. Talent shows for young
people are always predominantly American in content. Looking back over top movies and popular
music for 1987, an Atlanta youth organization
newsletter was content to list the top money
makers. None, of course, were Indian (Indian Youth
of Atlanta Source, January 1988). Except for
cases in which vegetarianism has been adopted for
health reasons (rather than because of Indian
culture or religion), most Indian youth are non-
vegetarian. Indian college students' use of alcohol is reportedly about the same as that of other
students, except for Indian Muslims and
Christians, who have been said to consume less.

There are exceptional individuals, of course,
(girls for the most part) who enroll in bharat
natyam and other dance and music instruction
courses. And there are other exceptions. Some

Indian college students have confessed, for example, that they <u>would</u> go to see a really big Bombay movie personality like Amitabh Bachan. And internationally known Indian music stars like Ravi Shankar would draw some Indian young people (although one older youth said he discovered Ravi Shankar through his interest in George Harrison).

A youth organization staged a young Indians' debate on arranged marriage in the spring of 1985 at the ICRC in Atlanta. What was said during the debate was rehearsed beforehand, it was definitely slanted toward parental listeners in the audience,[1] and it was run like a standard debate in which the young people argued the point of view they were assigned. Still, the debate content did express their views insofar as it was clearly intended to change parents' opinions by using the pressure they could exert as a group of about two dozen youth in a public forum. One of the ideas young Indians wanted to get across was that dating is for fun and that dating has no necessary relationship to marriage or sexual activity. The message was that parents should not get alarmed if their children date non-Indians--because it portends nothing definite about future spouses.

Some of the complaints articulated during the debate were surely genuine. Objections to the double standard used in treatment of boys and girls were repeated several times. Rules for girls are often much stricter than for boys (of course, this is often true in American families also). Many young men, like this one, had a much easier time dealing with parents about dating than their sisters did: "It didn't bother me about dating because they were more strong on her [my sister] because she was a girl, not on me." There were also objections to matrimonial advertisements as a device for arranging marriages because the advertisements seemed to be putting girls up for sale like commodities. There was also impatience that parents sometimes treat caste and other criteria important in India as though there were important in America.

In general, second-generation students on both sides of the issue identified basically with the interests of their families. Disagreement tended to be about details, rather than really substantive issues. Objections to parental cooperation and/or ratification of their marriage choices were really not very strong. The second generation expects to operate within extended rather than merely nuclear families, and they are still functioning, willingly, in a much wider network of kinship. Conflict occurs over disparate notions of dating, marriage, fun, and personal fulfillment. But children generally agree with their parents on questions of family, education, financial success, and personal drive and ambition.

Some young Indians have argued that more males are ready to go along with the parents' wishes to arrange or partially arrange their marriages than are females. Certainly, there are instances in Atlanta in which young men have asked their parents to make the arrangements. Young people of both sexes have indicated that they would like to know help is available if they need it. Some are shy. Others feel as though they might be too immature to make such an important decision and want their parents to contribute their know-how. And there are some young Indian women I know who are acquiescing in their parents' intent to arrange marriage. They do not date and stay very close to their families.

Other young women have told me that they are relieved to have arranged marriage as a fall-back plan if finding a mate on their own by dating does not work out. This is an especially attractive alternative for women who do not expect to finish professional training until they reach their upper twenties. They have read statistical predictions suggesting how difficult it currently is for older women to get married in America. Some, like this young woman, are obedient to parents' wishes, but not very happy about them:

> F1: Probably the biggest thing [problem with parents] for me is dating and marriage. . . . My mother has been, like, since sixth grade, has been, like, saying, "Don't get involved with anyone." Until this day [approximately age twenty] she says this to me.
> Q: She does not let you date? Do you sneak around and do it anyway?
> F1: No. . . . She is still trying to decide when she is going to arrange my

marriage.

F2: I would die! . . .

Q: So you are expecting an arranged
marriage at whatever time that turns out
to be?

F1:   I am expecting a lot of conflict.
That's what I am expecting a lot of.
. . . The way my mom said it--she said
that she would probably find guys for
me. And that I would probably go and
meet them. Not just, you know . . .
[pick   one   for   me--without   any
consultation].

Another young woman found it difficult initially:

> I found it hard, lots of times, because
> I could see my friends going out on
> dates, you know, staying out really
> late--things that are, I guess, normal
> here. They weren't so normal to my
> parents. Eventually, they got used to
> it. . . . It was really hard. And I'd
> have to try to convince them that, you
> know, it is OK, this and that.
> Eventually--I'm sure they're not fully
> used to it--they've accepted it.

Some children play out a role of sham obedience
for their parents, but then they find ways to get
around the dating restrictions even while they are
in high school. Dating without the parents' per-
mission becomes much easier once they leave home
for college. One young woman told about another:

> This girl I was telling you about. . . .
> Her mother is really, really strict
> . . . She hasn't changed with the times.
> Her dad is never at home really. And
> when she is with her mom, her mom is
> very strict with her. And she [the
> girl] sneaks around all of the time.
> You know, [she says], "Mom, I'm going
> out with this girl or this girl. We're
> going to the movies." You know, she
> really has a date.

Several young people suggested that Indian chil-

dren routinely work around their parents' wishes
by dissimulating, "pleasing" them, or manipulating
them and that the children generally get their own
way if they persist. They also said that honest
communication between parents and children is
ordinarily difficult and sometimes impossible (cf.
Desai and Coelho 1980, pp. 374-76).

The perceived threat to "ethnic values" seems
greatest to parents at the time children are ready
to marry. Ethnic boundaries shift depending on the
situation and the decision to be made (Barth
1969). Indians belonging to other Indian religious traditions may sometimes be within the
boundary and so may be regarded as potential
spouses, and sometimes they are understood to be
outside the boundary. An ethnic sense of other-
ness is sometimes reinforced by projections of the
questionable behavior of the "out" group. At times
the divisions may run along lines of religious
identity, at other times the functional divisions
in America are national. Muslims may not consider
non-Muslims as proper mates. Hindus may exclude
Muslims from consideration. Sikhs have strong
tendencies to marry among themselves. Sometimes
the unsuitability of outsiders is described as
behavioral problems--unreliability, excessive
indulgence in alcoholic beverages, and so forth.
(In fact, several Sikhs and Hindus own liquor
stores in Atlanta.)

Most parents I have talked with would strongly
prefer an Indian mate for their children. The
children are generally aware of their parents'
preferences, and they tend to agree with them, as
these two young men make clear. The first said:

> I could see a lot of friction from a lot
> of angles if I married a non-Indian.
> And that would be a big problem. I
> think it would cause a lot of problems
> for the marriage in general--just the
> stability of it. But I can't say what I
> would do.

The second (who several years later did marry a
second-generation Indian) said:

> In general I would think that marrying

an Indian girl would work out much more.
But I'm not saying that it would never
work with anybody else but an Indian
girl.   It   could   work. . . . First
generation would be, I mean, it would be
two totally different people.   If I
would marry an Indian girl, it would
probably have to be a second-generation
person. You know, somebody who has gone
through the same thing.

Conflicts over marriage choices have, on a
few occasions, led to strife between parents and
children. In one case the parents eventually came
to accept a second generation Indian Muslim spouse
for one daughter but refused to accept a native
American (presumably a Christian) for the other
daughter. While relative social status was probably a factor, non-Indians are apparently perceived as much more likely to divorce, more likely
to cheat maritally, and more likely to abandon or
divorce their wives in a short time. In another
case the father in one family objected vehemently
to the marriage of two second-generation Indians,
both of whom had Hindu backgrounds, because he
considered the girl's family to be of low social
status. A goodly number, perhaps as many as half
of the first wave of the Atlanta second generation
(those who have already finished college), have
married non-Indians. (In many of the cases the
Indian spouse was female. In the first generation
the Indian spouse is typically male.) Local scarcity of suitable Indian spouses was probably a
contributing factor. Several of these marriages
ended in divorce in less than five years.
    The size of the marriage-age group will in-
crease markedly in the next few years, and rates
of marriage outside the Indian population should
decrease noticeably in the near future. Indian
youth tend to congregate together more as their
total numbers increase. Dating is a primary factor, and it may be presumed that prospecting for
possible spouses is also a factor. Of course, it
is much more likely that some aspects of Indian
culture and religion will be preserved if intermarriage rates are low.
    Indian Youth of Atlanta (IYA) is popular
primarily because it makes it easy to mix with

Indians of the opposite sex. The organization started in 1986 to meet the obvious need of Atlanta Indian young people to socialize among themselves. Once it had come into existence, IYA stimulated interaction among young Indians, including some whose parents do not participate in the India American Cultural Association. IYA activities during 1986 and 1987 included three parties, a talent show, a formal debate on arranged marriage, a sports tournament, outings, group participation in Atlanta area community projects, staging (and winning first prize for) a college campus international festival, and setting up a college preparatory room in the India Cultural and Religious Center. A newsletter, IYA Source, is distributed monthly. Membership in IYA, which includes some non-Indian friends of Indians, was about 170 persons aged thirteen to twenty-five years in early 1988.

IYA participants come from Hindu, Jain, and Christian backgrounds, as well as from families deriving from different parts of India. Muslims, however, tend to join the Muslim Student Association instead of the Indian Youth of Atlanta. One parent commented with satisfaction: "This younger generation was able to transcend the regional differences of their parents and achieved the Indianism which we as grown-ups have yet to achieve." Concern with Indian rather than regional identity should, in any case, increase with time among the second generation, and in the long run, the common Indian background will be more important than regional origin.

THE FUTURE OF THE RELIGIOUS TRADITIONS

Close parallels from the past for the permanent transplantation of Indian religious traditions in America are not available. What the European immigrants brought with them were ethnically local forms of Christianity or Judaism. Little organized religious tradition has survived among Chinese Americans, who have either converted to Christianity or become secular. Fragments of Chinese religious traditions do survive in ethnic folk celebrations and tourist festivals, and there has also been some revival of

Chinese Buddhist and Daoist associations with the
new wave of immigration of the late 1960s (Lai
1980, p. 229).

The experience of the Japanese does show that
Asian immigrants who are neither Christians nor
Jews can maintain their religious traditions in
America. By the third generation, according to
Kashima (1977), one third had become Christian,
and another third were more or less secular, but
about one third of the Japanese immigrants and
their descendents still adhered to Japanese Buddhist traditions. At the very least, it can be
said that Asian religious traditions outside the
American mainstream can be maintained in America.

Religion is <u>one</u> of the cultural values Asian
Indian immigrants want to conserve in America.
But it is one cultural value among many for the
immigrants; it is not their strongest concern; and
for some immigrants transmitting the religious
tradition is a matter of indifference. In my
1984-1985 Atlanta survey (see Table 8), "religion"
came in third as the "<u>most important</u>" cultural
value. However, at 30 percent "religion" was the
most frequently chosen "<u>next most important</u>" cultural value to preserve in America. Over half of
the parents indicated that their children participate in group worship at least once each month,
and 80 percent of the respondents who had children
claimed that they were giving some form of religious education to their children. However, 22
percent of the survey population did not even
mention "religion" as one of the cultural values
they were interested in preserving.

Hindus

Hindus did not differ significantly from other
respondents in the Atlanta questionnaire survey in
giving the highest importance to preserving
"family" as a cultural value and to "Indian character" as the next most important value ahead of
"religion." "Religion" was the top choice for
"next most important." Cultural Hindus (see Chapter 2), however, ranked "religion" in fourth place
as the "most important" cultural value and, as the
"next most important" cultural value, preferred
"cultural arts," "Indian character," and "language
and regional culture" ahead of "religion."

Cultural and religious transmission to the Hindu second generation occurred primarily by means of what they could pick up at home until about 1985, when Sunday classes were introduced. Children who take part imbibe a strong emphasis on family values, good moral character, and fragments of the religious traditions. Older children, some of whom were born in India, often have a practical, concrete, or passive ability in the regional Indian language of their parents, although they usually cannot discuss any complex topics. This Hindu man expected that his children would automatically pick up what they need from their home environment, just as he believed that he did:

> That is one of my beliefs--that the children will learn Tamil by listening to parents; they will learn English. There is no question about it. No problem. They will be brought up in a dual language setup. And I hope to pass on to them as much of the way of life, religion, or philosophy, or however much of whatever I have learned, to them, so that they will have some kind of hold on what is God and what is religion, what man needs, and things like that.

A Hindu mother stressed that the religious tradition was being successfully transmitted in her home by the parents' telling traditional stories to the children:

> My children know mythological stories. . . . My husband particularly enjoys telling these stories to younger children. . . . From time to time, whenever possible, their father would narrate one episode from the <u>Mahabharata</u> or <u>Ramayana</u> before the children go to bed. I do it when I get home. And, boy, do they enjoy it!

Some young Hindus saw their situation quite differently. They suggested that parents talk about cultural transmission a great deal and describe what they wish were going on--as if it were happening. Parents seem to believe that Indian tradition will <u>somehow</u> continue without any effort from them. (One youth half-seriously suggested that Hindu parents may be waiting for divine intervention to get the job done.) It may be simply that parents naively expect the children to learn religious tradition the way they did--by just being around. But the mechanisms for effective transmission have not been there. Even when well done, family religion can't survive alone (cf. Dotson and Dotson 1968, pp. 106-10).

Parents' wishes to give religious education to the children has, for most of the older youth, not been translated into effective action. Religion is all pervasive in India, but here it is practiced just one hour a week in group worship (at most). Most second-generation Hindus in Atlanta have only superficial knowledge of and little concern for the survival of specifically Hindu religious tradition. The children typically understand neither the ritual nor the language used in worship. Often enough, the children are not even in the same room in which group worship occurs, although they do show up in time to eat. Girls pick up somewhat more of the religious tradition in this fashion than boys.

Hymns (bhajans) are more widely known by young people, but even these are generally sung from rote memory without comprehension, as two young men testified:

> Q: Are you able to participate in the puja?
> A1: Parents usually force you, usually when you are younger. . . . You don't really know what is going on, and you're are not really interested. You are just sitting there, you know, listening to this person talking.
> A2: You go there for dinner.

Questionnaire results from the quite small sample of Indian youth in my Atlanta survey and from a survey of forty-four second-generation Indians in 1987 by one of my students[2] showed that 56 to 57 percent indicated that they consider themselves religious. About one third said they do some form of individual worship daily, and another third do individual worship at least once a week (This

figure is undoubtedly too high.) About 32 percent
of the respondents attended group worship at least
once in two weeks ("attend" is meant loosely).
Young people below eighth grade in school said
that they do not enjoy puja and that they are
forced to attend by their parents. Children show
up for arati and prasad (just like some of the
parents). High school and college students do not
take puja very seriously and participate very
little.

A number of the children, like this young
woman, said that group worship is primarily a
social occasion for the parents and that there is
more talking than worship:

> They have pujas at people's homes. And
> I never like that because I found that
> it didn't seem like it was really
> significant in terms of religion. It
> seemed like it wasn't very serious. It
> seemed like it was (these are strictly
> my impressions) just a social gathering
> with religion as a front. . . . I didn't
> get that much out of it, except the fact
> that it was a social gathering and that
> the children were made to sit quietly
> for one hour. After that, you got to
> eat, and you got to run around and play.

Many of the young people in the first wave of the
second generation could be accurately described as
moral in some general sense and/or also religious
in a very general sense but with little specific
content. Indian <u>cultural</u> tradition is clearly
more important than religious tradition for some.
This young man of the second generation echoed
sentiments of many in the first generation:

> My dad is always saying, "Well, you know
> you don't have to believe in God, but
> [do believe in] the Indian tradition--
> such as the way you bring a person up or
> the way you act around other people.
> And just the way to live is really a
> good part of it.

When questioned about their religiosity, four
young men replied as follows:

A1: My parents almost admit to me
that they share my ignorance in terms of
religious tradition or religious philosophy. . . . They have instilled in me,
if nothing else, a strong faith in God,
which is very compatible with a Hindu
viewpoint. And now and then, I am involved in personal worship. I guess the
extent of the worship I am ever involved
in is just with my family, or on very
rare occasions.

A2: I guess it's just that they are
passing on their ignorance in a sense.
They can't teach what they don't
know. . . . They definitely tend to say,
"Yes, there is a God, and you should
believe in Him." But they don't go to
the extent of telling you who this God
is, or how to pray to Him. They just
say, "You can make your own personal
decision."

A3: You know, we have got all of these
forms of God. But once you have faith
in God, you have faith in God, not Ram.
I think the more devout people tend to
pray to the one God. . . . I used to
pray a lot--when I was young and when I
first came from India. . . . But slowly
and slowly, next you knew about
Christianity. . . . It turned into God
[more generalized]. Slowly [it became]
the pantheistic nature [of God]. Now it
is more a sense that there is God inside
me.

A4: I think I'd be more apt to spend
time exposing my kids to Boy Scouts and
Little League and stuff like that, and
camping. Seriously. Because I've
gotten more out of those activities and
a much greater growing experience out of
that than I have had out of the Indian
community.

A fifth young man was even more disaffected
from Hindu religious tradition:

Q: What kinds of differences do you see

between yourselves and your parents?
A: Probably religion. Because my mom
is very religious. As for me, I don't
even bother with it. My mom's like,
every day arati, every day, like yoga or
meditation. She tells <u>me</u> to do it. But
I'm just not interested in it.   It's
just like she wants me to quit eating
meat, because everyone in my family is
vegetarian. She also says it is bad for
you and all that, and "Just don't eat
it." To me it is just overbearing.

Most Hindu young persons think that conversion
to some other religious tradition is, for them,
not very likely.   They presume (in neo-Hindu
fashion, like this young man) that genuine spirituality is the same in all religious traditions
and that there is no credible reason to change
from one to another:

A lot of Hindus will just meditate. And
that is religion for them. So there is
no sense in converting.   You   don't
really feel like it is changing from one
religion to another. So you have no
need to convert.

Other Indian youth believe that some minimum
of specifically Hindu ritual will be needed to
provide a religious identity for Hindus   in
America--even if the second generation does not
understand the ritual very well. According to this
female college student, spirituality in general
won't be enough:

You can't just, say, meditate. You
can't do that.   You have to expose
children to the rituals first.   Then,
once they get old enough to understand
what the ritual is about, they can split
off and do it on their own. . . . A
Hindu child . . . can't compare himself
to what Americans go through in church.
You have to have something tangible to
hold on to. You have to be able to say,
"Well, I go to church also. We have our
own form of church." And that gives you

a certain amount of pride also.

Some of the older Hindus of the second generation have begun to regret how little they have
learned about their culture and religion. A few
have taken college courses in world religions and
even in Hinduism as a partial fill-in. This young
lady hoped the India cultural center would enable
her to absorb somehow as an adult what she did not
get as a child:

> I used to be not interested. . . . But
> now that I am getting older [nineteen]--
> which is exactly what my parents
> predicted: "Now that they are getting
> older, they are going to want to know."
> I know when I tell my children, like, if
> I do marry an American, I don't know
> what he is going to want to tell them.
> I don't know what I'm going to tell
> them, you know. Are they going to say,
> "Well, am I Indian? Am I American?"
> Even I have a hard time knowing, with
> both of my parents being Indian. I
> think just having a knowledge of what it
> is. You don't have to do everything and
> just be devout and "to the T"
> everything. Well, I think [the India
> center] will be important just to know,
> just to be aware.

The interest of Hindu parents in teaching
religion to children has recently increased. Now
the myth of their return to India has yielded to
their realization that they are going to stay in
America permanently. They have also seen the
first wave of the second generation grow up ignorant of Indian culture and religion, and they are
belatedly disappointed. They are more affluent
than they were initially, more numerous, and they
have become more concerned with the quality of
their lives instead of simply getting started and
getting ahead.

Since about 1985, there have been more con-
certed efforts to educate the children. In addition to older programs of short courses and occasional summer camps, encouraging children's
participation in worship, community events, and

entertainments, there are three regular weekly or biweekly children's programs in Atlanta. Not only are the children being given, for example in the Swadhyaya group, simplified mantra forms for personal devotions in classes, but many children are learning to follow the basic sequence of events in traditional puja. Hindi language is also being taught regularly to a small number of children.

Educating the children has become something of a national movement with much more highly struc- tured educational programs already in place in cities with large Hindu populations. The January 1988 issue of Hinduism Today, for example, lists schools, weekend sessions, and summer camps available in eleven locations. The Hindu Heritage Summer Camp run by the Rajarajeshvari Peetham in Stroudsburg, Pennsylvania, has been a national leader in this regard for some years. Hindu chil- dren in the second wave should be better versed in their tradition.

In addition to launching more serious teaching efforts, some aspects of the Hindu religious tradition itself will probably have to change in America if it is going to be vital for the second and subsequent generations. The language employed in worship, for example, necessarily will have to be predominantly English (See Williams 1984, p. 203). The passive spectator follow-along ability to which this young person testified will not be sufficient:

> Q: Can you understand the bhajans?
> A: Some of them I learned because my parents taught me when I was younger. They taught me what they meant. But I couldn't just pick it up. . . . We know the superficial meanings. . . . Like the purpose, we don't really know.

More than two thirds of the older first-wave young Indians I have talked with had no idea what was going on in Hindu puja. The responses of these seven young Hindus show that even an English-language outline of the steps in the pro- cess of worship would be of great value:

> Q: In worship, would it help if you had

an English outline about what is
happening?
A1: It would be helpful.
A2: With an explanation, OK?
Q: Would you like to have the whole
worship translated into English?
A3: Maybe the most important parts.
A4: I think the intent of the worship
should be for people to understand what
is going on. It's senseless if you
don't know what is going on--if you are
simply going through the motions. . . .
I really doubt that my children would
know whatever language, Sanskrit or
anything like that. And for them to get
the benefit of the worship, it should
probably be in English.
A5: I think, wouldn't it be neat also
to have some exposure to the Sanskrit
part of it because that is the
foundation upon which this religion
developed.
A6: Most of the Jains here are Gujarati
speaking. And the only thing I
understand is Hindi.
Q: Can you even follow what is going on
in worship?
A7: Little bits of it.

Indian religions are still taught to children
in an Indian idiom--even when English is used--
despite the children's saturation in American
public and private school teaching techniques.
Teaching styles may have to change somewhat. The
emphasis on memorization, teaching by repetition,
and by katha (storytelling) may be primarily left-
overs from oral-aural cultural tradition. What
is taught needs to be in line with the worship
life of the community. If elaborate rituals are
to be done, children need to be taught to understand and to appreciate them, and ways need to be
developed to increase their active participation.
Composite, simplified ritual patterns of shorter
duration have already developed quickly among the
first generation in local areas of the United
States, thereby providing a basis for uniquely
American forms of Hindu worship. Many in the
first generation, like this man, see the need to

reinterpret rituals as an opportunity for positive
religious development:

> Unless   it   is   reinterpreted,   these
> traditions   will   not   survive.   And
> that   is the reason why it is so   impor-
> tant   for   the   interpretation. . . .You
> know everyone is an individual. And you
> have a right to interpret things in the
> way you want. . . . Those people who try
> to   keep   the tradition   in   India,   you
> know, they literally killed the religion
> and any substance of the religion.   So
> that   is   why traditions   are   changing,
> happily.

If   only   to meet the religious needs of new
immigrants who will arrive periodically, traditional   ritual forms will survive to compete with
and/or complement more liberalized forms. But even
second- and subsequent-generation Hindus will find
a function for distinctively Hindu symbolic enact-
ments, even if the rituals mystify them. A traditional Hindu temple in Atlanta would provide
strong support for Indian ethnic identity, as this
young woman recognized:

> [If you have a temple] now you can go
> somewhere like my American friends who
> go to church, or Jewish friends who go
> to synagogue. I feel like there is some
> place that I can go, you know, where you
> will feel right. Indians are such new
> immigrants to this country. It is just
> good to know that at least your heritage
> is being continued. Because that's the
> thing that is really important for us.

Another young woman also recognized the role a
temple would play in social identity: "The temple
will draw people and so forth. Even in that sense
I would think that the temple would serve more of
a social function than a religious function."
The temple planned for the Atlanta area will
not make much difference for most of the second
generation unless there are swamis (teachers)
and/or pujaris (priests) in residence who will
teach and minister to what will amount to Hindu

"congregations." For second-generation Hindus most important will be the swami, then the temple--with the ritual possibly being little more than symbolic background.

The continuing influx of new adult Indian immigrants in future years will help to keep Indi-an cultural centers and temples operational, and their arrival will continue to reintroduce and to reinforce traditional forms of Hindu religion. But as the years pass, new immigrants will consti-tute smaller and smaller percentages of the total Indian population, and the influence of new immi-grants will decline. The immigrant forms of Hin-duism now being developed, with some yet-to-be-determined mix of the Indian heritage with Indian American culture, will then predominate.

Jains

Differences among local Jains in Atlanta (bet-ween the Digambara and Shwetambara subtraditions) are of little functional importance. The inclu-sion of a Mahavira image in the predominantly Hindu India Cultural and Religious Center Temple appears to constitute a form of religious paral-lelism, the image of Mahavira being just another murti in the temple. Puja in the center is on a schedule, but organized Jain group worship has otherwise been sporadic. Mahavira's birthday has not been celebrated every year, although there are indications that observance will be regular in the future.

The number of Jains in Atlanta is not expected to increase very quickly in the next ten years, and where numbers are small, as in Atlanta, Jains may in part be absorbed into Hindu practice. Jains from Gujarat already take part in Gujarati Hindu festivals, and presumably other Jains will do so increasingly. Jain group behavior could become largely indistinguishable from that of Hindus, except for occasions of special religious importance to Jains.

There are Jain cultural centers and temples in other American urban centers where the Indian population is much larger than in Atlanta, such as New York City (Fisher 1980, p. 148) and southern California, and educational programs are in place there. There is also the Arhum Yoga summer camp, which is operated by the International Mahavir Jain Mission. But home and family religion carry almost the entire burden of transmitting the tradition to Jain children in Atlanta. There is no systematic religious education for Jain children, and they have only occasional opportunities to participate in group worship.

Sikhs

Sikh religious tradition has proved to be highly portable and durable outside India, except when conditions are extremely difficult--as they were in California prior to the end of World War II. There is ample reason to expect the tradition to be vigorous where local Sikh populations are large, such as southern California and the New York metropolitan area, and for it to be sustained even when, as in Atlanta, total numbers are low.

Despite the universal character of the Sikh religious tradition, ethnicity and religion are more closely interwoven among Sikhs than among followers of any of the Asian Indian religious traditions in America. Sikhs are "disciples" of the True Name who de facto are almost exclusively of Punjabi stock. The ethnic structures of Sikh tradition together with the extended family and nationalist linkages in North America, overseas, and in India provide a strong social foundation for Sikh life in America as it has in other countries (See La Brack 1979, pp. 139-40). The Sikh sense of peoplehood is based on a determination to continue as a separate, faithful tradition of disciples, even when the local population is relatively small (as in Atlanta).

The Atlanta Sikh population will remain fairly small for the near future, but it may be feasible for Sikhs to build a gurudwara at some point within the next decade. Atlanta Sikhs have no formal education programs for the children. Children's participation in group worship in Atlanta is limited, as it is for Hindus. They are usually in the vicinity of group worship but are not really involved.

Sikh children traditionally learn largely by imitation and participation rather than by formal

instruction. This procedure transmits the funda-
mentals of personal devotion, the procedures for
family worship before the Granth, and the behavior
appropriate for group worship reasonably well, but
without supporting educational mechanisms, such
learning tends not to go much deeper than gestures
and symbolic affirmation of the five k's.   Some
Sikh boys are pakka (wearing turbans and uncut
hair), while others are not. A Sikh woman indicated that she will educate her son as best she can
and then let him decide:

> I am going to teach him [my son] first.
> . . . I am not going to take him to a
> barber and make him sit and cut his
> hair. But I am going to let him grow up
> and teach it. And if he were to feel
> that is the group he is going to go
> with,   I would let him.   I   would
> encourage him and tell him our reasons
> for sticking with it. But if he feels
> that he will follow the religion, but he
> could   not   abide by   the   physical
> appearance rules for certain reasons, I
> will allow that.

Some of the larger Sikh associations, such as
the Sikh Cultural Society of New York City, include classes in Sikh doctrine and the history of
the Sikh faith. There is also a Sikh camp and
retreat in the vicinity of Pittsburgh. But theology, ethics, and deeper understanding of the
tradition are much harder to transmit, and when
there is formal schooling, it sometimes consists
of Punjabi language practice and memorization of
Punjabi hymns (cf. James 1974, pp. 48-52; Cole and
Sambhi 1978, pp. 164-66).

Although Sikh tradition is carried by only one
sacred language in addition to Gurmukhi, Cole and
Sambhi questioned whether the next generation in
Britain will be able to use Punjabi. On the one
hand, the same doubt arises in America, especially
in communities without formal schooling. On the
other hand, Gurmukhi, the language of the Granth,
is a problem even for first-generation immigrants,
as this woman admitted:

> Frankly, half of the sermons, I mean

half   of the <u>Guru Granth Sahib</u>, I   don't
even   understand the meaning of   it.   I
understand the basic concept behind   it.
It gives me satisfaction.   I know it   is
something good that I am doing.   But if
you asked me to explain word for word, I
could not do it. . . . Every puja we do,
there   are   people   there   who   do   not
understand   the   meaning   of   the   <u>Guru</u>
<u>Granth Sahib</u>. . . . <u>Guru Granth Sahib</u>--
it   is a very difficult language   and   I
can   assure you that 90 percent   of   the
people in there could not translate that
for   you,   although they would   get   the
gist of the general thing.

New   Sikh immigrants and strong   connections   with
the homeland and with extended families will   help
to   keep   the   language alive, but the   second   and
subsequent   generations will probably need to   use
some English in the worship.

Muslims

The   international   Muslim   population   in
America,   which already constitutes a   substantial
American   religious minority, is expected to   continue growing, and expansion at the national level
should   also strengthen local Muslim   communities.
While Indian and Pakistani Sunni Muslims may   have
some   tendency   to organize mosques   along   ethnic
lines in places where they are numerous, there are
ideological   as well as contextual reasons to   expect that there will be countervailing   tendencies
for   Muslims   to unite   along   pan-Islamic   lines.
Unless   the   Muslim population increases   a   great
deal   more, mosques in Atlanta should continue   to
maintain a pan-Islamic rather than an ethnic character.
A   recent   immigrant, who felt   isolated   from
Muslim   society during the early 1980s,   was   very
concerned about the fate of his children and eager
for Muslims to become better organized:

The   first   responsibility   in   this
country--I   mean   Muslims   in   this
country--is, if you want to restore your

traditions and the ways you believe, the first thing that comes up against it is that there is no community. Because people coming from other countries, like the Middle East--that's so different. . . . Even in India, although Islam is a minority group, still the society is intact. . . . Only a few people in this area [of Atlanta are Muslim], maybe one or two families, and we may be meeting maybe once every couple of months. . . . Our children . . . they don't see this cultural and Islamic way of life every day or every moment. . . . We have come to this country after being matured in India. So, if we want, and if we have enough strength of mind, we can retain those traditions as well as Islamic ways, if we want. . . . So, the basic thought, the basic idea, of these organizations of the Muslim community is to develop sort of a continuation of Islamic tradition and Islamic way of life among ourselves . . . and to promote it to our children.

The Al-Farooq Masjid of Atlanta now has a reasonably effective religious education program in place for a small fraction of the Muslim children. The school was said to have about 150 children enrolled in early 1988 for classes on Saturdays and Sundays. There are also classes for both children and adults after 6:30 P.M. Tuesday, Thursday, Saturday, and Sunday. Construction for a separate school building next to the Atlanta masjid will begin in the near future. Muslim schools are intended to teach faith, the duties and obligations of a Muslim; Qur'an reading, recitation, memorization, and understanding; Islamic history; and pride in being a Muslim. Islamic schools are a long-standing Muslim tradition, and it is to be expected that religious education institutions will be set up in the United States generally and that educational efforts will improve and expand to reach more children in Atlanta.

Second-generation Muslims tend to be more

liberal and religiously open-minded than their
parents and are generally less observant of Muslim
obligations than their parents. A small sample of
second-generation college age Indian Muslims
showed that all were observant of Islamic practices to some degree, and they averaged attendance
at a mosque or other group worship once in two
weeks, but none performed the prayers five times a
day.[3] However, second-generation Indian Muslims
have little difficulty understanding and assimilating the basic beliefs and practices of Muslim
tradition. For them identification with international Islam is, in the long run, likely to be
of as much or more importance than identification
with India or South Asia.

Partly because of the experience of expulsion, which some experienced in East Africa, Ismailis emphasize that they are true immigrants,
not sojourners. (They believe that they had
little choice about leaving Africa.) They are
committed to stay in America and to develop an
American form of the Islamic-Ismaili faith.

Ismailis stress their continuity with tradition at the same time that they emphasize their
adaptability and progessiveness. In their view, I
was told, true faith must evolve and, it is at
least in part yet to be seen just what form Islamic faith will develop in confrontation with the
issues of modernity in America. Traditional
Ismaili cultural forms that are unsuitable to
America can be changed. The availability and
authority of the imam as religious interpreter is,
in this respect, a major adaptive advantage.

Based upon what Ismailis reported to me, it
appears that the Ismailia Cultural Association has
the largest and most extensive religious education
program for children of any of the religious
groups from India in Atlanta. Children almost
always come to worship with their families, and in
conjunction with worship, the children receive
some religious education every day. There are
systematic classes, and the transmission of the
faith to the next generation is given high priority among Ismaili center programs.

Ismailis recognize that there are problems
regarding the content of the teaching and the
training of teachers. There is no such thing as
an "Islamic" education that would be different in

form and content from "good" education. There is only education toward the truth or poor education. Since there is also no conflict between natural science and faith, truth may emerge from both directions. The natural world is full of "signs" of God's will.

Intermarriage with persons outside the faith is not forbidden to Ismailis. It occurred in Africa and in England to some extent and happens also in America. In some cases the non-Ismaili spouse becomes part of the community and in others not. Intermarriage will no doubt become more common in the second generation.

Ismailis have strong religious, cultural, and financial institutions, organizational unity, and flexibility and can be expected to continue with vigor. Future growth of Ismailis will be largely by immigration and reproduction. Atlanta Ismailis foresee only moderate growth in the size of the community over the next generation.

Christians

I expect Indian Christians to lose touch with Indian culture more than the second generation of any of the other Indians, a process that should be largely complete by the third generation. Indian Christians will be absorbed into existing Christian churches except in urban areas in which Indian Christian churches continue because of large local congregations. Continued immigration could produce such a constituency in Atlanta in the future, but none is currently in place.

Despite the origin of the majority of Christians in a single Indian region, the southern Indian state of Kerala, second-generation Indian Christians will more likely be Indian than regional, and Indian Christians will probably assimilate into American culture faster than persons from other Indian religious classifications. Morality, good character, Christian faith, and family loyalty are more important for most Christians than Indian culture. Second-generation intermarriage with non-Indians will also be rather common and can be expected to occur at a higher rate than among other Indians because they will, in fact, have less opportunity to socialize with

Indians. Many informants, like this North Indian man, doubted (in the early 1980s) that the second generation's sense of being Indian will be very deep:

> We could lose the Indian community in one generation. And you go back the next generation, there is no Indian community. Once my daughters grow up, they probably won't marry in the Indian community in the first place.

One Christian man felt that he did not have enough Indian culture in common to be able to share with other Indians:

> One of my closest friends . . . he is from . . . South India, and I am from the North. And North Indians know nothing about South Indians. . . . He speaks a different language completely. He looks very different from me. I can't communicate with him without English at all. The only thing we can say is that we came from the same subcontinent. Everything was different. His value system was different. We were Indians. . . . He had a certain pride about the work of Gandhi. . . . That was the only thing that I felt was common between us. There was nothing else about us being Indian, except that we came from the same subcontinent.

The strictness in doctrine and behavior with which Indian Christian parents were raised tends to carry over with the children, as this father stated:

> We believe what we believe very strongly, and we expect our children to believe and follow us. Sometimes we make them to understand, sometimes we fail to make them to understand what we believe. Because after a certain [amount of] education the children will develop their own philosophy.

Second-generation Christians gravitate with their parents toward native American Christian organizations that tend to be conservative in belief and practice. This should continue, provided these churches do not develop any racist prejudices against Indian Christians. In general, thorough assimilation into Christian and into general American culture is the most likely future for Indian Christians. Christians could, however, develop a tradition of parallel but separate Indian observance of annual Christian celebrations, such as Christmas, which will serve as occasional reminders of their Indian heritages.

NOTES

1. Some young Indians opined that public debates when parents are present cannot be honest expressions of what young Indians think. In such circumstances, young people say what they think they should say in front of their parents. Others reported that in their experience young Indians get together to discuss what they should say to get the right effect when they have to voice their opinions before the first generation. They do not even consider planning to say what they really think.

2. This information was collected for a project conducted in spring 1987 by Anuj Paul Manocha for an undergraduate course at Emory University.

3. This information was collected for a project conducted in spring 1987 by Shelena Charania for an undergraduate course at Emory University.

Conclusion

This study has given a description and interpretation of the transplantation of Indian
religious traditions to America. Each of the
major religious traditions represented among the
immigrants has its own individual developmental
sequences, but transplantation generally begins
with personal and family praxis. Worship groups
develop more slowly, and permanent dedicated religious buildings are instituted last.

Indian immigrants are, on the whole, about as
religious as the average native American. Those
immigrants who are religious have found it fairly
easy to continue the individual forms of worship
they practiced in India, and most have reported
little change in the patterns of their individual
worship. Family worship has also been comparatively easy to arrange even when, as for some Hindus
or Jains, no one in the family is adept at ritual
performance. Family rituals have been made possible through the use of recordings or printed rubrics, through rituals performed by qualified nonprofessionals, through long-range communication
with distant temples, jurists, and spiritual
guides, and by placing greater emphasis on nonritualistic forms of religious devotion and celebration for the family, for friends, and somewhat
larger groups. During the first years, when the
number of immigrants was still low and newly

arrived immigrants were busy with the more immediate concerns of making a place for themselves,
arrangements for religious observances tended to
be temporary and unelaborated.

But religious traditions are difficult, if not
impossible, to sustain without supporting social
structures. Voluntary religious associations have
to be put in place in America to provide substi-
tutes for the missing religious context of the
Indian homeland. Traditions with a strong emphasis on congregational worship tend to develop
group worship associations and stable religious
institutions earlier than the others, but given
time, all of the religious traditions will organize or they will not survive. Different types of
voluntary associations have been developed, but
all adapt to the American context.

The transition from temporary associations for
group worship to permanent worship institutions,
such as temples, mosques, jamaat khanas, and gurudwaras is an important symbolic and real change.
When permanent places of worship are instituted,
they evidence the transformation of sojourners
into immigrants, and they situate the land the
immigrants have chosen into a meaningful universe.
Temples and mosques also require an investment of
resources, which commits the immigrant to a future
in this place, not only for himself, but for his
children and for the children of his fellow com-
municants. Investment tends to strengthen commitment and to attract further investment from others
of like mind. Once temples and mosques have become
operational, they acquire greater ethnic purpose
leading to greater support and participation even
from persons who are only marginally religious.

The plight of the second immigrant generation
is a powerful motivation for establishing permanent places of worship complete with educational
facilities for the children. In most cases children's programs have been developed only after
considerable delay, and many of the older children
have grown up largely uninformed and indifferent
to the religious traditions of their parents.
Children below twelve years of age are now receiving better religious education, but current
programs are not very comprehensive and do not
reach all of the children. The job is not
finished, but it is clear that the religious

traditions can be transmitted to the children if
Indian immigrants have the will to do it. All of
the Indian religious traditions face challenges to
their resolve and their resourcefulness.

In principle, any religious tradition could be
transplanted to America. The difficulties that
some Indian immigrants have faced were due to
other factors, such as the hostility of native
Americans during the first decades of this
century, rather than to intrinsic characteristics
of the religious traditions they carried with
them. The transplantation processes now occurring
with Indian religious traditions are, in fact,
similar to those for the European religious traditions of earlier immigrants to America, and there
is no compelling reason that Indian religious
traditions should be less successful. Successful
transplantation depends on the will of the people
transmitting the tradition.

Asian Indians will still be a small minority
in America at the turn of the next millenium. But
there is reason to believe that their influence
will exceed their numbers. This is especially the
case with Indian religious traditions. The American religious situation has already been fundamentally altered. The new pluralism is, I
believe, enriching. It brings possibilities for
fruitful exchange among people of different religious commitments and opportunities for genuine
learning from each other.

Bibliography

Abdul-Rauf, Muhammad. 1983. "The Future of the Islamic Tradition in North America." In <u>The Muslim Community in North America</u>, eds. Earle H. Waugh, Baha Abu-Laban, and Regula B. Qureshi, pp. 271-78. Edmonton, Alberta: The University of Alberta Press.

Abu-Laban, Baha. 1983. "The Canadian Muslim Community: The Need for a New Survival Strategy." In <u>The Muslim Community in North America</u>, eds. Earle H. Waugh, Baha Abu-Laban, and Regula B. Qureshi, pp. 75-92. Edmonton, Alberta: The University of Alberta Press.

Allen, Shiela. 1971. <u>New Minorities and Old Conflicts</u>: <u>Asian and West Indian Immigrants in Britain</u>. New York: Random House.

Amarasingham, Lorna Rhodes. 1980. "Making Friends in a New Culture: South Asian Women in Boston, Massachusetts." In <u>Uprooting and Development</u>: <u>Dilemmas of Coping With Modernization</u>, eds. George V. Coelho and Paul I. Ahmed, pp. 417-44. Current Topics in Mental Health. New York: Plenum Press.

Anand, K. 1965. "An Analysis of Matrimonial Advertisements." <u>Sociological Bulletin</u> 14: 59-71.

Andrews, K. P., ed. 1983. <u>Keralites in America</u>: <u>Community Reference Book</u>. Glen Oaks, New York: Literary Market Review.

Arasaratnam, Sinnappah. 1979. <u>Indians in Malaysia and Singapore</u>, rev. ed. Institute of Race Relations. Kuala Lumpur: Oxford University

Press.

Babb, Lawrence A. 1986. Redemptive Encounters: Three Modern Styles in the Hindu Tradition. Comparative Studies in Religion and Society. Berkeley: University of California Press.

Barot, Rohit. 1987. "Caste and Sect in the Swaminarayan Movement." In Hinduism in Britain: The Perpetuation of Religion in an Alien Cultural Milieu, ed. Richard Burghart, pp. 67-80. London: Tavistock.

Barth, Fredrik, ed. 1969. Ethnic Groups and Boundaries. Boston: Little, Brown.

Basham, Arthur Llewellyn. 1959. The Wonder That Was India: A Survey of the Culture of the Indian Sub-Continent Before the Coming of the Muslims. New York: Grove Press.

Becker, Laura L. 1988. "Ethnicity and Religion." In Encyclopedia of the American Religious Experience: Studies of Traditions and Movements, ed. Charles H. Lippy and Peter W. Williams, pp. 1477-91. New York: Charles Scribner's Sons.

Benedict, Burton. 1965. Mauritius: The Problems of a Pluralistic Society. London: Pall Mall.

Bharati, Agehananda. 1972. The Asians in East Africa: Jayhind and Uhuru. Professional and Technical Series. Chicago: Nelson-Hall.

Bhatti, F. M. 1980. "A Comparative Study of British and Canadian Experience with South Asian Immigrants." In Visible Minorities and Multiculturalism: Asians in Canada, ed. K. Victor Ujimoto and Gordon Hirabayashi, pp. 43-61. Toronto: Butterworths.

Bhukary, Somdath. 1972. Profile of the Hindu Community. Port Louis: Mauritius Printing.

Bilge, Barbara J. 1987. "Islam: Islam in the Americas." In The Encyclopedia of Religion, vol.7, ed. Mircea Eliade, pp. 425-31. Chicago: The University of Chicago Press.

Booth, Newell S., Jr. 1988. "Islam in North America." In Encyclopedia of the American Religious Experience: Studies of Traditions and Movements, ed. Charles H. Lippy and Peter W. Williams, pp. 723-729. New York: Charles Scribner's Sons.

Bowen, David. 1987. "The Evolution of Gujurati Hindu Organizations in Bradford." In Hinduism in Great Britain: The Perpetuation of Religion in an Alien Cultural Milieu, ed. Richard Burghart, pp. 15-31. London: Tavistock.

Bradfield, Helen Hayes. 1971. "The East Indians of Yuba City: A Study in Acculturation." M.A. thesis, Sacramento State College.

Buchignani, Norman, and Doreen M. Indra with Ram Srivastiva. 1985. Continuous Journey: A Social History of South Asians in Canada. "A History of Canada's Peoples." Toronto, Ontario: McClelland and Stewart with Ministry of Supply and Services, Canada.

_____. 1982. 1980 Census of Population, vol. 1, Characteristics of the Population. General Population Characteristics, part 12, Georgia. Tables 30, 50. (PC 80-1-B12.)

_____. 1983a. 1980 Census of Population, vol. 1, Characteristics of the Population. General Social and Economic Characteristics, part 1, United States Summary. Tables 160-65. (PC 80-1-C1.)

_____. 1983b. 1980 Census of Population, vol. 1, Characteristics of the Population. General Social and Economic Characteristics, part 12, Georgia. Tables 58, 93-98. (PC 80-1-C12.)

_____. 1983c. 1980 Census of Population, vol. 1, Characteristics of the Population. Detailed Population Characteristics, part 12, Georgia. Tables 195-98. (PC 80-1-D12.)

_____. 1984. 1980 Census of Population, vol.

1, <u>Characteristics of the Population</u>. <u>De-tailed Population Characteristics</u>. part 1, United States Summary. Tables 254-57, 264. (PC 8-1-D1-A.)

Burghart, Richard. 1987a. "Conclusion: The Per-petuation of Hinduism in an Alien Cultural Milieu." In <u>Hinduism in Great Britain</u>: <u>The Perpetuation of Religion in an Alien Cultural Milieu</u>, ed. Richard Burghart, pp. 224-251. London: Tavistock.

_____. 1987b. "Introduction: The Diffusion of Hinduism to Great Britain." In <u>Hinduism in Great Britain</u>: <u>The Perpetuation of Religion in an Alien Cultural Milieu</u>, ed. Richard Burg-hart, pp. 1-14. London: Tavistock.

Burr, Angela. 1984. <u>I Am Not My Body</u>: <u>A Study of the International Hare Krishna Sect</u>. New Delhi: Vikas.

Carey, Sean. 1987. "Initiation into Monkhood in the Ramakrishna Mission." In <u>Hinduism in Great Britain</u>: <u>The Perpetuation of Religion in an Alien Milieu</u>, ed. Richard Burghart, pp. 134-56. London: Tavistock.

Chakravorti, Robindra C. 1968. "The Sikhs of El Centro." Ph.D. diss., University of Minnesota.

Chandras, Kananur V. 1978. "East Indian Ameri-cans." In <u>Racial Discrimination Against Neither-White-Nor-Black American Minorities (Native Americans, Chinese Americans, Japanese Americans, Mexican Americans, Puerto Ricans and East Indian Americans</u>), ed. Kananur V. Chandras, pp. 80-96. San Francisco: R and E Research Associates.

Chandrasekhar, Sripati. 1984. "Some Statistics on Asian Indian Immigration to the United States of America." In <u>From India to America</u>: <u>Immigration From India to the U.S.</u>, ed. Sri-pati Chandrasekhar, pp. 86-92. La Jolla, Calif.: Population Review Books.

Chawla, Raj. 1981. "A Trip Down Memory Lane."

Voice of India, 6 (October):17-19.

Clarke, Peter. 1978. "The Ismaili Sect in London." _Religion_ 8:68-84.

"Classifieds - Matrimonials." 1986. _India Abroad_, December 12, p. 34.

Clothey, Fred W. 1983. _Rhythm and Intent: Ritual Studies From South India_. Madras, India: Blackie and Sons.

Coelho, George V., and Paul I. Ahmed, eds. 1980. _Uprooting and Development: Dilemmas of Coping with Modernization_. Current Topics in Mental Health. New York: Plenum Press.

Cole, William Owen, and Piara Singh Sambhi. 1978. _The Sikhs: Their Religious Beliefs and Practices._ Library of Beliefs and Practices. London: Routledge and Kegan Paul.

Coward, Howard, and Leslie Kawamura, eds. 1978. _Religion and Ethnicity_. Waterloo, Ontario: Wilfred Laurier University Press.

Cross, Malcolm. 1972. "The East Indians of Guyana and Trinidad," Report no. 13. London: Minority Rights Group Publication.

Dadabhay, Yusuf. 1954. "Circuitous Assimilation Among Rural Hindustanis in California." _Social Forces_ 33 (December): 138-41.

Daniels, Roger. 1976. "American Historians and East Asian Immigrants." In _The Asian American: The Historical Experience_, ed. Norris Hundley, Jr., pp. 1-25. Clio Books/Pacific Historical Review Series, no. 3. Santa Barbara, Calif.: American Bibliographical Center, Clio Press.

Das, Rajani Kanta. 1923. _Hindustani Workers on the Pacific Coast_. Berlin: Walter DeGruyter.

Desai, Prakash N., and George V. Coelho, 1980. "Indian Immigrants in America: Some Cultural Aspects of Psychological Adaptation." In _The New Ethnics: Asian Indians in the United_

<u>States</u>, ed. Parmatma Saran and Edwin Eames, pp. 363-86. New York: Praeger.

de Vries, Jan. 1967. <u>The Study of Religion</u>: <u>A Historical Approach</u>, transl. by Kees W. Bolle. New York: Harcourt, Brace and World.

Dikshit, Om. 1975. "The Impact of Mahatma Gandhi on Martin Luther King, Jr." <u>Negro History Bulletin</u> vol. 38 (February-March):342-44.

Dotson, Floyd, and Lillian O. Dotson. 1968. <u>The Indian Minority of Zambia, Rhodesia, and Malawi</u>. New Haven and London: Yale University Press.

Dutta, Manoranjan. 1986. "Asian Indian Americans: Search for an Economic Profile." In <u>From India to America</u>: <u>A Brief History of Immigration; Problems of Discrimination; Admission and Assimilation</u>, 2d ed., ed. Sripati Chandrasekhar, pp. 78-84. La Jolla, Calif.: Population Review.

Elkhanialy, Hekmat, and Ralph W. Nicholas. 1976. "Racial and Ethnic Self-Designation, Experiences of Discrimination, and Desire for Legal Minority Status Among Indian Immigrants in the U.S.A." In <u>Indians From the Indian Subcontinent in the U.S.A.</u>: <u>Problems and Prospects</u>, eds. Hekmat Elkhanialy and Ralph W. Nicholas, pp. 41-50. Chicago: India League of America.

Fennell, Valerie I. 1977. "International Atlanta and Ethnic Group Relations." <u>Urban Anthropology</u> 6:345-54.

Fenton, John Y. 1983. "What is Religion?" In <u>Religions of Asia</u>, ed. John Y. Fenton, pp. 3-23. New York: St. Martin's Press.

_____. 1988. "Hinduism." In <u>Encyclopedia of the American Religious Experience: Studies of Traditions and Movements</u>, vol. 2, ed. Charles H. Lippy and Peter W. Williams, pp. 683-98. New York: Charles Scribner's Sons.

Fisher, Maxine P. 1980. The Indians of New York City: A Study of Immigrants From India. Columbia, Mo.: South Asia Books.

Fluret, Anne K. 1974. "Incorporation into Networks Among Sikhs in Los Angeles." Urban Anthropology 3:27-31.

Gallup, George, Jr. 1985. "Religion in America." In Religion in America Today, ed. Wade Clark Roof, pp. 167-74. The Annals of the American Academy of Political and Social Science, vol. 480. Newbury Park, Calif.: Sage.

Gardner, Robert W., Bryant Robey, and Peter C. Smith. 1985. Asian Americans: Growth, Change, and Diversity. Population Bulletin, vol. 40, no. 4 (October). Washington, D. C.: Population Reference Bureau.

Ghai, Yash, and Dharam Ghai. 1971. The Asian Minorities of East and Central Africa. report no. 4. London: Minority Rights Group.

Ghayur, M. Arif. 1981. "Muslims in the United States: Settlers and Visitors." Annals of the American Academy of Political and Social Science 450:150-63.

Gillian, K. L. 1962. Fiji's Indian Migrants. Melbourne: Oxford and Australian National University.

Gilroy, Paul. 1982. The Empire Strikes Back: Race and Racism in 70s Britain. London: Hutchinson Company in association with the Centre for Contemporary Cultural Studies, University of Birmingham.

Gupta, Santosh Prabha. 1969. "The Acculturation of Asian Indians in Central Pennsylvania." Ph.D. diss., The Pennsylvania State University.

Guthikonda, Ravindranath, K. P. Ananthpadmanabhan, C. P. Kamath, and P. Ramanathan, eds. 1979. Indian Community Reference Guide and Directory of Indian Associations in North America.

Livingston, N.J.: Orient Book Distributors.

Haddad, Yvonne Yazbeck. 1978. "Muslims in Canada: A Preliminary Study." In Religion and Ethnicity, eds. Harold Coward and Leslie Kawamura, pp. 101-14. Waterloo, Ontario: Wilfred Laurier University Press.

_____. 1979. "The Muslim Experience in the United States." The Link 12:1-12.

_____. 1983. "The Impact of the Islamic Revolution on the Syrian Muslims of Montreal." In The Muslim Community in North America, eds. Earle H. Waugh, Baha Abu-Laban, and Regula B. Qureshi, pp. 165-81. Edmonton, Alberta: University of Alberta Press.

_____. 1984a. "Islam." In The Canadian Encyclopedia. ed. James H. Marsh. Edmonton, Alberta: University of Alberta Press. vol. 2:905-7.

_____. 1984b. "Muslims in America." In Islam: The Religious and Political Life of a Community, ed. Marjorie Kelly. New York: Praeger Press.

_____, and Adair T. Lummis, eds. 1987. Islamic Values in the United States: A Comparative Study. New York: Oxford University Press.

Handlin, Oscar. 1951. The Uprooted: The Epic Story of the Great Migrations That Made the American People. Boston: Little, Brown.

Hazareesingh, K. 1966. "The Religion and Culture of Indian Immigrants in Mauritius and the Effect of Social Change." Comparative Studies in Society and History 8:241-57.

Helweg, Arthur Wesley. 1979. Sikhs in England: The Development of a Migrant Community. Delhi: Oxford University Press.

Hess, Gary R. 1969. "The 'Hindu' in America: Immigration and Naturalization Policies and India, 1917-1946." Pacific Historical Review

38:59-79.

_____. 1976. "The Forgotten Asian Americans: The East Indian Community in the United States." In The Asian American: The Historical Experience, ed. Norris Hundley, Jr., pp. 157-77. Clio Books/Pacific Historical Review Series, no. 3. Santa Barbara, Calif.: American Bibliographical Center, Clio Press.

Hill, Carole E. 1975. "Adaptation in Public and Private Behavior of Ethnic Groups in an American Urban Setting." Urban Anthropology 4:333-47.

_____, ed. 1976. Atlanta International Problems and Prospects. Atlanta: Georgia State University Printing Office.

Hogbin, Murray. 1983. "The Socio-Religious Behavior of Muslims in Canada: An Overview." In The Muslim Community in North America, ed. Earle H. Waugh, Baha Abu-Laban, and Regula B. Qureshi, pp. 111-26. Edmonton, Alberta: The University of Alberta Press.

Horowitz, Michael M. 1963. "The Worship of South Indian Deities in Martinique." Ethnology 2:339-45.

Hoyt, Edwin P. 1974. Asians in the West. New York: Thomas Nelson.

Hudson, Lynn. 1987. "Invoking the Law to Fight Discrimination." India Abroad, December 25, pp. 12-13.

Indian Youth of Atlanta Source. January 1988. Smyrna, Georgia: Indian Cultural and Religious Center.

Ivanow, Wladimir. 1953. "Ismailiya." In Shorter Encyclopedia of Islam, ed. H. A. R. Gibb and J. H. Kramers, pp. 179-83. Leiden: E. J. Brill.

Jacoby, Harold S. 1956. "A Half-Century Appraisal of the East Indians in the United States."

Sixth Annual College of the Pacific Faculty Research Lecture. Stockton: University of the Pacific.

_____. 1977. "East Indians in the United States: The First Half Century." Unpublished manuscript.

Jain, Usha R. 1964. "The Gujaratis of San Francisco." M. A. thesis, University of California, Berkeley.

Jaini, Padmanabh S. 1979. The Jaina Path of Purification. Berkeley: University of California Press.

James, Alan G. 1974. Sikh Children in Britain. London: Oxford University Press.

Jayawardene, Chandra. 1966. "Religious Belief and Social Change: Aspects of the Development of Hinduism in British Guiana." Comparative Studies in Society and History 8:211-40.

_____. 1968. "Migration and Social Change: A Survey of Indian Communities Overseas." Geographical Review 58:426-449.

Jensen, Joan M. 1969. "Apartheid: Pacific Coast Style." Pacific Historical Review 38:335-40.

_____. 1980. "East Indians." In Harvard Encyclopedia of American Ethnic Groups, ed. Stephan Thernstrom, pp. 296-301. Cambridge, Mass.: Harvard University Press.

_____. 1988. Passage From India: Asian Indian Immigrants in North America. New Haven: Yale University Press.

Johnson, Julian P. 1980. The Path of the Masters: The Science of Surat Shabd Yoga, 12th ed. Beas, India: Radha Soami Satsang Beas.

Juergensmeyer, Mark. 1979. "The Ghadar Syndrome: Immigrant Sikhs and Nationalist Pride." In Sikh Studies: Comparative Perspectives on a

Changing Tradition, ed. Mark Juergensmeyer and N. Gerald Barrier, pp. 173-90. Berkeley Religious Studies Series. Berkeley, Calif.: Graduate Theological Union.

Kalkunte, Sheila J. 1986. "India-Backed Nominees Won." _India Abroad_, November 14, pp. 1, 9.

Kapany, Narinder Singh. 1979. "Sikhs Abroad." In _Sikh Studies: Comparative Perspectives on a Changing Tradition_, ed. Mark Juergensmeyer and N. Gerald Barrier, pp. 209-10. The Berkeley Religious Studies Series. Berkeley, Calif.: Graduate Theological Union.

Kashima, Tetsuden. 1977. _Buddhism in America: The Social Organization of an Ethnic Religious Institution_. Contributions in Sociology, no. 26. Westport, Conn.: Greenwood Press.

Klass, Morton. 1961. _East Indians in Trinidad: A Study of Cultural Persistence_. New York: Columbia University Press.

Knott, Kim. 1987. "Hindu Temple Rituals in Britain: The Reinterpretation of Tradition." In _Hinduism in Britain: The Perpetuation of Religion in an Alien Cultural Milieu_, ed. Richard Burghart, pp. 157-79. London: Tavistock.

Kondapi, C. 1951. _Indians Overseas, 1838-1939_. New Delhi: Indian Council of World Affairs.

Kuper, Hilda. 1960. _Indian People in Natal_. Natal, South Africa: University Press.

La Brack, Bruce W. 1979. "Sikhs Real and Ideal: Discussion of Text and Context in the Description of Overseas Sikh Communities." In _Sikh Studies: Comparative Perspectives on a Changing Tradition_, ed. Mark Juergensmeyer and N. Gerald Barrier, pp. 127-42. Berkeley Religious Studies Series. Berkeley, Calif.: Graduate Theological Union.

_____. 1980. "The Sikhs of Northern California: A Socio-Historical Study." Ph.D. diss., Syracuse University.

_____. 1986. "Immigration Law and the Revitalization Process: The Case of the California Sikhs." In From India to America: A Brief History of Immigration; Problems of Discrimination; Admission and Assimilation, 2d ed., ed. Sripati Chandrasekhar, pp. 59-66. La Jolla, Calif.: Population Review.

Lai, H. M. 1980. "Chinese." In Harvard Encyclopedia of American Ethnic Groups, ed. Stephan Thernstrom, pp. 217-34. Cambridge, Mass.: Harvard University Press.

Leonard, Karen. 1986. "Marriage and Family Life Among Early Asian Indian Immigrants." In From India to America: A Brief History of Immigration; Problems of Discrimination; Admission and Assimilation, ed. Sripati Chandrasekhar, pp. 67-76. La Jolla, Calif.: Population Review.

Lipton, Michael, and John Firn. 1975. The Erosion of a Relationship: India and Britain Since 1960. London: Oxford University Press.

Littleton, C. Scott. 1964. "Some Aspects of Social Stratification Among the Immigrant Punjab Communities of California." In Culture Change and Stability, ed. Ralph L. Beals, pp. 105-16. Los Angeles: Department of Anthropology, University of California at Los Angeles.

Lopate, Phillip. 1986. "Zoroaster in the New World." The New York Times Magazine, October 19, pp. 83-85, 100-1.

_____. 1987. The Rug Merchant. New York: Viking.

Lovell, Emily Kalled. 1983. "Islam in the United States: Past and Present," In The Muslim Community in North America, ed. Earle H. Waugh, Baha Abu-Laban, and Regula B. Qureshi, pp. 93-110. Edmonton, Alberta: The University of Alberta Press.

Lyman, Stanford M., ed. 1970. The Asian In North America. Santa Barbara, Calif.: ABC-Clio Books.

Madelung, Wilferd. 1987. "Shiism: Isma'iliyya." In The Encyclopedia of Religion, vol. 13, ed. Mircea Eliade, , pp. 247-60. Chicago: The University of Chicago Press.

Malik, Yogendra K. 1971. East Indians in Trinidad: A Study in Minority Politics. London: Oxford University Press.

Mayer, Adrian C. 1973. Peasants in the Pacific: A Study of Fiji Indian Rural Society, 2d ed. Berkeley: University of California Press.

Melendy, H. Brett. 1977. Asians in America: Filipinos, Koreans, and East Indians. Boston: Twayne.

Melton, John Gordon. 1986. Encyclopedic Handbook of Cults in America. Garland Reference Library of Social Science, Vol. 213. New York: Garland.

_____. 1987a. The Encyclopedia of American Religions, 2d ed. Detroit: Gale.

_____. 1987b. The Encyclopedia of American Religions, 2d ed. supplement. Detroit: Gale.

Miller, Randall M., and Thomas D. Marzik, eds. 1977. Immigrants and Religion in Urban America. Philadelphia: Temple University Press.

Muhammad, Akbar. 1984. "Muslims in the United States: An Overview of Organizations." In The Islamic Impact, ed. Yvonne Yazbeck Haddad, Byron Haines and Ellison Findly, pp. 195-218. Syracuse, N.Y.: Syracuse University Press.

Mukherjee, Bharati. 1981. "An Invisible Woman." In Saturday Night, vol. 96 (March):36-40.

_____. 1985. Darkness. Ontario, Canada: Penguin Books Canada.

Muthanna, I. M. 1975. People of India in North America, Part 1. Bangalore: Lotus Printers.

Naby, Eden. 1980. "Zoroastrians." In Harvard Encyclopedia of American Ethnic Groups, ed. Stephan Thernstrom, pp. 1031-32. Cambridge, Mass.: Harvard University Press.

Nanda, Swami Jyotir Maya. 1985. "Valedictory Speech." In Hindu Vishwa: Vishwa Hindu Parishad 2nd Southeastern Regional Conference: July 5, 6, 7, 1985, Atlanta, ed. Aniruddha Lokre, pp. 39-42. South Glastonbury, Conn.: Vishwa Hindu Parishad of America.

Nanji, Azim. 1974. "Modernization and Change in the Nizari Ismaili Community in East Africa." Journal of Religion in Africa 6:123-39.

_____. 1978. The Nizari Ismaili Tradition in the Indo-Pakistani Subcontinent. Delmar, New York: Caravan Books.

_____. 1982. "Ritual and Symbolic Aspects of Islam in African Contexts." In Islam in Local Contexts, ed. Richard C. Martin, pp. 102-9. Contributions to Asian Studies, vol. 17. Leiden: E. J. Brill.

_____. 1983. "The Nizari Ismaili Muslim Community in North America: Background and Development." In The Muslim Community in North America, eds. Earle H. Waugh, Baha Abu-Laban, and Regula B. Qureshi, pp. 149-64. Edmonton, Alberta: University of Alberta Press.

_____. 1987. "Isma'ilism." In Islamic Spirituality: Foundations, ed. Seyyed Hossein Nasr, pp. 179-98. World Spirituality: An Encyclopedic History of the Religious Quest, vol. 19. New York: Crossroads.

Narayanan, Vasudha. 1984. "Becoming Hindu Outside the Aryan Land." Paper presented at the annual meeting of the American Academy of Religion. Chicago, December 10, 1984.

Nasr, Seyyed Hussain, ed. 1977. Ismaili Contributions to Islamic Culture. Tehran, Iran: Weidenfeld and Nicolson.

Niehoff, Arthur, and Juanita Niehoff. 1960. East Indians in the West Indies. Publications in Anthropology, no. 6. Milwaukee: Milwaukee Public Museum.

"Number of Foreign Students in U.S. Rises 0.5 Pct. to a Total of 343,777." 1986. Chronicle of Higher Education, October 22, pp. 31, 34.

"Ohio Jain Federation Introduces the East to Other Faiths." 1987. Hinduism Today vol. 9 (August):5.

Owen, Roger. 1985. Migrant Workers in the Gulf. Minority Rights Group Report No. 68. London: Minority Rights Group.

Pais, Arthur. 1987. "Celebrations of Hanukkah With Songs and Oil Lamps." India Abroad, January 9, pp. 1, 14.

Parthasarathy, Malini. 1982. "Affluent, Yet Insecure." The Hindu, May 9, p. 17.

Pattabhiram, B. 1986. "Hindu Temple Priests in America." Hinduism Today, vol. 8 (November/December):13.

Perry, John. 1987a. "Indians in Jersey City Harassed by 'Dotbusters.'" News India, October 2, pp. 1, 20.

_____. 1987b. "Mounting Attacks in Jersey City." News India, October 9, pp. 1, 20.

Petersen, William. 1980. "Concepts of Ethnicity." In Harvard Encyclopedia of American Ethnic Groups, ed. Stephan Thernstrom, pp. 234-42. Cambridge, Mass.: Harvard University Press.

Pocock, David F. 1957. "Factions in Indian and Overseas Indian Societies, II: The Basis of Faction in Gujerat." British Journal of Sociology 8:295-306.

_____. 1973. "Preservation of the Religious Life: Hindu Immigrants in Britain." Contributions to Indian Sociology, New Series 20:341-65.

Preston, James J. 1983. "Creation of the Sacred Image: Apotheosis and Destruction in Hinduism." In Gods of Flesh, Gods of Stone: The Embodiment of Divinity in India, eds. Joanne Punzo Waghorne and Norman Cutler, pp. 9-32. Chambersburg, Penn.: Anima.

Pye, E. M. 1969. "The Transplantation of Religions." Numen 16:234-39.

Qureshi, Regula B., and Saleem M. M. Qureshi. 1983. "Pakistani Canadians: The Making of a Muslim Community." In The Muslim Community in North America, ed. Earle H. Waugh, Baha Abu-Laban, and Regula B. Qureshi, pp. 127-48. Edmonton, Alberta: University of Alberta Press.

Qutub, Musa. 1987. "Editorial." The Invitation vol. 4 (February):1-2. Des Plaines: Islamic Information Center of America.

Ramchandani, Ram R. 1976. Uganda Asians: The End of an Enterprise: A Study of the Role of the People of Indian Origin in the Economic Development of Uganda and Their Expulsion 1894-1972. Bombay: United Asia.

Ramcharan, Subhas. 1982. Racism: Nonwhites in Canada. Toronto: Butterworths.

Rao, Pemmaraju Venugopala. 1977. "Taking Care of Our Cultural Traditions". Paper presented at the First Telegu Conference of North America, New York, New York. May 28.

_____. 1984. "Guest Editorial." Voice of India Inauguration Special, July/August, p. 5. Smyrna, Georgia: India American Cultural Association.

_____. 1985. "Do We Know What Our Culture Is?" Paper presented at the Fifth North America

Telugu Conference, Los Angeles, California. July 6.

Rice, Marion J., Purnima Kumar, and Manorama P. Taliaver. 1984. "Adjustment of Asian Indians in Atlanta, Georgia." Paper presented at The Southeastern Conference of the Asian Studies Association, Atlanta, Georgia. January 13.

Richardson, E. Allen. 1985. East Comes West: Asian Religions and Cultures in North America. New York: Pilgrim Press.

Saran, Parmatma. 1980a. "New Ethnics: The Case of the East Indians in New York City." In Sourcebook on the New Immigration: Inplications [sic] for the United States and the International Community, ed. Roy S. Bryce-Laporte, pp. 303-11. New Brunswick, N.J.: Transaction Books.

_____. 1980b. "Patterns of Adaptation of Indian Immigrants." In Uprooting and Development: Dilemmas of Coping With Modernization, ed. George V. Coelho and Paul I. Ahmed, pp. 375-400. New York: Plenum Press.

_____. 1985. The Asian Indian Experience in the United States. Cambridge, Mass.: Schenkman.

_____ and Edwin Eames, eds. 1980. The New Ethnics: Asian Indians in the United States. New York: Praeger.

Sarma, Jotirmoyee. 1969. "Puja Associations in West Bengal." Journal of Asian Studies 28:579-94.

Schermerhorn, R. A. 1978. Ethnic Plurality in India. Tuscon: University of Arizona Press.

Schwartz, Barton, ed. 1967. Caste in Overseas Indian Communities. Chandler Publications in Anthropology and Sociology. San Francisco: Chandler.

Sethi, S. Prakash. 1987. "The New 'Assimilative' Immigrants: An Opinion-Attitude Survey of

Asian-Indian Influentials in the United States: Executive Summary." Unpublished manuscript. New York: Baruch College Center for Management Development and Organization Research.

Smith, Wilfred Cantwell. 1957. Islam in Modern History. New York: The New American Library of World Literature.

Solanki, Ratilal. 1973. "Americanization of Immigrants: A Study in Acculturation of Asian Indians in the State of Colorado and the Educational Implications Thereof." Ph.D. thesis, University of Denver.

Sorcar, Manick. 1982. The Melting Pot: Indians in America. Golden, Colo.: Sorcar Enterprises.

Swarap, Ram. 1986. "Ramakrishna Mission Wins Non-Hindu Status." Hinduism Today vol. 8 (March):1, 11, 21.

Tandon, Yash, and Arnold Raphael. 1984. The New Position of East Africa's Asians: Problems of a Displaced Minority. Minority Rights Group Report, no. 16. London: Minority Rights Group.

Tatla, Darshan Singh. 1983. "Sikhs Abroad: A Research Bibliography." Journal of Sikh Studies 10:138-42.

Taylor, Donald. 1987. "Charismatic Authority in the Sathya Sai Baba Movement." In Hinduism in Great Britain: The Perpetuation of Religion in an Alien Cultural Milieu, ed. Richard Burghart, pp. 119-33. London: Tavistock.

"Temple Services in North America." 1988. Hinduism Today vol. 10 (January):11.

Thapar, Romila. 1966. A History of India, vol. 1. Baltimore: Penguin Books.

Thompson, Gardner. 1974. "The Ismailis in Uganda." In Expulsion of a Minority: Essays on Ugandan Asians, ed. Michael Twaddle, pp. 30-

52. London: Athlone Press.

Thottathil, Pelis A., and Parmatma Saran. 1980. "An Economic Profile of Asian Indians." In The New Ethics: Asian Indians in the United States, ed. Parmatma Saran and Edwin Eames, pp. 233-46. New York: Praeger.

Thundy, Zacharias P. 1983. "Kerala: People and Culture." in Keralites in America: Community Reference Book, ed. K. P. Andrews, pp. 11-90. Glen Oaks, N.Y.: Literary Market Review.

Tinker, Hugh. 1971. "Indians in Israel: The Acceptance Model and Its Limitations." Race 13:81-84.

_____. 1977. The Banyan Tree: Overseas Emigrants From India, Pakistan, and Bangladesh. New York: Oxford University Press.

Twaddle, Michael, ed. 1975. Expulsion of a Minority: Essays on Ugandan Asians. Commonwealth Papers, no. 18. London: The Athlone Press.

U.S. Congress. House. 1986. Congressional Record, 99th Congress, 2d sess., V. 132: HR3737.

Vempathy, Krishna M. 1984. "Discrimination: An Overview." In North American Directory and Reference Guide of Asian Indian Businesses and Independent Professional Practitioners, ed. Thomas Abraham, p. 44. New York: India Enterprises of the West.

Venkateshwaran, S. 1988. "Spurring Political Involvement." India Abroad, January 30, p. 7.

Vijay, Kamlakant. 1987. "India Cultural and Religious Center." IACA Directory, pp. 18-19. Smyrna, Ga.: India Cultural and Religious Center.

Vora, Batuk. 1987. "Sikhs of Yuba City: Pattern of Change Over Generations." India Abroad, February 27, pp. 1, 8.

Wadley, Susan S. 1983. "Vrats: Transformers of

Destiny." In Karma: An Anthropological Inquiry, ed. Charles F. Keyes and E. Valentine Daniel, pp. 147-62. Berkeley: University of California Press.

Ward, W. Peter. 1978. White Canada Forever: Popular Attitudes and Public Policy Toward Orientals in British Columbia. Montreal: McGill, Queen's University Press.

Waugh, Earle H. 1980. "The Imam in the New World: Models and Modifications." In Transitions and Transformations in the History of Religions, ed. Frank E. Reynolds and Theodore M. Ludwig, pp. 124-49. Leiden: E. J. Brill.

_____ 1983. "Muslim Leadership and the Shaping of the Umma: Classical Tradition and Religious Tension in the North American Setting." In The Muslim Community in North America, ed. Earle H. Waugh, Baha Abu-Laban, and Regula B. Qureshi, pp. 12-26. Edmonton, Alberta: University of Alberta Press.

Waugh, Earle H., Baha Abu-Laban, and Regula B. Qureshi, eds. 1976. Ethnic Information Sources of the United States. Detroit: Gale Research

Wenzel, Lawrence A. 1966. The Identification and Analysis of Certain Value Orientations of Two Generations of East Indians in California. Ph.D. thesis, University of the Pacific.

_____. 1968. "The Rural Punjabis of California: A Religio-Ethnic Group." Phylon 29:245-56.

Williams, Raymond B. 1984. A New Face of Hinduism: The Swaminarayan Religion. Cambridge: Cambridge University Press.

_____. 1986a. "The Guru as Pastoral Counselor." The Journal of Pastoral Care 40:331-40.

_____. 1986b. "Reshaping the Tradition: Asian Indian Religious Organizations in the United States." Unpublished manuscript.

_____. 1986c. "Translating Indian Christianity to America." The Christian Century 103:889-90.

Wilson, Jim G. 1983. "Fijian Hinduism." In Rama's Banishment: A Centenary Tribute to the Fiji Indians 1897-1079, ed. Vijay Mishra, pp. 86-111. Portland, Oreg.: International Specialized Book Services.

Wood, Louise Ann. 1966. "East Indians in California: A Study of Their Organizations, 1900-1947." M.A. thesis, University of Wisconsin.

Index

About the Author

John Y. Fenton has been engaged in college and graduate teaching and research concerned with Hindu and Buddhist religious traditions, cross-cultural mysticism, and cross-cultural theology for 20 years at Emory University in Atlanta, Georgia. He taught previously at the Pennsylvania State University. He has conducted research on the Indian immigrant population of Atlanta since 1979. He wrote the article on Hinduism for The Encyclopedia of the American Religious Experience (1987) and composed articles concerning Asian religious traditions for the Abingdon Dictionary of Living Religions (1981). He also edited and contributed chapters to the first and second editions of Religions of Asia (1983 and 1987). Professor Fenton earned his Ph.D. at Princeton University and has engaged in post-doctoral studies at the University of Chicago and the University of Washington in Seattle.